Founded in 1807, John Wiley & Sons is the oldest independent publishing company in the United States. With offices in North America, Europe, Asia, and Australia, Wiley is globally committed to developing and marketing print and electronic products and services for our customers' professional and personal knowledge and understanding.

The Wiley Corporate F&A series provides information, tools, and insights to corporate professionals responsible for issues affecting the profitability of their company, from accounting and finance to internal controls and performance management.

Supply Chain
Transformation

Supply Chain Transformation

Practical Roadmap to Best Practice Results

RICHARD J. SHERMAN

WILEY

John Wiley & Sons, Inc.

Cover image: © *diegocervo/iStockphoto*
Cover design: *John Wiley & Sons, Inc.*

Published by John Wiley & Sons, Inc., Hoboken, New Jersey.
Published simultaneously in Canada.

For general information on our other products and services or for technical support, please contact our Customer Care Department within the United States at (800) 762-2974, outside the United States at (317) 572-3993 or fax (317) 572-4002.

Wiley publishes in a variety of print and electronic formats and by print-on-demand. Some material included with standard print versions of this book may not be included in e-books or in print-on-demand. If this book refers to media such as a CD or DVD that is not included in the version you purchased, you may download this material at http://booksupport.wiley.com. For more information about Wiley products, visit www.wiley.com.

Library of Congress Cataloging-in-Publication Data:
Sherman, Richard J., 1950-
    Supply chain transformation : practical roadmap to best practice results / Richard J. Sherman.
        p. cm.— (Wiley corporate F&A series)
    Includes bibliographical references and index.
    ISBN 978-1-118-31444-9 (cloth); ISBN 978-1-118-41992-2 (ebk); ISBN 978-1-118-42174-1 (ebk); ISBN 978-1-118-43413-0 (ebk)
    1. Business logistics.   I. Title.
    HD38.5.S554 2013
    658.5—c23

                                                                              2012022693

Printed in the United States of America.

10 9 8 7 6 5 4 3 2 1

To my wife, for driving me to, for the first time ever, beat a deadline and "git 'er done" ahead of schedule. And to my family who have supported me through years of travels, ups and downs, and life in general.

Contents

Foreword

AS CEO'S, WE ARE reminded daily of the critical role supply chain plays in driving value. Please consider:

- Consumer loyalty is a by product of our ability to get innovative product to market quickly and efficiently and to maintain the highest affordable levels of in-stock possible.
- Shareholder satisfaction will follow the enterprise's actual success to achieve lean . . . and to focus not just on working capital but that capital that doesn't work.
- Management teams thrive when an integrated approach to supply chain delivers great results through seamless execution of a long-range strategy linking your business objectives, systems, and logistics capabilities.

Supply chain excellence truly is at the core of our need to be lean, customer-driven organizations that collaborate for the highest and best use of capital.

So we are all fortunate that Rich Sherman, a truly distinguished international supply chain thought leader, has written this book. Unlike so many academic approaches, you will find his work to be refreshing, practical, insightful, and helpful in every respect. It is authentic, as it is grounded based on practices in real companies across a number of vertical businesses with conclusions that go far beyond mere theory.

It is also thought provoking.

After 40 years in the retail industry, having held senior positions in five different companies and board experience with ten companies with heavy reliance on supply chain success, Rich's work made me really think again. It raises some fresh questions that we must all answer:

- What are the organizational mis-alignments that block improved performance? Are they cultural? Are they ego-driven?
- Does your dashboard adequately address the right business drivers?
- Do your rewards systems properly reinforce supply chain performance?
- Are your execution shortfalls a result of poor planning? Poor forecasting? Poor operations? Poor vendor collaboration? Are structural or leadership changes in order?

- Do your processes identify and address products that seldom move? Especially those that are highly seasonal and those with strong climatic variables?
- What systems enhancements are necessary to achieve speed and accuracy at low cost?
- With a focused change agenda, how much capital can be unleashed for higher returns and subsequent reinvestment?
- Does your board membership include deep expertise in this discipline?

Sherman provides us with a valuable roadmap to help guide us, challenge us, and answer these and other questions that are certain to be raised. It is a read to be shared by your top team to revisit (or perhaps elevate) your supply chain strategy and create a fresh approach that can lead not just to improved performance but also to differentiation in your vertical space.

Wishing you success as you read, reflect, and react!

Marty Hanaka
Austin, TX

Mr. Hanaka is Chairman and CEO of Golfsmith International and formerly served as Chairman and CEO of The Sports Authority as well as COO and a Director of Staples, Inc. His retail career spans forty years. He also has served on the Boards of five public companies as well as numerous private boards and as a National Governor of the Boys and Girls Clubs of America.

Preface

FACING UNPRECEDENTED GLOBAL competition and economic volatility, companies must turn their attention to the strategic leverage and value locked in traditional supply chain management. The supply chain impacts virtually every financial metric included in the company's balance sheet and income statement, and supply chain operations excellence can create gains of more than a 35 percent increase in return on capital employed. According to APQC's Open Standards Research benchmarks, best-in-class companies outperform their median competitors by a 50 percent or more supply chain cost advantage across all industries—a gap that hasn't closed in more than 25 years. Transforming your supply chain management into a journey for continuous performance improvement and operations excellence is no longer an option; it's a strategic mandate.

For the past 30 years, I have been "infotaining" audiences around the world with presentations both informative and, at least I think, entertaining. Commonly, though, across all of the feedback I receive following a conference or symposium, is the comment that people felt a bit "fire hosed." Despite the great content, fast pace, and a few chuckles, they wished that they had had more time to digest the material. So, I started breaking up my presentations into more digestible topics and scope, and kept the pace and chuckles, but I was less satisfied. The problem is that the intricacy of the complexity of supply chain management can't be captured in sound bites, or panel discussions, or even necessarily case studies. Certainly, the solution isn't a 40-minute case study concluded by "We had executive sponsorship."

Surveying the literature, I found lots of great "how-to" books, textbooks, technical dissertations, and, quite frankly, pretty dry material on what I think is a very dynamic, exciting, and virtually endless career . . . supply chain management. It has also frustrated me that the gap between the Leaders and Laggards continues to be so large, especially when I know what the leaders do; I know what the technology is capable of; I know the difference is often corporate culture; and I know that the justification is there to garner executive sponsorship!

When Wiley approached me about writing a book on supply chain transformation, my first inclination was to call it "Why Do We Have to Wait for People to Die?" The story behind that, based on a meeting with Professor Jay Forrester, is in Chapter 1. Fortunately, Tim Burgard from Wiley convinced me otherwise. But I really wanted to write more than a "how-to" book. I hope that you will find this more of a "why to" book. It's not that people are unwilling to change or to improve their performance or to transform the organization. Most of them just don't know why. There is a level of transformation maturity in every company's culture that needs to evolve to influence behavior. Transformation is perceived as being a lot of work. The reality is that the Laggards work every bit as hard as the Leaders. I'd rather be working on winning than losing. Wouldn't you? The difference between Leaders and Laggards is output, not input.

As I guide you through the "why's" of transformation, my hope is that you will see, as I have experienced, that the transformation journey, building a House of Excellence, and living in Leader City can be satisfying work and any organization can take the journey. As Ron Johnson, CEO of J.C. Penney, stated upon his appointment, "The journey is the reward." It's actually a lot of fun. Working for success, winning, growing, in a culture of learning and self-actualization is a heckuva lot more fun than just "showing up."

So, for once, I can give a presentation that has no time limit. I can speak to as many supply chain challenges, processes, approaches, and solutions from end to end, no matter how complex, as I want to. And you can take as little or as much time as you want to digest the material. The pace, though, will be rhythmic; there will be stories (I am a storyteller); and there will be, I hope, a few chuckles. I love being in the supply chain . . . real work, real people.

Collaboration is the key to Leader City and I will share with you my experiences cross-functionally, working in and with sales and marketing, R&D, finance, procurement, production, and logistics. I will also share my experience across the channel with retailers, distributors, manufacturers, suppliers, and growers. Did you know the corn cost content of a box of cornflakes is about 10 cents on a dollar? It's like waking up one morning and finding out Santa Claus spent 10 times as much on the wrappings as he did on the gift inside.

You can't break down the silos. It's how work is organized to achieve business goals. But processes cross those silos, and you have to know the points of intersection for people to collaborate to ensure a synchronous flow of goods, information, cash, and capital from their source to consumption and back again. And you need to know and understand your processes and their contribution to your success to be able to evaluate outsourcing opportunities. I have seen the third-party services industry grow up, and I have had the opportunity to work with many of the leaders over the years.

My experience spans virtually every industry and nearly every continent and is just deep enough to understand that globalization is a game changer. I am going to share with you not just why every case study ends with the need for management commitment and support; I am going to share how to get it! Don't skip to Chapter 7!

The supply chain is a pipeline of opportunity, essential to civilization (we do feed, clothe, and shelter the world), an unlocked chest of free cash flow and return on invested capital—and it will never go away (Chapter 2). So I wanted to write this book so that everyone and anyone can and should be able to gain an understanding of the strategic value of supply chain, how it works, and its value to the organization and to global commerce, and why, for many, it is and will be a great career choice. This is not a textbook, but it can be the reason why students want to open their textbook. It should be why every executive will want to spend some time understanding the financial levers and fulcrums of supply chain management and operations. It should by why every supply chain professional will want to jump on that journey to supply chain transformation. And it's why everyone at the cocktail party should buy a drink for the supply chain professional to say "Thank you." I told you it's a "why to" book! Enjoy! And send me a note when you "git 'er done!"

Acknowledgments

I T HAS BEEN A LONG career journey with lots of people contributing to my growth and inspiring me. While the dedication is to my wife and family, I would be remiss not to acknowledge the inspiration of my mother for my "stage presence," theatrical aptitude, and positive outlook . . . her optimism has moved me through the years.

When I was getting a bit full of myself for scoring in the 99th percentile in aptitude tests, my father pointed out to me that it meant that 1 percent of the population was as smart as or smarter than me. While I may not be a math major, I've learned there are a lot of smart people out there. If I were one in a million, there would be at least 6,000 or more as smart or smarter people than me in the world. We all have an aptitude for greatness in some aspect of our lives, and the really smart people are the ones who look for it in everyone they meet.

That came from my father's inspiring and guiding me to always keep learning and be humble in my learning. He always told me that regardless of the diversity in the people I would meet in my life, there was always something I could learn from each of them. And, as I have met many different people in my career, I have learned, been influenced by, and inspired by all of you past, present, and future. Thanks, Dad, for opening me up to the wonder of people.

I am particularly thankful to Robert Meshew, a Microsoft colleague, for introducing me to Michael Hugos, author of *Essentials of Supply Chain Management* (Wiley, 2011). Michael introduced me to Tim Burgard at John Wiley & Sons, who was amazingly supportive and helpful to me in preparing the book proposal and subsequently obtaining approval. And, of course, thanks goes to Stacey Rivera, development editor and Chris Gage, production editor, at Wiley, for the guidance and suggestions in developing the content.

Throughout this book, I will introduce many people who have influenced and inspired my thinking on supply chain management. I am particularly grateful to the academic community: the late Don Bowersox at MSU; Pat Daugherty at MSU; Dale Rogers at Rutgers; Glenn Richey and Alex Ellinger at Alabama; Bud LaLonde, Doug Lambert, and Martha Cooper at Ohio State; Ray Mundy and John Langley from Tennessee and now at Missouri and Penn State, respectively; Bob Novack, John Coyle, and Skip Grenoble at Penn State; Jack Crumbly at Tuskegee University; John White at Georgia Tech; the late Don Taylor at MSU; and George Wagenheim, Bixby Cooper,

Keith Helferich, Nick Little, and Dave Closs at MSU; Mary Holcomb, Jim Foggin, Lloyd Rineheart, Rhonda Barton, Bric Wheeler, and Ted Stank at Tennessee; Tom Speh at Miami of Ohio; John Gaski at Notre Dame; Karl Manrodt at Georgia Southern; Yossi Sheffi, Peter Senge, and Larry Lapide at MIT; Arnie Maltz at ASU; Madhav Pappu at Texas A&M; Mike Hasler and Doug Morrice at Texas; and the many students, staff, and faculty at the many universities and colleges that have opened their classrooms and minds to me over the years.

From the many people I have worked for and with over the years, Mike Prusha at Burroughs and DEC; Dave Alcala at EXE and Pelion; Andre Martin and the late Jim Andress at IRI; Hank Phelps at DEC; and Bob Sabath at AT Kearney, Mercer, and now at Trissential have been great leaders, mentors, and influencers in my management thinking in particular. They inspired me to be a good leader and mentor to the people on my teams, at least based on how many of them still keep in touch, such as Rob Gilson, Ron Griggs, Dave Montgomery, Keri Schoonderwoerd, Patricia Bertoni, Sue Hoxie, Steve Goldsmith, Laura Twite, Erin Burr, and Kim Pacheco. Scotty and Katrine at Comedy Industries are real inspirations. They made every trade show a major success. I really want to acknowledge my co-workers. There are too many to name; but each of you have a special place in my heart and I thank you for the person you inspired me to be.

To the many business associates, clients, and pundits that I have worked with over the years, especially Gus Santelli, Doug MacLean, and the late Mike Bonelli from Lead Time Technology whose work on end-to-end supply chain decision support has been truly inspiring. Thanks to Jeremy Geiger, founder of Retailigence, who has given me the opportunity to participate in a game-changing new market segment, data as a service and Big Data. Also, special thanks to the late John Fontanella whom I worked with at Digital, Microsoft, Skyway, and later when I was a client of AMR. John was a great colleague and thought leader. Certainly, Bob Ferrari, Greg Aimi, John Bermudez, Roddy Martin, Simon Jacobson, Michael Di Pietro, Rob Cerulle, Bob Saltz, Tony Friscia, Kevin Doyle, Dwight Klappich, and Jeff Woods at AMR/Gartner; Steve Banker, Andy Chatha, Adrian Gonzalez, Greg Gorbach, Ralph Rio, and Dick Slanski at ARC; Ed Toben at Colgate; Nick Lahowchic at Colgate, BD, and the Limited; Nancy Haslip at DEC and CSCMP; Joe Andraski at Nabisco and VICS; Rick Blasgen at Nabisco, Kraft, and CSCMP; Hoon Chung, Ed Sitarski, and Brian Nickerson at Numetrix; my good friend and colleague in thought, Ron Richter; Rich Cialabrini, Rob Getz, and Tom Alioto at "The Band"; Michael Goodman and Bill Latshaw at Innovation Associates; John Perry, Tom Costello, and Mike Pajakowski at Burroughs; Tom Sharpe at WERC; Dave Simbari at IMI and Optum; Jeff Langley at Fletcher Challenge, EXE, and KPMG; Trevor Barrows at EXE; Nari Viswanathan at Aberdeen and Steelwedge; Joe Francis, Melinda Spring, and Caspar Hunsche at the Supply Chain Council; Kate Vitasek at Supply Chain Visions and University of Tennessee; Mike Massetti at AMD; Mike Gray at Dell, Penn State, and Oliver Wight; Lou Boudreau, Ralph Drayer, and Tom Ford at P&G; Ted Rybeck, Ann Grackin, and Jane Biddle at Benchmarking Partners; Dave Gleditsch at Pelion; Chris Sellers, Mike Cassettari, and Matt Johnson at Syncra; Tom Brunnell at Avicon; Ed Nieuwenhuis at Meijer; Bob Parker and Simon Ellis at IDC Manufacturing Insights; John Faldetta at Gillette; Marty Hanaka from Staples, The

Sports Authority, and Golfsmith/Golf Town for the insight into what drives CEOs; my former roommates at ND, the late Mike Zikas for his inspiration and great friendship, Mike Murphy for conservative insights, and Paul Michaels for consumer marketing insights. Dave Anderson at TBS and Andersen Consulting; the late Bill Copacino at Andersen Consulting; Paul Fulchino at Mercer; Jim Morehouse and Mike Moriarty at A.T. Kearney, especially for "exacerbated"; Elcio Graccia at Integrare; Narayan Laksham at Ultriva; Ann Drake at DSC Logistics, Cliff Otto at CHEP and Saddle Creek; Dave Malenfant at Alcon; Enrique Carillo at IBM and Wipro; Ed Lange at Burroughs, Andersen Consulting and SAP; and many, many others, thank you for helping me shape my thoughts on this wonderful industry.

CHAPTER ONE

Change Is Inevitable, Growth Is Optional

CHARLES DICKENS MAY HAVE been the first supply chain industry analyst. Back in the 1800s, he wrote: "It was the best of times, it was the worst of times, it was the age of wisdom, it was the age of foolishness, it was the epoch of belief, it was the epoch of incredulity, it was the season of Light, it was the season of Darkness, it was the spring of hope, it was the winter of despair. . . ." Sound like another day in the life of a supply chain professional? Nowhere in industry is there a profession that has so much volatility, variability, and certain uncertainty. And nowhere in a company is an organizational structure (you may say function) that has as many levers on free cash flow, return on invested capital, and shareholder value. Quite simply, if you can't ship it, you can't bill it. Create, Market, and Sell all you want; but if you can't Source, Make, and Deliver it, it will never be capital or revenue to Invest, Measure, and Value. And the total cost it delivers (landed) determines its profitability.

And, as Dickens's novel is titled *A Tale of Two Cities*, so, too, we can call the supply chain a tale of two cities; cities that we can call "Leaders" and "Laggards" with a channel of doubters between them. For nearly 25 years, I have been leading most of my presentations with a graphic of industry benchmarks (see Figure 1.1). Don't worry about the date. It doesn't matter. While I ask my friends at APQC to refresh the data each year, even though the raw numbers may vary a bit, the gap between top, median, and bottom percentiles has remained the same. "Best-in-class" companies outperform their *median* competitors with more than a 50 percent cost advantage! And the gap between the Leaders and Laggards is even more significant.

Why is it that despite advances in performance improvement methodologies, tools, technologies, and education, lagging and even median performers haven't been able to close the gap on supply chain costs? As we will see in later chapters, the gap among other metrics can be close. But, in the total cost metric, there remains a

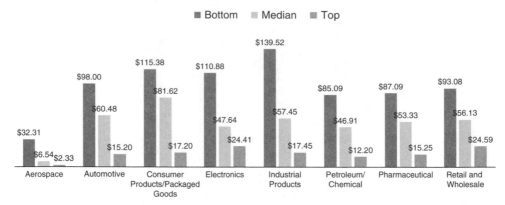

Supply Chain Management Costs per $1,000 Revenue

FIGURE 1.1   Superior Supply Chain Performance Has Long Been a Source of Competitive Advantage

significant gap—a gap that has been sustained for more than 25 years. It begins with supply chain complexity and trade-offs. To excel in total, one must be excellent in total. There are too many cost trade-offs between time, mode, distance, speed, service, and other attributes of the supply chain (to name a few) that to excel in all requires a high level of integration, education, systems, and commitment that most companies have not been willing or able to make. Companies that are unwilling to transform their operations to adopt best practices and adapt to a changing marketplace will continue to inhabit the city of Laggards.

Throughout this book, we'll explore why that is, but, if companies think it's size, cost, or level of financial investment, they are wrong. Working again with APQC (they maintain extensive open standards research on industry metrics and benchmark data), we have not been able to find any correlation between performance and revenue or investment. Companies of all sizes, level of investment, and industries have been able to achieve high performance results sustainable over time by continuous improvement and best practices adoption. And, similarly, companies with what appear to be brand and financial equity populate the median and even the Laggards' metrics. So why is this? Why does such a gap exist?

The good news about being considered an industry visionary is that you can use the same slides for 25 years and they will still be current. The bad news is that many companies' operations processes and systems have not progressed significantly in those same 25 years despite the fact that they have probably invested millions in enterprise applications (i.e., enterprise resource planning, or ERP) and systems integration. And it's not that the world hasn't changed in that time; *au contraire*, the world has seen more change in the past 25 years than in the past 250 years. It just seems that organizational paradigms (i.e., culture) are defined in such a way that it is very difficult to move an organization, let alone transform it, without real leadership from the head office.

Well, it doesn't have to be that way. And while I'd like to think the executives at the top are reading this to drive their organizations forward, this is a road map for everyone in the organization. While it really helps to have transformation driven from the top, we cannot necessarily wait for or expect that every senior executive will be driven toward operations excellence or necessarily understand what it is. *You*, regardless of your rank in the company, can garner top management commitment more easily than you think, and in the coming pages we will explore not only how, but why.

 ## GLOBALIZATION CHANGES THE GAME

Globalization is not only changing the competitive landscape but also the way companies will compete and collaborate with one another. Yes, collaborate. For, if we don't collaborate to eliminate waste across all dimensions, the twenty-first century may be the beginning of the last millennium. From new product development, commercialization, marketing, and sales to how you plan, source, make, and deliver your products in a sustainable manner, to capital acquisition and deployment, cost structure and performance, all functions of the organization contribute to increasing shareholder value.

Before I began my business and research career, I was a theology and English teacher. As an English major in college, one of the first things I learned was the definition of research: *"To steal from one is plagiarism; to steal from many is research!"* As an industry researcher, I have been "stealing" practices, best and worst, from many sources, colleagues, and companies that I have engaged throughout the years, heard present at numerous industry conferences, attended executive programs, and occasionally shared war stories over a beer. Of course, I will acknowledge their contribution to my research base accordingly.

What's interesting, though, is how few people have connected the dots over the years. When I was at Digital Equipment Corporation (DEC), I had the opportunity to work with Peter Senge, author of *The Fifth Discipline: The Art and Practice of The Learning Organization*,[1] and his colleagues at Innovation Associates (founded by Charlie Kiefer), especially Michael Goodman and Bill Latshaw. At DEC, we were developing the "Digital Logistics Architecture." We were using Senge's teaching in system dynamics and utilizing the Beer Game to teach the conundrums of supply chain. That project brought us all together. More about the Beer Game in Chapter 3.

It was while working with Senge and his colleagues that systems thinking really began to have an impact on the analysis of all of the industry practices I was "stealing." It's not necessarily the practices, advances, and changes individually that bring revelation and transformation. It's how all of the end-to-end activities, *as a system*, impact behavior. Change is a dynamic system of people, processes, and technology impacted by organizational structure and activity (see Figure 1.2).

That is where the impact of books like Thomas Friedman's *The World Is Flat* is realized.[2] It's not the individual impact of the 10 "flatteners" that Thomas Friedman speaks about in his book; it's the dynamic convergence of those flatteners that changes

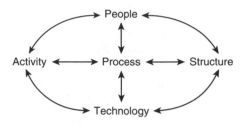

FIGURE 1.2   The Dynamics of Change

the world. What's important about his work is that several billion new consumers and tens of thousands of new businesses are entering the global commerce consumption *and* competitive markets.

All of those new consumers and competitors have real-time global communication and commerce capabilities at very low cost—*virtually!* New software applications that leverage limitless computing power, what (Gordon) Moore's Law (Intel, early 1990s) states: "Every 18 months computing power doubles and its price drops in half," is being developed more rapidly and inexpensively due to open source code collaboration, business process management, cloud technology deployment, and business process management software tools. And it's a challenge to the electronics supply chain . . . computers have a shorter shelf life than a gallon of milk!

Communicating on a global basis is as common as talking across the fence to your neighbor; as Bill Gates in the early 1990s said, "We'll have infinite bandwidth in a decade's time." What he didn't forecast is how inexpensive it would be. I communicate with colleagues all over the world *virtually* for free using Skype. Using "telepresence" technology from companies such as Cisco and Polycom, I recently sat "across" the table in a client meeting in Decatur, Illinois, and from colleagues in London, England, *virtually*. Toss in the fact that it can all be done through your personal communication device (including all commercial broadcasts), wirelessly, and anywhere, anytime, and well, yes, Tom Friedman, the world is not only flat but always on and in HD 3D. It won't be long before "telepresence" is holographic; thank you, Princess Leia.

However, of great importance to you is not only the emergence of a flat world paradigm changing the playing field; it's changing the game and how your company will compete in the twenty-first century. Companies are unlocking the value of their supply chains, outsourcing more and more noncore processes (not just for cost but for flexibility and agility), deploying more of their sales and marketing operations as well as production to the geographic point of the most profitable response, and leaning themselves into rapidly adapting, customer-responsive global competitors that see your business as their lunch. Innovation is the breakfast of champions, market leadership is for dinner, and dessert is increased shareholder value. Apple, for example, traditionally tops Gartner's Top 25 Supply Chains list, and they outsource just about all of their supply chain operations' execution capability.

PARADIGMS DRIVE ORGANIZATIONAL BEHAVIOR AND CULTURE

Transforming your organizational paradigm to a customer-responsive smart supply network (see accompanying "The Smart Supply Network") is the new strategic imperative for competing in the years ahead. While we hear of some successes, the major challenges to implementation are managing change and leveraging technology to empower your people to capitalize on the opportunities that a new world economy creates. Companies must adapt and tech-enable their business processes to the new global playing field to create game-changing strategies for market leadership against new and fierce global competitors, or be voted off the island. And it doesn't have to cost millions or require an army of consultants and integrators. You have the capability within your own company. Why not "unleash the hounds"?

Everett Rogers, in his 1962 book *The Diffusion of Innovations* (which has been widely adapted), suggests that the degree to which an innovation (something perceived as new or a change) is perceived (by its opponents) as being better than the idea it supersedes has a direct impact on the likelihood of adoption.[3] What that really means is "no pain, no gain." Change isn't easy. It's hard work. People aren't likely to accept a change to their comfort zone unless the innovation is perceived as being vastly better than the status quo.

One of my good friends and professional colleagues is Rick Blasgen. We first met when he was a planner at Nabisco and I was at Information Resources (IRI). Blasgen is now the CEO of the Council of Supply Chain Management Professionals (CSCMP), which was called the Council of Logistics Management (CLM) when I joined. At the 1997 CLM Annual Global Conference in Chicago, Blasgen presented on supply chain management at Nabisco.

One of the major barriers to Nabisco's supply chain transformation, he said, was that the "company was mired in a successful way of doing business. . . . "

Think about that. Your first reaction is to say, "Don't fix it if it ain't broke." Status quo, especially successful status quo, creates a comfort zone that is difficult to change. But, as the market around the company changes, as Blasgen pointed out in his presentation, if the company is not adaptive to change, its success can be fleeting.

The reality is that the *organization* creates the comfort zone, and it's called *culture*. The first step in any transformation or even a project initiative is to understand the culture. Transforming operations means transforming the culture. It's also the hardest thing for people to communicate. Visiting hundreds of companies over the years and asking people to describe their culture, I get hundreds of blank stares first, followed by deep thought, followed by some glib description of emotional attributes like *enthusiastic, regimented, highly disciplined, hierarchical,* and so on. It varies from "we have a culture of continuous improvement," "pursuit of excellence," to simply "it's like the Wild West."

Years ago at another CLM Annual Global Conference, the keynote speaker was Joel Arthur Barker and he was promoting his book, *Future Edge*.[4] My takeaway from his talk, which has stuck with me for many years, was that people live in paradigms. He defined a paradigm as "a set of rules (written or unwritten) that does two things: (1) it establishes or defines boundaries; and, (2) it tells you how to behave inside the

THE SMART SUPPLY NETWORK

What if everyone in your supply chain is connected in real time? What if every shipping unit is "labeled" with electronic AutoID (automatic identification) and RFID (radio frequency identification)? What if every transport container is GPS (global positioning system) enabled and can be monitored and tracked?

Every person in the network has the capability to share his or her local expert knowledge to manage and respond to change at any time and anywhere. As change occurs, perhaps a promotion or sales initiative, congestion around a major highway, severe weather, or other disruption or variable, ("oops, they bought the other company's product this time") the impact (considering all variables and aggregations) of the change is communicated across the network.

If the change is outside preset limits for material flow, cost, time, or other performance criteria, each person responsible for that variance is notified of how conditions at other locations (nodes) will or might directly affect them, and what operational adjustments need to be made to ensure timely response to the customer's request/order.

Upon notification, the person has graphical information with event drill-down capability to locate, utilize, and communicate the information needed to respond profitably to the change. The presence of everyone impacted is displayed so that live communications and collaboration are initiated to ensure compliance in response to the change. Information to support the necessary decisions is shared and displayed in multiple dimensions across any media anywhere in the world in real time. Data are collected from the transmissions of the RFID and GPS (telematics) devices located on all materials, containers, and transport resources throughout the network.

Everyone and every system in the network is guided by a measurable plan to keep the business on track and synchronized to respond to actual demand to achieve strategic business goals and create shareholder value. And it's not just for one company but for all the participants collaborating in the network.

Customers, suppliers, and outsourced service partners participate directly in the decision-making process and share in the value to extend the effectiveness of the organization and improve service and responsiveness while managing variability and uncertainty. Schedules, resources, and capacity, including labor, materials, machines, distribution, and capital, are synchronized to respond to demand with maximum effective agility across the enterprise and channel, leading to optimal response and maximum value creation for the network as a whole. Not possible, you say? *Business as usual has been canceled . . . Welcome to supply chain management in the twenty-first century and the Smart Supply Network. Are you, your people, and your systems up to the challenge?* ■

boundaries in order to be successful." This simple definition has helped me with assessing and understanding the culture of a company. Company culture establishes the rules of behavior inside the company. Culture is the company's paradigm.

Companies create operating paradigms through their policies, procedures, and culture. At the end of the day, a "culture" is a "paradigm." We all live in paradigms of some sort, both in our business lives and our personal lives. If your behavior is within the rules or boundaries of the culture, then you will ultimately be successful (for the most part) within the company. The culture largely determines the perception people will have of the new idea or innovation that is being presented to them. If it is within the boundaries, the likelihood of adoption is great. If it's outside the boundaries and is perceived as potentially disruptive or a challenge to the culture, it will be resisted.

The greatest resistance to change is the result of past success. The biggest factor in not moving forward is comfort with the status quo, and the best offense to combat change is its inherent lack of "proof" or evidence of success in the market. It's the reason that for more than 25 years the cost gap between Leaders and their median competitors has not changed. Figure 1.3 is the "Perfect Order" benchmark provided by APQC. Perfect orders are a measure of total supply chain performance and service. Across industries the gap between Leaders and their median competitors are relatively close, certainly closer than the cost gap.

The median competitors are executing as *efficiently* as the Leaders, but the Leaders are executing more *effectively* at a lower total cost! That's the difference between Leaders, the median, and the Laggards. Leaders have learned how to assess and leverage change as an opportunity, not a threat. They look for innovation and will risk failure for a greater reward. They work to win!

I remember a story (whether it's true or not, I don't know) about the former chairman of IBM, Thomas Watson, Jr. According to the lore my IBMer friends related to me, one of his direct reports made a decision costing the company around $200 million. As Watson called the executive in for a discussion to explain his actions, most of his colleagues expected him to come out of the meeting with his "pink slip." Instead, he came out of the meeting with a promotion. When asked why he didn't fire the executive, Watson responded, "Fire him? I just spent $200 million to educate him." Transformational cultures are learning cultures. If the company culture is not transformational, neither will be its performance.

ASSESSING YOUR COMPANY'S CULTURE

So how do you assess a culture to determine how it can evolve to be transformational? One of the more practical approaches to assessing a culture that I have found useful over the years has been a hybrid of Abraham Maslow's "Hierarchy of Needs"

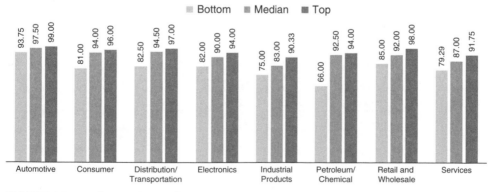

FIGURE 1.3 Perfect Order Performance

from his article "A Theory of Human Motivation" and French and Raven's "The Bases of Social Power."

I have adapted the concepts over the years to be my 5 Ss of transformational (cultural and managerial) maturity matrix (see Figure 1.4). The matrix can be used to assess relatively rapidly where a company's culture is in transformational maturity and what the likely managerial attitudes and response will be to change.

By the way, ever notice how every industry pundit has a "maturity model" of some kind? Well, I am no different, except unlike most pundits' maturity models that never have anyone at the highest level (so that they can have a never-ending series of consulting engagements) my highest level is not only achievable, but it's also the level I have found most leaders to be at. Senge calls it a "Learning Organization." In my model, it's Maslow's self-actualization level.

Horizontally, the table represents French and Raven's bases of power: referent, expert, legitimate, reward, and coercive. Vertically, the table represents Maslow's needs: self-actualization, self-esteem, social, security, and survival. How much time and detail you spend on the analysis is up to you. In my experience, you can assess overall culture pretty rapidly from interviews and observations across various functions in the organization. On a scale of 1 to 10 with 10 being the strongest or more frequently observed influence or behavior in the organization, you rate your assessment of the organization across the various dimensions and total them. In this example (Figure 1.4), I have rated what I have observed to be a very common state of cultural or transformational maturity. Social, with a value of 35, is the best descriptor of the state of the culture for this organization.

Assessing this successful company, as with most organizations, legitimate power, or the respect for authority or responsible management level is the strongest power base observed. For the most part, people feel they belong to the organization and are part of the team, but they are also not necessarily out for a lot of recognition or desire to stand out. Professional development programs are not aggressively encouraged or provided, nor are people requesting them.

People are generally appreciated for their specific areas of expertise or competency and there is a healthy respect, especially among peers, for one another when it comes to looking for someone to lead a project or initiative. But projects tend to be initiated due to an operational need or problem rather than because of piloting or testing a new idea, technology, or approach.

Ranking on scale of 1–10; 10 being strongest influence

French & Raven/ Maslow	Referent Power	Expert Power	Legitimate Power	Reward Power	Coercive Power	Total
Self-Actualization	3	7	10	2	1	23
Self-Esteem	3	7	10	4	2	26
Social	7	7	10	7	4	35
Security	5	5	10	8	6	34
Survival	2	5	10	5	7	29

FIGURE 1.4   The 5 Ss of Transformational Maturity Matrix

Management routinely applauds success and there may be evidence of incentives in the form of bonuses or the suggestion box, but it's more archetypal than as a formal program or process. People are generally comfortable that if they work toward achievement of their objectives and reach acceptable levels of performance, they will continue in the company's employ, and they are generally satisfied that their overall compensation is competitive and fairly applied throughout the company. There does not seem to be much adversity or coercion (fear) in the company. The status quo is acceptable. There are a few go-getters and people seeking to move up the ladder, but initiatives tend to be evolutionary versus revolutionary or disruptive. Sound familiar?

When I interview and observe people in a company, I look for how open people are. Are they forthcoming with information? Is their body language relaxed? Are they listening and probing? Asking questions? Or are they closed, restrained? Is everything about cost? Is there a fear of saying the wrong thing or volunteering information? Is the organizational structure command and control? Is everything governed by policy and procedure? Do you see what I mean? I used to learn a lot about an organization, back in the day when I smoked, because I would head to the break room for a smoke with the troops. You can learn a lot from just listening to the break room chatter and throwing in a question or two.

For example, necessity is the mother of invention. We were on a project and having a hard time figuring out why line fill was down, but there was plenty of inventory and on-time ship was great. Through the interview process we couldn't figure out why line fill was so off the mark. I took a break for a smoke with the boys and nonchalantly asked them what they were working on. Innocently, I found out that they were staging trailers (prebuilding loads) to match with orders as they came in . . . kind of a "no-no" from at least an accounting perspective. When we dug a little deeper—well, as I mentioned, if you can't ship it, you can't bill it. More supply chain managers get fired for not shipping against orders and meeting revenue than anything.

Since, at this company, most orders came in right at the end of the period and often exceeded the loading capacity at the warehouse, this enterprising management team, noting that many customers ordered full truckloads of certain products and also had pretty regular order patterns, scheduled loads to be built according to the patterns and parked in the yard. As orders came in, they matched them to the closest "fitting the order" loads and had the carrier "drop (the empty) and hook (the load)" so that they could ship the highest number of orders to make revenue. Since they weren't "picked and loaded to order," they often didn't match orders perfectly, resulting in poor line fill metrics. A couple of my colleagues picked up smoking (at least on projects) after that. I may not smoke anymore, but I still hang in the break room from time to time when I am on a project.

LEVELS OF CULTURAL MATURITY

There is also a lot of truth to the old notion of "managing by wandering around," coined by Thomas Peters and Robert Waterman in their book *In Search of Excellence*, based on an interview with then president of HP, John Young,[7] in 1980.

Let's look at some of the characteristics and power bases influencing cultural maturity.

Level 1: Survival

At the most basic level of culture is the need to survive. It may not be at Maslow's physiological level but, clearly, people want to be employed. They don't want to risk losing their job. They want a fair wage and to come to work without fear that they will be fired. Unions came to be based on these needs in the workplace. There are surprisingly a lot of companies that are on the day-to-day survival level, especially small- to midsized companies and relatively new companies. Many companies are being acquired or merging and jobs will be lost. It's not unusual for managers to be threatening to employees. If they don't perform at a certain level, they will be replaced. Costs drive behaviors. Every activity is evaluated on cost and efficiency.

Transformation, let alone innovation, will be tough when people are more concerned about maintaining their job than anything else. Why?

At this level, people are governed largely by fear. They're worried about making mistakes, worried about their jobs, worried about what will happen. Power within this level is primarily coercive, according to French and Raven, based on the employee's (used intentionally instead of associate) perception that the supervisor (used intentionally instead of manager) has the ability to mediate punishments for the employee. If you don't do what you're told, you will be fired. There is generally not a lot of discussion.

Note that in business, for the most part, nearly all levels of cultural maturity leverage "legitimate" power, according to French and Raven, based on the associate's perception that the manager has a legitimate right to prescribe behavior to the employee. While organizational authority is generally accepted by most employees, at survival level or in a union environment, it can be adversarial. The structure is generally vertically command and control, policies are strictly adhered to, and there is little room for creative response to problems. The usual means or motivation to change at this level is a burning platform. Competitive, financial, and/or customer pressures place the organization at the crossroads.

We are going to have to initiate a program of transformation that will have to begin with moving people to the next level or we will go out of business.

Level 2: Security

People need to have some sense of security in their workplace in order for any type of real process improvement or transformation to begin let alone be sustained. They want to have a reasonably stable employment, competitive wages and benefits, and to be respected for their contributions. This level is a management commitment level. Management has to begin moving away from the fear of coercive power to the exertion of reward power, according to French and Raven, based on the associate's perception that the manager has the ability to mediate rewards and/or recognition for the associate. With this level of cultural transformation maturity, management evolves away from coercion to encouragement. You don't have to change the incentive system (though it may be helpful), but you have to mete out encouragement, congratulate or celebrate success, and in some way reward associates for exhibiting the behavior you want in your operations.

It's all about taking fear out of the equation and acknowledging positive outcomes. You want them to feel secure that if they perform their responsibilities well, they will be acknowledged; and, more importantly, employed. But it requires a commitment from management to initiate. Over the years I have seen everything from formal incentive systems and policies to pizza parties and coffee cards. But management must initiate the transformation.

Ever been to an industry conference or event? Sure you have. And at every event there are case-study presentations. It's an inexpensive way to gather information on industry challenges and practices. What does every case-study presentation have in common? C'mon, that's right; every case-study success begins and ends with "management commitment." Without management commitment, the speaker says, the project will not succeed. Well good news, bad news. First, the bad news. You probably have never heard any of those presenters tell you *how* to get management commitment. They just tell you how important it is. Now, the good news. As you progress through this book, you will learn how *you* can get management commitment. In fact, Chapter 7 is devoted to it. In the meantime, let me tell a story about why management commitment will eventually be necessary for transformation. You don't have to start with management commitment but you will have to win it at some point.

People's paradigms often get in the way of progress. Whether it is management or floor people, if people do not feel secure in their ability to embrace change and take a risk, the likelihood of any positive outcome is slim. For example, the editor in charge of business books for Prentice Hall in 1957 is supposed to have said this about the emergence of data processing: "I have traveled the length and breadth of this country and talked with the best people, and I can assure you that data processing is a fad that won't last out the year." There are lots of attributed "blunder" quotes about technology out there, like Tom Watson of IBM in 1943 saying there is "a world market for about five computers." Or, in March 1949, *Popular Mechanics* saying "Where a calculator on the ENIAC is equipped with 18,000 vacuum tubes and weighs 30 tons, computers in the future may have only 1,000 vacuum tubes and perhaps weigh $1^1/_2$ tons."

For me, though, the Prentice Hall editor's quote has always been significant in that it was published in 1957. What's the significance of 1957? (Not Sputnik, though that's significant, too.) Nineteen fifty-seven is the year that Jay Forrester, the MIT Sloan School of Management professor and pioneer in computer engineering, was completing his research on the impact of change to a multi-echelon supply chain, leading to his publication of "Industrial Dynamics: A Major Breakthrough for Decision Makers," in which he wrote:

> Management is on the verge of a major breakthrough in understanding how industrial company success depends on the interaction between the flows of information, materials, money, manpower, and capital equipment. The way these five flow systems interlock to amplify one another and to cause change

and fluctuation will form a basis for anticipating the effects of decisions, policies, organizational forms, and investment choices.

Reprinted by permission of *Harvard Business Review* (1958). Excerpt from "Industrial Dynamics—A Major Breakthrough for Decision Makers," by Jay Forrester, Volume 36, Issue 4.

Professor Forrester's work on the breakthrough in management decision making enabled by data processing led to the development of the field of system dynamics. One of his colleagues was Peter Senge. As I mentioned earlier, while I was at DEC, we were working both internally and externally on the development of a logistics architecture that would internally guide our logistics strategy and operations and externally enable us to lead our customers to achieve operations excellence. In addition, it would be the guide for us to recruit partners into our logistics (*supply chain* was not a prominent term at the time) solution ecosystem. As part of that project, we were working with Innovation Associates and Peter Senge.

So here it is, 1957, and we have the editor of Prentice Hall business books saying data processing is a fad and won't last the year, and Professor Forrester writing that it's about to cause a major breakthrough in business decision making. Two very different paradigms, and depending which way you go will determine which city you will live in . . . Leaders or Laggards. Well, it's at the first Systems Thinking in Action conference in Cambridge that I have the opportunity to meet Professor Forrester. Senge invited him to be the keynote speaker, and I listened with fascination as he spoke about the evolution of the field in the 30-some years that had passed since his *HBR* article was published.

Of course, when it came time for the Q&A, I had to ask the professor why, after some 30 years, so few business professors had embraced the principles of system dynamics and weren't teaching it as a methodology for understanding the dynamics of logistics and ultimately organizational behavior and decision making.

He responded quite quickly and simply said, "We just have to wait for people to die."

Holy cow! I was flabbergasted. We have to wait for people to die? Well, as you can imagine, we were in the big tent and follow-up questions were not permitted. But I had to meet the professor and ask him to explain. Fortunately, Senge invited me to a more private session later that day, and I was able to ask the professor for an explanation.

The professor explained to me that Max Planck, the pioneering German physicist, said in 1936, "An important innovation rarely makes its way by winning over its opponents. . . . What does happen is that its opponents gradually die." Professor Forrester went on to explain that academics all have their theories and hypotheses on business, and their prominence is dependent upon the adoption of their teaching over their peers' teachings. And academics have tenure, so there is little to lose by not adopting a peer's hypotheses . . . So, he said, "We just have to wait for the opposing academics to die and hope that my students take their place."

This was one of the biggest learning experiences I had in organizational behavior, not to mention academic politics. Unless you can develop a plan that addresses the culture of the "as is," identifies how the changes you are proposing in the "to be" will impact the perception of gain over pain to the "as is" culture, and put forth a plan to communicate the perceived gain, you may have to wait until people die before the transformation will be able to proceed!

Simply put, you have to be able to tell management and peers alike that they will be significantly better off with the transformation than they are without it. Senge calls it building a shared vision. Yes, it's tough. But it's not insurmountable and *you* don't have to die trying. You just need to convince the company it may die if it doesn't transform.

So, now you know why, in every case study, people will tell you the most important success factor in any transformation is executive sponsorship and commitment. If the "to be" factors are not in the paradigm of senior management, it's unlikely to be instituted into the culture of the company and unlikely to succeed. It is the single most critical barrier to change in an organization. In Chapter 7, we'll look in detail at just how we can communicate that to senior management as a component of their paradigm. Why? Because in this millennium, we just can't wait for management to die. Until they buy in, however, if people are not secure in their ability to adopt the changes that the transformation will bring, they are unlikely to mature to the next level.

Level 3: Social

As we develop our transformation strategy, we will have to begin instituting changes to the culture to promote more of a team strategy (i.e., transforming from the notion of "supervisors and employees" to "managers and associates" and self-managed work teams). It isn't easy. There may be years of conditioning to the old culture to overcome but, until people become comfortable with speaking to one another, opening up to the process, and looking for support, transformation is just too big a bite to swallow. It's really hard work to make these changes, especially within the context of operations that have been around for a while.

Take, for example, the case of Procter & Gamble's implementation of high-performance work systems (HPWS) at their manufacturing plants worldwide. I will be referring to experiences I have had with Procter and Gamble (P&G) people (P&Gers) over the years, as P&G is probably one of, if not the most, transformational and innovative companies I have ever observed. They are always moving their organization forward with an aggressive pursuit of excellence and competition.

Okay, that said, let's look at the case. It was at the second Systems Thinking in Action conference held at the Mount Washington Hotel, Bretton Woods, New Hampshire, hosted by Pegasus Communications. One of the invited speakers was Charlie Eberle, retired former head of P&G worldwide manufacturing, conducting a session on the implementation of HPWS at their facilities worldwide. Eberle spent about 45 minutes detailing their journey and timeline for the implementation.

At the end of the presentation, I added up the timeline and asked a simple question: "Charlie, excuse me for asking, but you've just detailed the superior performance gains that you made at each facility that you implemented HPWS at, yet, when I look at the timeline, why did it take 15 years to implement at all of P&G's plants worldwide?"

Eberle responded almost immediately, "Because it took me 15 years to be promoted to vice president of worldwide manufacturing!" and, he added, "Quite frankly, when I got to my office in Cincinnati, overlooking the river, I didn't want to do it either."

Eberle went on to explain that implementing HPWS was not that easy. It was transformational and required a different cultural mind-set (paradigm) than existed at most P&G plants. HPWS empowered people and changed the supervisory relationship. Employees became "associates" or "technicians" and participated in self-managed work teams with interchangeable roles that were responsible for improving the processes, operational decision making, and so on.

So while it was great for new P&G facilities, "greenfield implementations," none of the preceding VPs of worldwide manufacturing wanted to endure the pain of retrofitting the existing plants. While the performance and productivity of the HPWS plants was far superior to the existing plants, the existing plants were already performing at a significant advantage over competitive benchmarks. The bottom line was that the gain did not exceed the pain of worldwide implementation.

Eberle said he at first didn't want to do it either. He said he took a fishing trip with Peter Senge, and together they decided that "it was the right thing to do." As he was promoted into the position, he embarked on the journey of worldwide implementation. And, as the last facility was finally converted, he retired. It was a great presentation and one that would be formative in my thinking and communicating both the challenge and the opportunity of implementing a change within an organization. If the organization cannot get beyond a culture of survival or security and into at least professional "social" interaction, transformation will be difficult at best.

 ## BUILDING A CASE FOR CHANGE

Generally, the most practical method of engaging people at this level is introducing process mapping, modeling, and other visualization techniques to the organization. It is the quickest way to begin defining what the "as is" business environment and processes are. In Chapter 4, we'll introduce in more depth the various mapping techniques and how to bring the organization into line and engage it. For now, why is process mapping so important?

Visualization techniques are great ways to direct people to gather information and data about their workplace in a nonthreatening manner. We map out the steps of the processes and gather data about the behavior and performance of those processes. We keep it objective and simply map out the way activities are organized and performed to achieve our objectives.

Process mapping is also a great way to communicate process behavior. People respond to graphical depictions. Most modeling techniques have "levels of detail" so that processes can be communicated at a very high level to senior management and at a very detailed level for operational execution. Most important, people can sit back and observe how activities contribute to the success of the operation or may inhibit or constrain the operation.

The most beneficial outcome of process mapping is that it takes the people out of the process. It objectifies the process. It's not the people who are good or bad; it's the process. Once you have people working together as a team, defining processes, activities, metrics, and so forth and gathering the data to support their maps, you have enabled more interaction and created a "social" culture conducive to analysis and change. The people don't need fixing; the process needs fixing. At this point, the need for improvement or change almost becomes self-evident and companies begin to exhibit the evolution to the next level of cultural maturity—the self-esteem level.

Level 4: Self-Esteem

As process improvements begin to take hold, successes occur and, generally, as I alluded to earlier, those successes should be celebrated and/or rewarded. For many companies, it doesn't have to be a heavy investment or formal incentive compensation plan. It can take the form of a team pizza party or luncheon or even passing out coffee cards. As associates observe the successes and recognition that goes with it, they also want to become involved. They begin seeking means to experience higher levels of self-esteem and personal worth. They also begin to acknowledge the value of their colleagues' contributions and teamwork. Expert and Referent power bases become more the norm than even Legitimate power. People become more team-oriented and self-managed. Coercive power is almost nonexistent, while Reward power is more a result than a lever.

While it is important to implement professional development programs early in a transformational initiative, it is within the maturity of the organization from social to self-esteem that it is most critical. And it is one of the key levers to maturing the organization to self-actualization. A professional development program with key courses, internal or external, that supports the company's transformation gets people on the same page, talking the same language, and builds relationships. Team learning, as Senge refers to it, becomes routine.

Level 5: Self-Actualization

This is the highest level of transformational culture maturity, and there are very few organizations that exhibit consistent self-awareness and personal and professional growth behaviors within their culture. At this level, the people in the organization, of course, recognize the formal structure and legitimate assignments of responsibility and management.

Legitimate power, however, is exerted more as a guide than a mandate and people feel empowered to do the right things, constantly looking for ways to improve themselves and the organization. Change is an opportunity to be exploited. People are re-inventors of the status quo and most interested in reaching their full potential. Leaders emerge and are rewarded with recognition. Self-esteem within the organization can be seen everywhere.

When you meet people from organizations at this level, you almost feel they are arrogant, but they're not. They're competitors and winners and self-aware and self-confident. They are also probably from top universities, were top in their classes, leaders in academics, and often in sports and extracurricular activities. Why? Because companies at this stage of maturity inhabit Leader City, they have the funding to generally build from within and "restock" by recruiting the top talent in the world. They are market leaders, highly recognized in their industries, and they continuously invest in their people, processes, and technology. The best and the brightest *want* to work for them. They take risks and look to the future relentlessly pursuing every innovation they can. They are, in Senge's terms, a "learning organization." Their greatest fear is being left behind, losing their leadership position, being taken by surprise. This is the learning culture that is the objective of transformation and it is why transformation is considered a journey . . . There is no end and the journey is as long as the time that has passed since you started.

■ PARADIGMS CAN ENCOURAGE OR CONSTRAIN INNOVATION

When I was at DEC and began working with Peter Senge and Innovation Associates, I enrolled in one of their workshop programs, Leadership & Mastery, that I think became part of the inspiration for Senge's book. The course was taught by Senge and was held in the executive education center at Babson College. I'll refer to some of the experiences and learnings from this program throughout the book; however, it was during the program that I learned about P&G's transformation and how it was being implemented, and subsequently this was reinforced in my conversations with Charlie Eberle at Bretton Woods and with other P&Gers whom I met at industry committee meetings and events throughout the years.

As with most workshops, we began by introducing ourselves, our companies, and our roles. There were about 15 people, give or take, in the class. As we went around the room, there were probably 8 to 10 of the attendees who came from P&G. As I learned from the conversations among classmates, John G. Smale, P&G's CEO at the time, pretty much mandated that every P&G manager go through the Leadership & Mastery program. The reason, I was told, was that Smale, as I later learned, was one of those "management commitment" executives who not only embraced change but was an agent of change. Upon his passing, in November 2011, the memorials, testimonials, and obituaries all heralded him as the leader of P&G's global expansion and transformation. In the company memoriam to John Smale it is noted that Ed Artzt, Smale's successor as CEO, observed, "The one thing that distinguishes John's career as the leader of our company has been his remarkable record as an agent for change."

In speaking with my workshop colleagues and later with others, Smale wanted the company to create a vision for itself that would take it to market leadership, and he needed its people to be aligned and share in that vision and execute as a team to achieve it. I believe it was Smale who first led P&G on its transformational journey to self-actualization; and, it's been on the journey for more than 30 years, as it is a journey that knows no end. To get everyone on the same page, to get everyone working together, Smale leveraged professional training programs to move P&G's social maturity level to self-esteem and eventually to self-actualization. Every manager went through Leadership & Mastery and learned the principles of *The Fifth Discipline: The Art and Practice of the Learning Organization.*[8]

They learned systems thinking, personal mastery, and how to experience self-esteem; they learned to create a vision and how to build shared vision. More important, they were speaking the same language, engaging in team learning, and joining the journey. John

Smale's paradigm and commitment led to P&G's emergence as a market leader and best practices leader that can be a model for any company seeking a basis for transformation.

On the other hand, as we have seen from earlier blunder quotes, senior management paradigms can impede the growth or success of a company. Before joining DEC, I spent about 10 years with Burroughs Corporation, which merged with Sperry Corporation and became UNISYS. The leadership of the company was in the process of taking two $6 billion companies and turning them into a $4 billion company. My mentor at UNISYS had recently joined DEC, which was in the midst of a major transformation both internally and externally.

DEC's rapid growth was largely the result of founder Ken Olsen's breakthrough engineering leading to the introduction of the mini-computer, initially for process control, and later leveraging network technology for distributed computing. We were successfully selling and deploying our technology as departmental solutions with partners providing industry-specific applications, surrounding the mainframe's "glass house" and competing quite well against IBM and the mainframe BUNCH (Burroughs, Univac, NCR, Control Data, and Honeywell). In the field and in marketing, we were actually saying "the network is the system."

To make a long story short, field leadership's five-year transformation strategy of deploying distributed computing as industry solutions did not fit into Ken Olsen's paradigm. Olsen's attributed all-time best technology blunder quote in 1977 was "There is no reason for any individual to have a computer in their home." How many computers do you have in your home? More and more homes have more computers than people.

His paradigm (obsession) was to beat IBM by replacing the glass house, not surrounding and unplugging it. Being a hardware guy, he did build a computer powerful enough to replace the IBM mainframes. But he underestimated the software part and, as it was not plug compatible, most companies wouldn't pay the cost of converting all of their applications just to get a comparable box. The investment in R&D to develop it and production costs of the initial run drained DEC's cash reserves and led to the decline of the company and its subsequent purchase by Compaq, ironically one of the early successes in the personal computer market. Compaq, of course, was bought by Hewlett-Packard, DEC's West Coast counterpart and fiercest competitor at the time. In the ultimate irony, Olsen's Way became the HP Way.

The major learning is that we cannot afford to wait for old ways to die. We have to constantly be monitoring and moving our company's culture forward toward market goals, not personal paradigms. The paradigm has to be driven by market and process innovation encouraged through transformation to self-actualization.

At the end of the day, *change is inevitable; growth is optional.* Supply chain transformation is not an option. If you want to live in Leader City, it will be, as P&G has learned, a continuous journey, which from my early conversation with Charlie Eberle, leaders such as P&G embrace and institutionalize into their culture. It has no end. The fall from the top can occur at any time and, if you're not constantly scanning the horizon for change, it can take you by surprise.

The point of all of this is that as Nobel Prize and Oscar winner George Bernard Shaw said, "Progress is impossible without change; and those who cannot change their minds cannot change anything." If a transformation is to be successful, it will be as much a cultural change project as it is a process improvement project and you will have to plan accordingly. It's why so many pundits speak of it as a journey. On the other hand, as P&G has demonstrated over the years, once the journey begins, it has no end. It's like planting an orchard. It takes time, effort, and investment to plant and cultivate the trees, but they will bear fruit for many, many years.

My initial experiences at DEC and with P&G led me to develop the techniques and tools for transformation that I later honed in a project at Colgate-Palmolive, working for supply chain technology providers and participating in various industry transformational initiatives such as Efficient Consumer Response (ECR) and Collaborative Planning, Forecasting, and Replenishment (CPFR®) as well as some forays into the DAMA project (Demand Activated Manufacturing Architecture) in apparel. Working as an industry analyst and being a member of the team that developed the SCOR® model and founded the Supply Chain Council, I have also had the opportunity to visit and live in both cities, Leaders and Laggards, and learn from both. Let's begin our journey with a look at the business.

 NOTES

1. Senge, Peter. *The Fifth Discipline: The Art and Practice of the Learning Organization*, Currency Doubleday, 1990.
2. Friedman, Thomas. *The World Is Flat*, Farrar, Straus, and Giroux, 2005.
3. Rogers, Everett. *The Diffusion of Innovations*, Simon and Schuster, 1962.
4. Barker, Joel Arthur. *Future Edge*, William Morrow, 1992.
5. Maslow, Abraham, "A Theory of Human Motivation," *Psychological Review*, 1943, vol. 50, no. 4, pp. 370–396.
6. Adapted from French, J. P. R. Jr., and Raven, B. "The Bases of Social Power," in D. Cartwright and A. Zander (eds.), *Group Dynamics*, pp. 607–623, Harper and Row, 1960.
7. Peters, Thomas J., and Robert H. Waterman, Jr. *In Search of Excellence: Lessons from America's Best-Run Companies*, HarperCollins, 1982.
8. Senge, Peter. *The Fifth Discipline: The Art and Practice of The Learning Organization*, Currency Doubleday, 1990.

CHAPTER TWO

Putting the Business in Perspective

B
ACK IN 1969, THE United States sent a man to the moon. Think about the computational power required to perform all of the calculations to consider all of the variables and unexpected changes necessary to execute that feat. Ten years later, virtually any business could be run with more computational power than NASA had had available to them. Ten years after that, more computational power was available on the desktop. Ten years after that, it was mobile and on our laptop. Today, we have more computational power, individually, in our pocket. And, along with the computational power, that pocket computer has global communications, location-based services, audio and video, Internet access, and commercial telecasts. Don't be surprised if we have simultaneous translation capabilities in those smartphones, thus eliminating language barriers, within the next ten years . . . maybe sooner. After all, you can get Web pages translated instantaneously; why not voice? If you can imagine it, it can happen.

During that same period of time, we have experienced many new industry initiatives and transformational strategies to leverage these gains in technology, communications, and information management. Industry initiatives, such as Quick Response (QR) in the apparel industry, Efficient Consumer Response (ECR) in the grocery/consumer packaged goods industry, the Automotive Industry Action Group (AIAG) in the automotive manufacturing industry, have all promised billions in cost savings in each of the respective industries. Transformation strategies such as Total Quality Management (TQM), just in time (JIT), continuous flow manufacturing (CFM), High Performance Work Systems (HPWS), Lean, Six Sigma, the Supply Chain Operations Reference (SCOR®) model, and others have all promised to enable companies to achieve operations excellence; reduce inventory, working capital, and costs; increase customer service, revenue, and profitability; and to sustain those results over time.

And lest we forget, remember Michael Hammer's mantra "Don't automate, obliterate," which resulted in the reengineering movement of companies investing millions to improve their business. Of course, I always like to talk about the popular definition of reengineering by holding up a glass partially filled with water. Optimists would say it is half full. Pessimists would say it is half empty. A reengineering team would say, "It has too much glass." That was followed by millions more invested in ERP (Enterprise Resource Planning) systems and even millions more to implement them (not to mention how many of those ERP modules are unimplementable "shelfware"). By the way, I am writing this to prove that ECR did not stand for "every consultant's retirement." That said, whether you were in Leader City or Laggard City, you paid a price for change regardless of how long or how hard you resisted it.

Yet, according to the State of the Logistics Report published by the Council of Supply Chain Management Professionals (CSCMP), inventories and logistics costs in the United States over the past 20 years were annually at all-time highs . . . until a recession took them down, and they are now back on their way up. More than a trillion dollars annually are consumed in inventory and logistics costs. Are we reducing supply chain inventories and costs or just moving them around?

Okay, so I like to speak about paradigms and paradigm shifts, culture, trends, and change. I've been doing it for 30+ years and companies still resist change. If transforming the business were easy, everyone would do it. What's different now? Fact is, winners win, competitors compete, and the winners, like P&G, continuously take risks, learn from inside and outside their organization, focus relentlessly on their customers and the business created by their customers, and innovate. They are continuously looking ahead and adapting their business to meet the opportunity the future presents to them. The laggards lag behind and the lucky ones survive on the chunks of the market the leaders leave behind. The not so lucky ones fade away. You can't avoid change. *Now is the time for you to step up.* Laggards work just as hard as leaders. Why work to lag behind, when you can be working to lead? As I said, transformation is a journey, continuous with no end.

The *Austin American Statesman* published an article entitled "New J.C. Penney CEO's Challenge: Bring Life Back to an Iconic Brand" on the new CEO of J.C. Penney coming on board from Apple.[1] In it, Ron Johnson speaks to his 15-year journey of transformation at Target and his 10-year journey at Apple. He said that J.C. Penney's "No. 1 competitor is ourselves and our way of thinking, which is informed by decades of experience. It's not another store; it's not another format like the Internet. Our competition is ourselves and our best friend is our imagination." Whether he will be granted the time to transform J.C. Penney or not; whether he will succeed or not remains to be seen. The point is that he is placing J.C. Penney on its journey. It's better to be on the journey to Leader City than lagging behind waiting for the end. Later in the article, he speaks to the fact that the change comes about "month to month" and "that the journey is the reward."

It's time to step back and think about a journey. When was the last time you took a business trip? Did you think about getting in an accident on the way to the airport? Did you check the airlines' safety record before booking? Did you request full disclosure on the training and background of all of the crew before boarding? Did you agonize the night before about whether this trip was really worth the investment? My guess is that you didn't. Yet most people are afraid to embark on, let alone take, the journey to operations excellence. Well, my friend, I am here to tell you that you don't have to fear the journey. *It's like the Three Stooges sketch "Niagara Falls," slowly I turned, one step at a time, step by step, inch by inch.* How do you eat an elephant?

If you put the business into perspective . . . if you set your vision . . . if you take it one step at a time, the transformation journey to operations excellence doesn't have to be painful and it will be its own reward. It doesn't have to be undertaken all at once. *It just has to be done.* It can be done from the bottom up or the top down; it's your choice. You can start with a little project and a little success. People will see the success, see that it's not that painful, and see the reward. You can start regardless of your level of transformational culture maturity. In fact, a little success will breed more success, and more people will want to join in. The culture will begin to mature and self-esteem will creep in. It just has to happen because *change is happening all around you and your company.* Hundreds, if not thousands, of companies have both started up and fallen down in light of the changes that occur over time. It's like the Framm oil filter guy: "You can pay me now, or you can pay me later."

The difference is that the early adopters, the companies that have adopted transformation as business as usual and are now at the fourth or fifth level of maturity, made the *commitment* to excellence early, and their change, their transformation, is being paid for by the benefits of leadership. They are not experiencing the pain of change—they are experiencing the rewards of change, of the journey they are on. And the reward pays for the cost of continuing the journey. So why wait? Just pack your bags and let's get this party started. *Today is the first day of your journey to Leader City.*

 ## DEFINING AND UNDERSTANDING BUSINESS OBJECTIVES

Theodore Levitt in his book *The Marketing Imagination* (Expanded Edition), said, "The purpose of business is to create and keep a customer. To do that you have to produce goods and services that people want and value at prices and under conditions that are reasonably attractive relative to those offered by others to a proportion of customers large enough to make those prices and conditions possible."[2] I have always felt that supply chain is as much marketing as any function in the business. In fact, over the years, the professors at the universities I most frequently worked with were in the marketing department of the business school. Of course, my subject-level experience, while very cross-functional and interdisciplinary, evolved more from logistics than other fields. But it has only been since "supply chain" became popular that every operations-oriented academic discipline (and professional association) now claims to be supply chain.

What Levitt and others have failed to expand on is that supply chain is more than just producing the goods and services. It's the capability to deliver the products and services to the delight of the customer that competitively differentiates companies in the market. After all, there are 4Ps in marketing: product, price, promotion, and place.

(Of course, in global marketing, as a former DuPont executive once told me, you have to add two more Ps, power and politics—subjects for another book.) Product is the procurement and production functions, and place is the distribution function of the supply chain. The challenge comes in managing the 4Ps within the context of integrating with the participants in the marketing mix, the 4Cs: company, channels, customers/consumers, and competitors (see Figure 2.1).

As with any performance management initiative, it is critical that you have an understanding of your company's business objectives and strategy. Supply chain management is all about trade-offs. Making the right trade-off decision will be driven by your business objectives.

I always used to say that the reason I didn't shop at Wal-Mart was because I could afford not to. At Wal-Mart, you pull into the parking lot, drive up and down the property looking for a place to park, then you walk half a mile, and, as you are about to scream as you enter the door, the greeter smiles just enough to calm you down. Actually, the greeter is there to screen you. But that's another story.

The greeter at Neiman Marcus, on the other hand, is the valet to park your car. It's all about trade-offs. If you're in supply chain at Wal-Mart, your strategy and decisions will be very different than if you're in supply chain at Neiman Marcus. Depending on the products, services, and economics of your business, you will make very different procurement, production, distribution, and financial decisions. You probably aren't going to start shipping sugar by air but that might make sense for time-sensitive, high-value electronics or pharmaceutical products.

The Limited, back in the day, used to ship products from Asia by ocean carrier. Then their merchandising and logistics folks did an analysis of time on water, margin lost from fashion cycle times, and markdowns. The trade-off decision was to incur a higher air transportation cost to reduce shipping lead time to offset the margin and opportunity cost of the fickleness of fashion life cycles. It paid off quickly. Think about what this also did for the air carrier's and ocean carrier's business. More on this in Chapter 3.

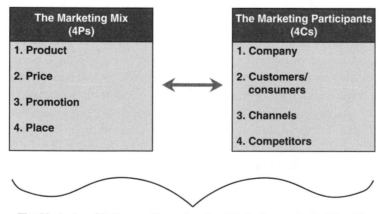

The Marketing Challenge: Managing the 4Ps in the context of the 4Cs

FIGURE 2.1 The Marketing Mix

Your transformation strategy will be based on aligning the people, processes, and technology in your supply chain to the business objectives of the company. From a supply chain perspective, you will have to consider and measure the following five attributes:

1. Reliability: how well you are performing to meet the customers' needs.
2. Responsiveness: your lead times and capabilities to meet changes.
3. Flexibility: how rapidly you can scale up or down globally based on demand and/or product changes.
4. Costs: how well you are operating within your margin goals.
5. Assets: how well you are generating the return on invested capital (ROIC) from operating your supply chain.

The ultimate goal of any transformational strategy is to improve the performance of the business, creating shareholder value (see Figure 2.2). We'll explore the financial details more in Chapter 7 . . . don't skip ahead.

The markets your company serves, the channels you operate in, your customers' expectations, and how you choose to differentiate your company from your competitors will drive your vision of where you want your operations to be in the next year to five years and what the trade-offs will be. In subsequent chapters, I will provide more insight and tools to develop supply chain strategy; however, understanding your business and the objectives of the company is the foundation for setting the vision and strategy.

Depending on your role in the company, you may be a senior manager or have access to them and will sit at the table to participate in the strategic planning process of your company. If not, your immediate management, the HR department, and the

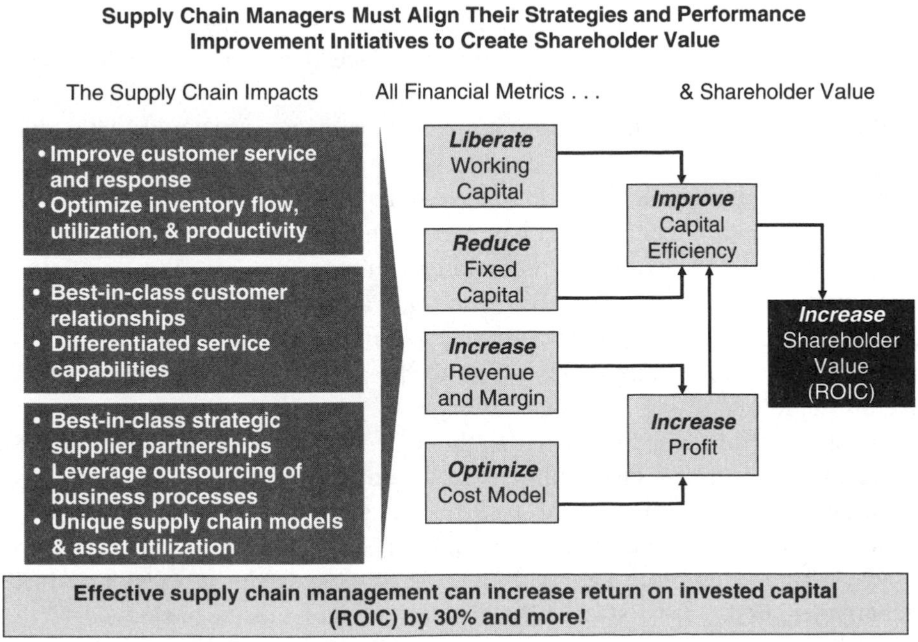

Supply Chain Managers Must Align Their Strategies and Performance Improvement Initiatives to Create Shareholder Value

FIGURE 2.2 The Ultimate Goal of Transformation

company website can provide valuable information on the company's business objectives, strategy, markets, customers, and partners.

DEFINING THE BUSINESS WITHIN THE CONTEXT OF THE MARKET

While every industry will have its own idiosyncrasies, it will be important to gather information on industry trends and the economy you are operating in. Is the company planning any new product introductions or developments? Based on the key attributes of your supply chain, what metrics will be most critical to supporting the company's objectives both in operations and financially? What channels do you operate in? Business to business, business to consumer, electronic or physical, bricks and mortar, company-owned or outsourced, or all of the above?

Where is the company headed? Are acquisitions or mergers in the strategic plan? Are there any major impediments or constraints that may change the business in the foreseeable future? The introduction of firearms eliminated an entire class of labor, swordsmen, and the business of producing swords at scale. The introduction of electronic word processing and the personal computer virtually eliminated typing pools, secretaries, and many of the office products to support them (e.g., typewriters that supported secretarial work). Lexmark is the transformation of the IBM typewriter business.

Regardless of your position in the company, you can obtain sufficient knowledge of the business objectives to guide your transformation initiative. And regardless of your position, having the ability to communicate your ideas within the context of meeting the business objectives is critical to your ability to secure management and peer buy-in to the initiative, regardless of the step you are on in your journey. So let's look at a technique that I have used for years in setting the stage for improvement initiatives and transformation.

While at DEC, I had the opportunity to meet with and work a bit with Charles Savage, author of an amazing book, *5th Generation Management.*[3] He challenged command and control structures and suggested that management in the future would hinge on self-empowerment and human networking. The key lesson for me from the book and what I began using in presentations and projects was that regardless of management style, ultimately, it's the people and knowledge capital of the company that will make up the culture and the level of maturity. You have to clearly understand where you are as an organization to create the process to achieve the vision that you have for the future.

So after several years, I also came to the understanding that trying to change, at least head on, a company's leadership management style was not a particularly good job continuance or project-winning strategy. So, I stopped referring to *5th Generation Management* and adapted one of his concepts to my own thinking. I called this adapted process "visioneering" (see Figure 2.3).[4] Visioneering is the process by which a company defines its "as-is" state of the business, understands its business objectives, and applies that understanding as the basis to develop its vision, not necessarily in that order.

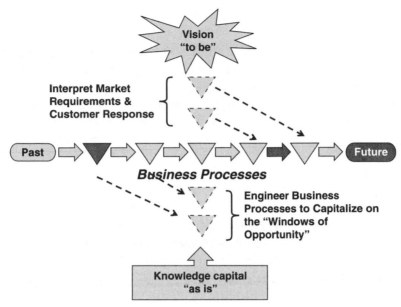

FIGURE 2.3 Visioneering
Adapted from Charles Savage, *5th Generation Management.*

As the gap between the vision and what Senge refers to as "current reality" is established, the company can empower its people to engineer its processes to close the gap and move closer to the vision. Over time the vision may change as the environment changes, but as the organization and culture mature to self-actualization, or as Senge calls it, a learning organization, the company will adapt and develop its response to the change profitably.

More important, it embraces change routinely and as an opportunity. In Chapter 4, I will explore business process management in more detail. But for me, visioneering can work with and accommodate virtually any management style or improvement methodology. And it can also be independent of what level of cultural maturity a company is at. It's a great way to step onto your journey. Let me take you through an easy-to-understand example and some stories.

 ## DEVELOPING YOUR VISION

You can use Visioneering to put any business into perspective, and it can be used at any level, both personally and professionally. For example, during the Leadership & Mastery course, Peter Senge had all of us sit quietly and think of what we would like to be in the next three to five years. What was our vision of where we wanted to be and what we would be doing? After several minutes had passed, he had us share our visions with the person sitting next to us. And then he did something that will always stick in my mind.

He said, "Okay, you've created a vision of where you want to be in five years. Why aren't you already there?"

We then spent the next time period thinking about "personal mastery" and the obstacles, or rocks in the road, on our journey to achieve our vision. If we could create a vision of where we want to go, why couldn't we also be able to articulate the path to get there? And if we could articulate the path, we should already be on the journey to get there, if that's where we want to be. Of course, none of us really thought of it as a journey to transform ourselves, and it impacted everyone in the class significantly.

Sure, we had goals and plans, but we had not really put forth a vision of our future state, let alone mapped a journey to continuously adapt and achieve. If we want to improve, we have to start the journey to improvement. It won't happen by itself. Think about that for a little while, and I hope it changes your perspective the way it did mine. Think about the group of P&Gers and other managers in the class. What would their attitude toward change and transformation be when they returned to work? *Time to start the journey? What are you waiting for?*

That little exercise led me to a trademark little gimmick that for the past 20 years I have been using in virtually every presentation that I give on supply chain management. It will serve well as an example of Visioneering that you can adapt to your purposes.

I ask the audience, "What do you think the perfect supply chain system is? I don't know about you; but I have been speaking for about 30 minutes now . . . and it's late in the afternoon . . . and, well . . . I could really go for an ice . . . cold . . . Bud! Beam me a Bud, Scotty!"

That's right; the perfect supply chain system, or business operating system, for that matter, would be that at the precise moment that a customer recognized the need for your product, in this case a beer, you could just beam it to them. Upon receipt of the product, the funds in payment would be beamed into your account. *Voilà!* The transaction is complete. It would be as near to a zero-latency business, supply chain, or whatever that you could design.

Impossible, you say? Well, as I said, I have been telling this story for many years, and you can imagine that people have some fun with it once in a while (I'll be relating more of those experiences later in other chapters). At one point, though, my PR firm in the United Kingdom thought it so clever that they found a book by a professor Lawrence M. Krauss, *The Physics of Star Trek*.[5]

Well, the book will tell you two things. The first is that the concept of teleportation is not impossible. In fact, in my own research, I found a *Scientific American* article that spoke about molecular disassembly and reassembly. I also read an article about an experiment with quantum teleportation that had been successfully completed at IBM. In both cases, the experiments were with very simple, basic matter, nothing as complex as a product or person.

Krauss explained that while teleportation is not impossible, it is improbable. The reason is that for even the simplest thing to be teleported, it would take a significant multiplier of the energy of the sun to accomplish it. So, until we get an alternative source of energy several times greater than the sun . . . don't start architecting the "beam me a Bud" supply chain just yet. Oh, and the second lesson from the book? Professors have way too much time on their hands.

Of course, the problem is that for the foreseeable future, we can't beam products to customers. While we like to think of the supply chain as a pipeline with product flowing smoothly and uninterrupted from source to consumption (and now disposal), the reality is that it isn't a pipeline as illustrated in Figure 2.4.

Before we discuss the challenge, though, let me ask you to think about something for a moment. Do you have running water in your house? Can you go to the tap and get a glass of water? Why can't it be beer? Wouldn't you like to be able to draw a beer anytime, right in your own house? Why isn't there a beer utility company?

Anyway, Visioneering can open up some real possibilities for you and your team to brainstorm the future of your operations. You can have some fun with it, especially if you have some pizza beamed in with the beer. So, we can't beam beer to the consumer, but let's look at what we can do in the meantime.

In reality, we have lines of fracture in our product flow. These lines of fracture are caused by physical boundaries between geographic locations or by organizational boundaries between customers and channel partners. In addition, we have to manage a variety of activities associated with moving the product through the supply chain. We have to procure materials, manage the materials through production, and then distribute them physically using warehousing and transportation. Of course, all of these decoupling points in product flow introduce uncertainty in the demand caused by the intersection of what I plan or forecast my customer demand to be and what the actual customer order turns out to be. Usually this requires a buffer of lead time, capacity, or inventory to ensure that we can meet the business's customer service objectives because, guess what? The forecast or plan is always wrong! We'll discuss this in more detail in Chapter 5. But wouldn't it be wonderful if customers behaved the way we plan?

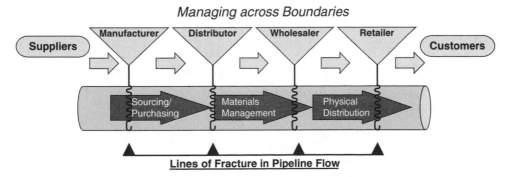

FIGURE 2.4 The Challenge: Managing a Disconnected Chain

Here's another little anecdote from my speaking about beaming beer. I was speaking at AMR Research's Annual Executive Conference in Boston back in the early 1990s. While I was on my way up to the stage, I saw one of our clients from Miller Brewing in the audience. When it came time in my presentation for the beaming analogy, I decided to "beam me a Miller Lite!" Afterward, he came up to me and expressed dismay that he didn't know I was going to use Miller Lite as the example. If he had known, he would have planned to have a bottle of Miller Lite in his bag to stick in my hand . . . those darn customers!

So, while you can create this vision of the perfect market response system to beam beer to consumers, there may be some rocks in the road that will prevent you from implementation. The Visioneering process lets you define your "current reality" and then formulate a vision of where you would like to be. Why not start with a vision of the perfect state? Let's try to engineer our business to approximate the vision of beaming beer to our customers.

As we begin to engineer our business to achieve the vision, lo and behold, there is an immediate obstacle in the journey . . . a big rock called the energy of the sun. As you develop your vision, you will identify rocks in the road . . . some big, some little. We are probably not going to place a big bet (investment) on developing an alternative source of energy to the sun but we can bet that we can load the beer onto to a vehicle and deliver it to the consumer.

But there is another rock in that journey . . . the cost of individually delivering beers to the consumer exceeds our profit goals. Another big rock (something, by the way, a lot of dot-com investors didn't consider deeply enough . . . the big rock that burst the bubble on a lot of Internet home-delivery businesses). I don't think building a transportation network and fleet big enough to deliver beer direct to the consumer is a good plan for us. The number-one issue in transportation is driver shortages, resulting in the number-two issue, driver quality. While customers may not be uncomfortable with who shows up at their warehouse, they will be much more concerned with who shows up at their home.

We may also want to consider the whole regulatory and liability rock. Maybe we should rethink this scenario?

Note: This example is for the retail beer market that we are playing in. Given different markets, products, and pricing/margin strategies, we might want to design an outsourced supply chain using third-party service providers (3PLs) such as UPS or FedEx to design a home delivery model. With Visioneering you can adapt your thought processes to many different scenarios. Think of the number of different business models Amazon went through, and they are still adapting to the challenges of physically delivering based on an electronic selling format. The key is that with each scenario, we think it out and identify the rocks and the bets we want to make to overcome the obstacle or constraint the rock poses. In supply chain, the devil is always in the details.

What if we deliver beer to a store owned by a retailer that will hold the beer until the consumer wants to come purchase it when they want it, and we will sell it to the retailer at a price that will enable a profit to be made for holding the beer for us and still be within our margin objectives? Of course, this is all dependent on whether our marketing group is developing promotional initiatives to communicate the availability of our beer to the consumer. Think about the poor Bud man in the audience when I used the Miller Lite example instead of Bud. We'll explore this little assumption in more detail in Chapter 5 as well. For now, we should be okay with a direct store delivery model, right?

Oops, if every company that makes beer delivers to the store, there will be no room in the parking lot for the consumers and that will make the retailer unhappy. Another big rock (now you know why most "direct store delivery" strategies to eliminate the middleman were not always successful. Direct store delivery (DSD) is largely dependent on the retailer's strategy, not the manufacturer's. (Investors should take operations courses!) And, while it is not as big a rock, we would still have to have a pretty good-sized network and fleet. Even working with 3PLs can pose some capacity/cost/margin issues for us with the DSD scenario.

Perhaps we could leverage a network of beer distributors to consolidate beers from many different sources to make a single delivery each week to the store, so that the store will be in stock and the retailer will be happy. We can adjust the price so that the distributor will also make a profit for providing us with the services we need. And we can do so while still maintaining our margin objectives. This is shaping up to be a feasible plan to support our vision. Are you coming to understand the visioneering process? Start with a concept or vision and decompose the steps to execute the vision to determine the feasibility and process of what you are proposing.

ADDING SWOT ANALYSIS PUTS THE BUSINESS IN PERSPECTIVE

As we go through the exercise of determining what the "as is" engineering needs to be to close the gap to become what "to be" state, we can collect and document what the strengths, weaknesses, opportunities, and threats (SWOT analysis) to the vision are and will be (see Figure 2.5). By creating a SWOT matrix while we go through the vision-eering process, we will identify what our risks to the scenario may be and assess what the competition's likely response will be. Don't forget, competition is a participant in our mix. For example, how does our performance measure up across the five attributes of our supply chain? How strong are we as a company in this market relative to the competition? How strong are our channel partners and our overall supply network? What are our strengths in price, product, and packaging? Do we have the promotional strength to compel customers? Or will we have to leverage other capabilities, such as price or packaging?

As we review our SWOT results, we can assess the overall merits of our business and strategy within the context of the market and existing competition. This will begin to formulate the baseline for the more detailed market analysis we'll examine in Chapter 3. We can list our weaknesses, where we need improvements, and what the rocks are that we will have to overcome. We can then determine what we need to do to improve, what will be the costs to overcome the barriers posed by the rocks, and where we want to place our bets (investments) and priorities. We have to start challenging any assumptions and asking what if, how much, and what's the risk?

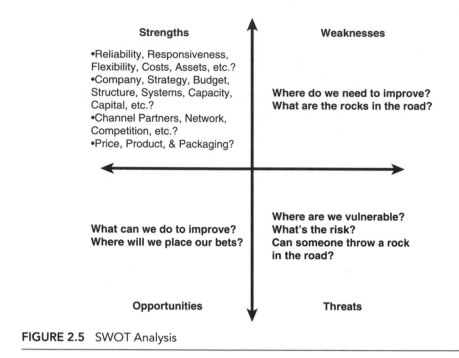

Strengths

•Reliability, Responsiveness,
Flexibility, Costs, Assets, etc.?
•Company, Strategy, Budget,
Structure, Systems, Capacity,
Capital, etc.?
•Channel Partners, Network,
Competition, etc.?
•Price, Product, & Packaging?

Weaknesses

**Where do we need to improve?
What are the rocks in the road?**

**What can we do to improve?
Where will we place our bets?**

**Where are we vulnerable?
What's the risk?
Can someone throw a rock
in the road?**

Opportunities

Threats

FIGURE 2.5   SWOT Analysis

By the way, there are many different approaches to risk management. It has become a major trend and many approaches are being developed. That said, I would like to share a quick thought from one of my experiences that may help guide you in some simple thinking about how to assess risk in general. Rick Blasgen is CEO of CSCMP. I first met Rick when he was a planner at Nabisco and I was at IRI's logistics venture, LogicNet. When I joined Numetrix several years later, Nabisco was also a customer using our supply chain optimization tool to model its own supply chain. When I asked Rick about the benefits, one of the more significant was that when they experienced failures in their supply chain, such as a plant or line going down, they could rerun the model without that facility or line in the plan, and the model would develop an alternative feasible plan at lowest cost to overcome the loss of the facility or line.

While in this case Nabisco was using it after the fact, expanding on their example, you can rapidly develop a risk assessment of your supply network simply by taking resources out of the model or your plan. What if we didn't have supplier A? What if we didn't have plant B? What if customer C no longer did business with us? A lot of companies spend a lot of time hypothesizing what may go wrong. In my experience, if you spend less time on why an asset or resource could be lost and just took the resource out to see what the impact would be, you would be able to assess risk to your plan more rapidly. It's not a substitute for a comprehensive risk assessment and planning process, but I have found it useful to challenge assumptions during general planning.

So let's get back to our hypothetical SWOT analysis. While our strategy of working through a network of distributors appears to have strengths, are there any weaknesses we need to consider? Remember, we need to measure our attributes of reliability, responsiveness, flexibility, costs, and assets. The process of using a distributor network is certainly within our cost structure. And the assets required can be a kept at a minimum as we will be leveraging distributor and retailer assets in the process.

We should be able to provide reliable and competitively responsive service but we will have to create some processes to minimize our exposure to variability in demand. What if the consumer doesn't buy into our product and our promotion plans? Do we have enough flexibility to adapt to changes in the market? What if that Sherman guy comes to town and uses our brand as his example? You know people are going to get thirsty . . . and one beer leads to another, pretty soon a party breaks out, and the whole conference starts asking for our brand. Do we have a local supply to meet that unanticipated upturn in demand? Maybe we should start tracking Sherman's speaking schedule.

What is our competition doing in the market? Do we have any supply chain vulnerability that a competitor may be able to exploit? Conversely, can we leverage any of our capabilities to create a competitive advantage?

What? Leverage supply chain for competitive advantage? I told you that supply chain management was marketing. For example, throughout the years, I have worked for a number of technology companies serving the consumer market and, as luck would have it, I worked with several brewing companies, which, based on that experience, led me to choose beer as the example product to "beam." We were also conducting a lot of Beer Games (more on that in Chapter 3), so that using beer as a product example actually provides a stream of consistency in my articles, presentations, and now this book. And, of course, many of you will also be familiar with consuming beer.

So, as you can imagine, I have heard and shared a lot of stories over a beer or two. One of the more fascinating stories I heard back in the day was the fear Anheuser-Busch (A-B) had with the entry of Coors Brewing into the national market. If you recall, Coors had a "mystique" about it. It was very hip and West Coast-ish. It was brewed with Rocky Mountain water and sold in vertically produced, stylish aluminum cans at Coors' own facility. But it was unavailable east of the Mississippi River. People would take driving vacations, stock up the trunk of their cars with cases of Coors, and peddle the beer for three to four times the cost when they returned.

Needless to say, there was a lot of pent-up demand and anticipation regarding the launch of Coors nationally. So, as the story goes, A-B set out on a mission to look at Coors' versus A-B's strengths, weaknesses, opportunities, and threats for vulnerability. Also at the time, beer in cans was very popular as the culture was becoming very mobile and cans didn't break. And, despite many bottle design attempts (remember the stubbies and snub nosed), cans were also more compact, fit in coolers better, and the market was very can-oriented.

So, just prior to the national launch of Coors, A-B launches a major advertising campaign announcing the availability of its products in "long-neck" throwback bottles, the kind of bottles that used to be served at the corner bar and required a deposit. They went away as disposables were introduced. There is some environmental irony there, I think. Oh for the nostalgia associated with sitting at your neighborhood tap sipping a cold one from those long-neck bottles of the past. We longed for the flavor of beer from glass versus the "tinny" taste of the can.

Needless to say, there was a huge demand created for beer in long-neck bottles, and nearly every brewery responded with its own long-neck bottled brew . . . except, of course, Coors. You see, Coors had a bottleneck . . . very limited capacity for producing bottled beer, let alone the long-neck variety. And, as they were very vertically integrated, they didn't have the strategic relationships with the glass packaging suppliers that the other breweries had. And, as Coors is not pasteurized, it required cooler space. As demand for "cold bottled beer" rose, the retailers started pulling cooler space for cans in order to make room for the long necks to get cold, and the canned beers, like Coors, were allocated floor space.

So A-B leverages a weakness in Coors' supply chain capability to create demand for product Coors can't supply. And it adds to the problem because now Coors will often be placed on the floor versus in the cooler, eroding its freshness and taste. Well, the rest is history . . . coincidence, you think?

Well, if you don't believe that A-B developed a conscious competitive initiative to exploit a weakness in Coors' supply chain, let me share another story. I told you that at Numetrix we were selling supply chain optimization solutions that can model, simulate, and solve highly complex supply chain problems. One of our customers, a commodity chemicals manufacturer, took the modeling to a different level. Not only did they model their supply chain; they modeled their competitors' supply chains.

It's a commodity business, so the manufacturing processes and formulas are not significantly different, and it's a price-sensitive, supply and demand–driven market. A company's success came from production economies, product availability, and service. By modeling the competitors' supply chains, the Numetrix customer was able to determine vulnerability in the competitor's supply chain. They could create demand for product (pricing incentives) in regions that they knew their competitors would have problems meeting locally (increased transportation cost). They could also optimize their run length to demand by region and often force their competitors into costly production changeovers and higher unit costs. Their entire market and margin strategy was based on leveraging their supply chain capabilities to a competitive advantage. That's marketing!

As you develop your vision and your plan, rocks will be found or placed in your path, gaps between the vision and current reality will widen, and tension will occur resulting in resistance. It's often the tension that's created that causes people to modify or even abandon their plan. And it's often that tension that keeps people from embarking on the transformation journey. As that tension develops, you have to be strong; you have to be prepared to respond to it. It is usually the biggest obstacle I have seen in change management projects.

 ## PRINCIPLE OF CREATIVE TENSION

Peter Senge introduced us to another concept about embarking on the journey to transformation. He taught us the principle of "creative tension." As I recall, Senge adapted the principle from his relationship with Robert Fritz and his book *The Path of Least Resistance.*[6] There will be a gap between the "as is" and current reality of your business and the "to be" and vision of where you want the business to be in the future. It's kind of like the gap you experience each year as you embark on your journey to accomplish New Year's resolutions.

Imagine that you're going to describe that gap the way you would describe the size of a fish you caught. Place the ends of a rubber band on each of your hands and stretch them out to represent the size of the gap between your current reality and your vision. As the gap widens, a tension develops from the rubber band—a "creative tension." Depending on the size of the gap, the tension will be easily tolerated or become excessive and even cause the band to break. There have been times that I have passed rubber bands out to my audience—a very brave feat for a speaker to arm his audience.

The tension is the same level of tension or resistance that you will experience as you begin your journey to transformation. There are two ways to resolve the tension. You can modify your vision to be a lot closer to the current reality (the path of least resistance). Or you can aggressively develop and communicate the critical success factors that will move your company on the journey of transforming itself into the business you envision. Managing the tension between current reality and what it takes to be a leader in your industry is what holds back most companies from beginning the journey. *Don't let it hold you back.*

Creating a vision, or Visioneering, doesn't have to take an enormous investment. Start with the outlandish, the improbable, or the perfect business outcome. Then decompose the process to execute on the vision to see if there are rocks in the road that may impede your journey. While I am making the process seem simple, it's really not. Business is complex. There will be a lot of rocks in the road.

Here's a simple road map or game plan to get your journey started:

Why Should We Change?

- Assess Current Operations—*Define* Your Supply Chain.
- Determine Market Benchmarks, Environment, and Challenges—*Measure*.

How Do We Change?

- Create a Strategy and Vision for the Future—*Analyze*.
- Map "As-Is" and "To-Be" Business Processes and Systems.

What Is the Value of Changing?

- Determine Critical Success Factors and Windows of Opportunity.
- Calculate Return on Investment.

Getting Management Buy-In and Investment

- Present the Solution Plan to Management.

Getting Operations Buy-In and Commitment

- Pilot Implementation "Proof of Concept" . . . Rapid Results—*Improve*.

Everyone Jumps on the Bandwagon

- Deploy Transformation Plan across the Enterprise—*Control*.

Sure, there will be rocks in the road and I'll offer some dynamite or detours as we go along. And there are often a lot of competitors that will be placing more rocks in the road. Some are big and you'll have to find a detour or an alternative source of energy to get around them (Management commitment? Don't skip ahead!). However, if you engage in a logical process, follow the roadmap, and execute the game plan, it doesn't have to be complicated and it doesn't have to stop you from trying. Remember, *the journey is the reward!*

And if you can get your colleagues, associates, and management to engage in this level of thinking, Visioneering will work to get your journey started. It puts the business into perspective.

 NOTES

1. D'Innocenzio, Anne, "New J.C. Penney CEO's Challenge: Bring Life Back to an Iconic Brand," *Austin American Statesman*, January 31, 2012.
2. Levitt, Theodore M., *The Marketing Imagination (Expanded Edition)*, Free Press, 1986.
3. Savage, Charles, *5th Generation Management*, Digital Press, 1990.
4. I have to confess that I didn't come up with the term *Visioneering*. One of the pitchers on our South Bend city softball team (ironically sponsored by Sherman's Cleaners . . . I wish I had kept that jersey!) was working for his father's engineering firm called Visioneering. For a case of beer, Jim "Keeb" Kistler wasn't going to send me a letter to "cease and desist" from using the term.
5. Krauss, Lawrence M., *The Physics of Star Trek*, Basic Books, 1995.
6. Senge, Peter, *The Path of Least Resistance*, Fawcett Columbine/Ballantine Books, 1989.

CHAPTER THREE

Market Drivers and the Dynamics of Change

S O, CHANGE IS INEVITABLE and we've put the business in perspective. We have established a road map and game plan, and we're ready to start on the yellow brick road to Leader City and our transformational journey. Becoming a resident of Leader City, though, requires innovative approaches to the market environment that we operate in. In my experience, most companies are entrenched in a culture of efficiency. They are at level three in transformational culture maturity, and they think that progress is driven by incrementally trying to squeeze cost out of the company's operations each year. And they assume it will never end.

The problem with level three is its comfort in complacency. People really like the security of level two and the good feeling from level three. Change may disrupt that feeling of comfort. So they resist it and try to control their environment and do everything in their power to maintain the status quo. In reality, the market cannot be controlled, as more than 80 percent—or 400 of the original Fortune 500 from 1955 that are no longer in that revered group can attest. If you aren't scanning the market for emerging trends and assessing the impact they might have on your business, you may find yourself among the many casualties of market dynamics . . . the collateral damage of change.

Leaders, as we have said, are often at level four or five in transformational culture maturity. They have the confidence and esteem to think outside the box and are driven more by the effectiveness of their operations than simply efficiency. They leverage their supply chain as they would any competitive initiative. They view it as an integral component of their marketing and business strategy. And they have the margin and funds to accelerate their journey and capitalize on market opportunities while generally thwarting the competition. Remember, Leader City residents have a 50 percent cost advantage over their *median* competitors!

But they don't beat their competition on cost or pricing actions. They are driven by profitable growth, by seizing opportunities their competition ignores or resists. They win through innovation, superior quality, and focusing on their customer and their customer's customer. They scan the market for the edge. What trends are stirring the market? What changes will open windows of opportunity? What can we learn from others? They take calculated risks with the promise of a sizable reward. They listen to their suppliers and competing vendors. They play in the sandbox with new technologies and pilots. They leverage their cost advantage for investment and research.

Building the business case and maturing the culture to enable and encourage transformation requires you to consider the dynamics of the market. Where's the edge? How can we adapt and respond to market changes? There can be no satisfaction with the status quo. Drink from the glass of victory, celebrate success, and esteem trumps complacency. Change isn't going to happen. It is happening. Your competition is already on the journey and is capitalizing on it. Aren't you tired of eating their dust?

In my experience, gaining an understanding of the market drivers that will breed change is not just the responsibility of the marketing department. Supply chain management has to be aligned to the company's business objectives and aware of how supply chain operations must proactively respond to the dynamics of the market environment as well as the other functions in the organization.

I remember when Efficient Consumer Response (ECR) became a major industry initiative. I was transitioning from Mercer Management Consulting to Information Resources (IRI). We had just published "New Ways to Take Costs Out of the Retail Food Pipeline: Making Replenishment Logistics Happen: A Study" for the Coca-Cola Retailing Research Council.[1] As part of the technology research, I came across Andre Martin, author of the original *DRP: Distribution Resource Planning.*[2] It turned out that the co-CEO of IRI was the late Jim Andress. Martin was Andress's distribution manager at Abbott Labs Canada back when Martin came up with the concept of DRP and later published the book.

Andress recognized the potential of all of the point of sale (POS) data that IRI was collecting in grocery stores for market analysis to be used to drive DRP. POS-driven DRP has always been a Holy Grail in the market. So IRI and Andre formed a joint venture called LogicNet and, as luck would have it, they needed an evangelist/marketing/sales executive to supplement Martin's evangelism in the market. Hence, my transition from Mercer and the beginning of several "bleeding" edge technology ventures I would become a part of.

I had the opportunity to work closely with Andress at IRI and I will never forget one piece of advice he gave to me. He was a West Point grad and spoke to me during the presentation of one of my "overthought, overanalyzed" concepts.

"Rich," he said, "remember what Napoleon used to say, 'Perfection is the worst enemy of the good enough.'"

Keep that in mind as you contemplate taking that first step.

So, that's the quick background. As part of our marketing strategy both at LogicNet and IRI, we wanted to get as many people as we could involved with various ECR committees and initiatives as possible. I became involved in the Continuous Replenishment Planning (CRP) committee and was a speaker at many ECR events and conferences. Here is the nugget from this story. Most companies in the market were just discovering the trend toward CRP and Vendor Managed Inventory (VMI) as a means to reduce cost and uncertainty in the consumer goods supply chain.

P&G, on the other hand, had not only been doing CRP for many years, but they had developed a CRP system and were co-marketing it with IBM. As I began to dig into the story, it seemed that more than five years earlier, P&G began piloting and designing a CRP process and later a system in conjunction with Wal-Mart and had already institutionalized it. They were a supply chain light year ahead of their competition. The competition didn't even understand the underlying benefits let alone how to leverage them.

The pundits were all heralding VMI, consignment inventory, as the way for retailers to reduce their inventories. And I was no exception, until I was speaking at a CLM conference and Joe Neal, then VP, Distribution of Lechmere (former discount retailer in New England), heard me speak and invited me to join him for dinner.

"You know that retailers really don't care about VMI, don't you?" he said at dinner.

"No, I think it's a great advantage, as I pointed out in my presentation," I responded.

"Well, Rich, think about this. For the most part, we sell our inventory faster than we have to pay for it. And, if it doesn't move, we generally have an agreement that we can return it to the manufacturer. The manufacturer's payment terms generally finances our inventory," he pointed out. "We really don't care about VMI. Check it out."

Well, it doesn't take a lot of electricity for my lightbulb to turn on. And the more research I did into the subject, the more I learned that the real benefit to the manufacturer from VMI was reduced transportation cost. You see, when P&G first recognized the trend to more frequent retail ordering in smaller quantities to increase gross margin return on investment (GMROI), a key retail finance metric, their transportation costs began going up.

With big box retailer customers, the manufacturer, in this case P&G, usually had substantial volume flowing to the retail distribution centers (DCs) on less than 20 transportation lanes. With that kind of volume concentration, P&G figured they should be shipping plant direct with higher SKU density to Wal-Mart and other big box customer DCs, in full truckloads (TL), optimizing capacity. Instead of maximizing capacity, they were shipping more and more less than truckload (LTL) quantities with higher SKU variability at a higher cost and complexity. This was just the opposite reaction to the volume concentration they should be experiencing.

How could they capitalize on this window of opportunity? Develop a continuous replenishment program that would enable P&G to control freight in while letting Wal-Mart withdraw inventory as needed to maximize GMROI, win-win. In essence, create a P&G "DC" within the customer DC. The reduced *cost per case* from optimizing transportation cost, combined with a healthy GMROI, made it attractive to the retail customer, not VMI in and of itself. The retailer sold the inventory before they paid for it, anyway. That was the part of the presentation P&G never shared in its CRP presentations. Of course, while the rest of the industry was figuring all that out, P&G reaped financial rewards and a stronger relationship with its customers, leading to continued market leadership. That's why it's important for supply chain to pay attention to a changing market, not just marketing.

SUPPLY CHAIN IS MARKETING: A TOOL FOR ANALYZING THE MARKET ENVIRONMENT IMPACTING THE SUPPLY CHAIN

A simple tool that I use for scanning the market for opportunities and threats is to place the marketing 4Ps into a visual context model with the 4Cs, as illustrated in Figure 3.1. It provides a template that allows me to brainstorm with colleagues and upper management, if possible, considering each person's perspective on the variables and drivers of market change and the company's business objectives. This provides the market "sanity" check to ensure we are keeping supply chain initiatives in line with the company's strategy. It builds on and identifies changes to the early SWOT analysis based on market drivers to the strengths and vulnerabilities (weaknesses) in the supply chain that may be leveraged by me or my competitors while considering the perspectives of my peers in other functional areas of the company.

The model also serves as a building block for analyzing organizational structures. Yes, there are silos! Live with it. We have wasted too much time and invested way too much money with consultants trying to break down silos that are only a symptom of the problem. Supply chain is not going to report to R&D or vice versa. After 30 years, guess what I learned? You can't really break down the silos. But we can create bridges and windows that enable cross-functional visibility and communication at the points of functional intersection—the lack of which is the root cause. But I have also learned that you need an organization development template for determining the right combination of vertical and horizontal inputs, outputs, structure, functions, and processes to effectively transform the company and enable people to collaborate more fluidly to

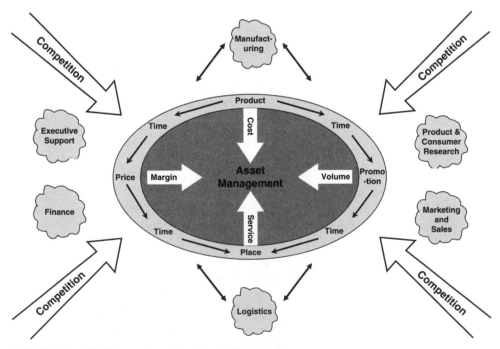

FIGURE 3.1   The Dynamics of the Marketing Environment

identify and respond to changing market dynamics. People are simply too busy to proactively call people in other departments as things change. You have to have processes and systems in place to enable collaboration.

The goal of most organizations is to invest capital in assets that can be leveraged as a business to provide a return on that invested capital (ROIC) or, in the case of distribution companies, a gross margin return on that investment (GMROI) in goods at a rate greater than any other investment of that capital would return. The organization's functions and the market will act separately and together from different perspectives to impact the company's assets. Think of the business as an operating system. No one function within the organization truly controls the ability of the business to generate a higher ROIC or GMROI, despite what many executives think.

For example, in many manufacturing companies, the day-to-day planners and schedulers are generally making million-dollar capital decisions. They determine what material inventories (working capital) are to be converted into finished goods inventory (working capital). Do you think they are consulting the business plan and operating budget as they determine the day's schedule? Do they call the board for approval on what they will produce today? The CEO? Chances are that they are making that million-dollar capital decision based on tribal knowledge and a custom spreadsheet.

Understanding the dynamics of the market and the potential impact to the organization are critical to managing company assets. Generally, manufacturing and logistics will have the controlling levers that drive much of cost and service capabilities that drive financial return. Research and development, marketing, and sales have the controlling levers that drive volume into the company. Executive and financial management are the most likely controllers of margin based on budgeting, pricing, and the strategic plan. However, operations will control the cost and revenue levers to manage margin as the year plays out.

It's critical to meet with colleagues, managers, and, if possible, senior executives across all of the functions of the organization to assess and identify trends, challenges, best practices, and benchmarks. Using the model in Figure 3.1, you can capture the market drivers from each function's perspective and chart the findings in a model like the one in Figure 3.2, Market Drivers. If you can't meet with functional colleagues, develop the chart from each function's perspective. It's always important to take a walk in the other person's shoes. Extend the concept of "Voice of the Customer" to internal constituencies as well.

Presenting the various challenges and trends the organization is or will be facing acts as a catalyst for transformational discussions. How will these challenges impact the company's competitive position, growth, business strategies, and so on? What can we do as an organization to capitalize on these opportunities? What will the financial impact be? People don't necessarily look for change; it just hits them. If you aren't nudging them to consider the changes now, they, and ultimately you, will be hit with a 2×4 of change sooner or later.

While every industry will have its own unique challenges and idiosyncrasies, there are market challenges common across industries that every supply chain manager faces. It has always interested me that, when market changes occur, the pundits all like to speak of the "new normal." When has anything in supply chain operations been

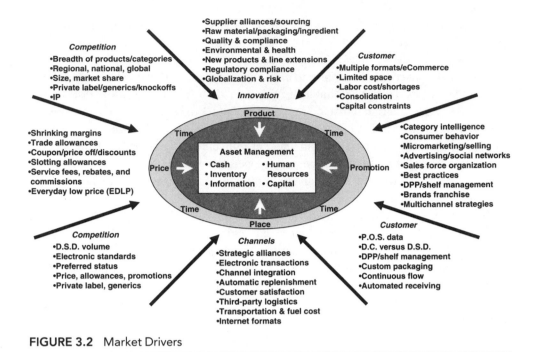

FIGURE 3.2 Market Drivers

normal? Supply chain management by its very nature is abnormal. Every time we think we're about to get to "normal," something new happens and, well, "normal" is to throw the plan out the window and figure out how to fight this fire before it burns down the forest. When I was young, I always wanted to be a fireman. When I chose supply chain as my career, I achieved that goal.

 ## SCANNING THE MARKET ENVIRONMENT FOR DRIVERS OF CHANGE

While every supply chain manager is charged with reducing total supply chain costs and providing superior and consistent customer service, there are also new pressures on measuring revenue and margin impact from operations. As a result, supply chain managers have to become more aware of what their counterparts in product development, marketing, and sales are planning. Changes in products, packaging, components, and product retirement directly impact supply chain planning and performance. Understanding the market drivers of those changes well ahead of introduction can be the difference between success and failure. It's critical to meet regularly (integrated business planning in Chapter 5; not just sales and operations planning) with cross-functional colleagues to ensure your strategy is aligned with the rest of the business and that you have the time to develop an effective operations response to those changes. You can't rely on them to take all of *your* variables into consideration.

I remember one consumer goods manufacturer whose operations team was handed down "detailed, well-thought-out" promotion plans for a major new suntan lotion launch. Everything was considered for the production and launch of the product, except for the lead times to develop the materials and graphics for the end aisle units that would hold the promotional product for display at the thousands of retail outlets planned for the distribution. It seems the marketer had "assumed" that procurement would just buy the displays off the shelf. How much lead time could there be for cardboard and printing? He wasn't aware that end aisle displays had to be not only custom ordered but also custom produced at asset-constrained supplier facilities.

To make a long story short, a local packaging supplier went from a contingency commodity supplier to strategic partner really fast. And, not only did the supplier get its largest contract ever (for a very profitable price), it also got a 10-year, volume-guaranteed contract for future products as a now strategic source supplier. Collaboration among functions, as we will see, is critical to operations excellence; it is one of the primary objectives of supply chain transformation. In Senge's context it is akin to "team learning and shared vision."

Another market impact that I don't see going away soon is the competition for capital. It is important to identify financial trends and the impact they will have on funding projects and initiatives. A couple of years ago, I was meeting with a project engineer at a tier-one automotive supplier. Taped to his wall was one of the most detailed and complex process maps I have ever seen.

I asked him, "Is this some new major supply chain process improvement initiative? A new product line production process, perhaps?"

He replied, "No, it's our capital appropriation and approval process."

Critical to your transformation plans are actions on inventory balancing, right-sizing, integration to production planning and scheduling, and supplier relationships designed to liberate working capital. You remember those planners and schedulers making million-dollar working capital decisions? The old way of doing it probably isn't good enough in today's market. I don't think we are going to see increases in capital availability changing soon. Capital is like oil, as we shall see in a moment; constrained supply, growing demand.

And then, globalization changes everything. Thomas Friedman's book, *The World Is Flat*, sure made that clear for everyone. You have to be prepared for change to come from anywhere at any time. It's not just a sourcing game anymore. It's also about consumption and new markets for our goods. As developing countries, once a source of cheap labor and goods, evolve, their economies create greater per capita incomes. With expendable income comes more consumption. Who would have thought that in 2010 General Motors would sell more vehicles in China than in the United States? In a press release issued on January 8, 2011, GM reported that in 2010 it sold a car or truck on average every 12 seconds in China.

As a supply chain manager, you have to be aware of the potential impact that expanding into a new global market area is going to have. The infrastructure and local laws, customs, and tax policies may have a direct impact on how you source, make, and deliver product. Today, a tax-effective supply chain management strategy is as important, if not more so, than traditional logistics network optimization strategies. In Chapter 2, I mentioned a DuPont executive adding two more Ps to the 4Ps: power and politics. Political instability and changes in the geopolitical landscape can change the game at any time. It's critical that you scan the market and discuss with your peers anticipated changes in the global landscape. It's critical to sourcing decisions, location decisions, and delivery options. It is at the core of determining whether to outsource an operation or not.

Are you taking advantage of the widening of the Panama Canal? The creation of new shipping lanes and lower rates are opening new alternatives for sourcing product from Asia and the west coast of South America to the east coast of North America and the Caribbean. Conversely, new markets are opening in Asia and the west coast of South America for North American suppliers, especially on the East Coast. It also changes labor assumptions as well as placing addition pressure on U.S. investments in infrastructure improvements.

Chuck Taylor, a "semiretired" supply chain veteran and a recipient of CSCMP's Distinguished Service Award (DSA), founded Awake! Consulting back in 2005 to awaken supply chain managers to the fact that the era of cheap oil was over. I have heard Taylor speak on the topic several times and, as most supply chain managers are experiencing, oil prices aren't going to stabilize ever, in all probability. The supply is finite and the demand is changing constantly, usually upward, around the world. All those vehicles sold in China? India? Brazil? Russia? Just to name a few countries having an impact on global oil demand. And fuel price volatility isn't the only petroleum-based consideration impacting supply chain structure and strategy. Nearly everything we produce and package has a petroleum component to it that will impact cost and ultimately price.

These macro global trends, while common across industries, have driven more emphasis on supply chain risk assessment. While I spoke about risk management earlier—and I don't intend to expand much more on it—you need to be keenly aware of risks to your supply chain operations across all global dimensions as well as changing regulatory compliance requirements. As companies are quickly learning, these decisions can impact their brand and corporate reputation as much as their supply chain.

Companies that are not regularly using supply chain modeling and simulation tools to test different scenarios are at a competitive disadvantage. Once only available to larger companies and operations research personnel, cloud computing and advanced analytic technology makes these tools available to companies of any size.

Supply chains are also more vulnerable than ever to security threats as the value of components increases the value of shipments.

John Faldetta, retired director of global logistics at Gillette and a good friend over the years, was the first logistics executive to make me aware of just how vulnerable supply chains can be to cargo theft. He told me the story of Gillette's introduction of the first disposable razor. Their distribution center was located in Andover, MA, less than 30 miles from their headquarters in Boston.

It was a landmark product launch and the company invited hundreds of press representatives to the news conference announcing the new razors. Faldetta's department was charged with packing up and delivering a truckload of samples to distribute to the press following the news conference. One problem: The truck was hijacked on its way into the city. Imagine the street value of a truckload of razors. Imagine how many razors and blades can be loaded on a truck . . . any wonder Gillette started producing shaving cream and other products with higher weight and cube and lower value than razors to reduce the value of a load?

As many stories as there are about cargo theft, think how many stories are not publicly reported. Losing $70 million of goods in a warehouse burglary or trailer hijacking is not something most companies want to see in the news every day.

Just as we are seeing the trend to more emphasis on supply chain risk management, supply chain resiliency and sustainability are becoming as critical to supply chain operations. As with risk management, I am not going to devote significant time to that either; however, your risk management plan has to include contingencies to mitigate risk and respond to instances when they occur, including estimates of the financial and market impact to your supply chain vulnerabilities. It goes without saying that sustainability and environmental compliance are beyond the early-adopter stage and have to be key operational strategies moving forward, especially as "cap and trade" policies and laws are enacted and carbon credits become as valuable to a company as its stock. Global ecological impact was also, ironically, one of the first projects coming out of Forrester's Systems Lab in the 1960s and is a perfect lead for why this is all so important to starting your journey to operations excellence.

I could go on about what's happening in the industry, and in more detail. But this isn't a book on future trends, and they all change, all the time. This is about packing your bags to get on that transformational journey. As I said in Chapter 1, "Business as usual has been canceled." Building the case for transformation, building a shared vision, establishing a basis for organizational learning, and leading to self-actualization stems from a common understanding of where the business fits in the market and how we will meet and respond to the challenges that we are facing.

What may change in the market may just change the game . . . you don't want to be a sword or typewriter manufacturer. I "Googled" Fortune 500 changes and found a blog by Toby Elwin, "The Cost of Culture: A 50% Turnover of the Fortune 500."[3] While he has written a quite insightful and complimentary blog, he cites data found on CNN Money for the Fortune 500 that shows that 238 of the 1999 Fortune 500 were not part of the 2009 Fortune 500.[4]

And you want your colleagues and management to experience that fear. Remember, no pain, no gain . . . no pain is worse than irrelevance. If we don't transform, we risk irrelevance.

 ## SYSTEMS THINKING: YOUR STRATEGY FOR MANAGING IN A CHANGING MARKET

One of the most basic transformational concepts that supply chain managers and any business person, for that matter, needs to have is at least a basic understanding of systems thinking. Of Senge's five disciplines, systems thinking is the foundation. I was first exposed to systems thinking when I was in graduate school at Notre Dame. My master's degree was in educational administration and one of the courses was Systems and the Environment. The side benefit of being an EdAd major was that the curriculum was heavily oriented to psychology and organizational development; hence the earlier references to Maslow, French and Raven, culture, and now systems thinking.

The course was, naturally, based on social/educational systems and the community environment. But it taught me to lay out visually all of the entities of a school district "system," so that I could see how the entities worked together and separately to cause change in the system as a whole. Learning to think holistically would serve me well; over the years, I observed that the supply chain leaders that looked at their supply network holistically and as a system, as in Figures 3.1 and 3.2, were always ahead of the rest of the competition.

In fact, it would serve us all well if all business leaders, if all leaders, if all people would develop a holistic systems view of the environment in which they work and live. Supply chain can save the world.

Looking holistically at a supply network is to look at it from end to end. My friends at Kimberly-Clark used to (maybe still do) refer to their supply chain as "stump to rump." I always used to say from "dirt to dirt" (my theology background) as most supply chains originate from materials from the earth that are eventually returned to the earth. Many of the pundits and evangelists of lean thinking would have you listening to the voice of the customer. In my mind, however, you should start by looking at the voice of the "end" customer . . . either the consumer or the customer's customer, depending on what industry you serve. If you are the point of material origin, you may have to listen to the customer's customer's customer's customer. It's important to know how your product fits into and creates value for your customer and the entire supply chain that you operate in. It is the foundation for developing a business operating system for your operations or company as a whole.

By understanding how your product contributes to your customer's product and success, you can develop initiatives and services to help them better utilize your product and add value. The more value you add, the more valuable you become. Think about that supplier of end aisle displays. The other learning from looking at your customer's customer, and how your customer uses your product to serve their customer, is that you can observe the customer's market and identify changes occurring in their market. You can think of the market as a system and each participant as a subsystem. All of the components are linked together into a network of systems creating and responding to change. Think of the game-changing moment that could have come had the sword manufacturer seen Indiana Jones end the sword fight with a squeeze of his revolver's trigger.

Nine times out of ten, a change to their market won't dramatically impact your business, but that one "surprise" is usually a "gotcha." And the "gotcha" often is the result of a combination of changes occurring at different times, influencing several components in the network with varying degrees of impact. The dynamics of system behavior introduce the concept that time delay and amplification can have on the behavior of a supply chain and the degree of impact based on where one is positioned in the supply chain.

The best example of this that I have heard is turning the faucet in the shower a little too far to the hot or cold side. For a moment, there is no impact and you might turn it a little further . . . surprise, the impact can be a real "gotcha." Kind of like the change to the market Anheuser-Busch created with the campaign for long-neck bottles and the resulting "gotcha" that Coors experienced.

While, by education, I have always thought holistically, in fact, one of my early articles published in *Transportation and Distribution* was entitled "Look Ahead to Integrated Channels."[5] It wasn't until I started working with Innovation Associates and experienced my first Beer Game that I began to really understand how systems thinking can impact the supply chain and the business.

My first meeting with P&G was with Lou Boudreau, a product supply manager or director in the food division, when I was with DEC.

He walked into the room, sat down, and said, "You have 15 minutes to share your vision with me. Then we will either continue with the meeting or I will leave."

I asked him instead to read the *Transportation and Distribution* article.

After reading it, he said, "Let's talk."

He then shared the P&G Food Division's vision for Total Systems and Packaging Logistics (TS&PL). We never did execute the project—another story for another time—but the next several months were a fabulous experience of building shared visions and team learning. It also gave me the opportunity to work more closely with Bob Sabath, then head of the supply chain practice at A.T. Kearney, who would later bring me to Mercer Management Consulting and also have a significant impact on my notions of supply chain management throughout the years.

It was 1990 and, as I would learn, P&G were well into their journey and, at the time, well ahead of the time, and their vision of a demand flow™ management network.

Notice the trademark on demand flow™? P&G always referred to demand flow management. When I founded and launched the Supply Chain Strategic Advisory Services for Advanced Manufacturing Research (AMR became AMR Research and is now Gartner Supply Chain), one of my first reports was on my interpretation of demand flow management. Of course, that was followed by a "cease and desist" letter from the John Costanza Institute of Technology (JCIT, now DemandPoint). To make a long story short, John Costanza, founder of the JCIT, had trademarked the term. When I queried P&G about their use of the term, I found out that like Leadership & Mastery, Demand Flow™ Technology (DFT) was another one of those classes many of P&G's managers were guided to. And Costanza would only allow people who paid a license fee to use it to any great extent, which is probably why this may be the first time many of you from a logistics background have ever heard of it.

So let's get back to the Beer Game. As you recall, Jay Forrester's computer simulation demonstrated the impact of demand change on a multi-echelon supply chain. As I had pointed out to him at the Systems Thinking in Action conference, it is a fabulous tool for experiencing and teaching what supply chain management is all about (see the accompanying "Simulating Supply Chain Dynamics: 'The Beer Game'"). Yet, at that time, it was not being widely leveraged for supply chain education or training. I was introduced to it as part of our overall development of the DEC Logistics Architecture based on the relationship our corporate logistics folks had with MIT. This led me to take the Leadership & Mastery workshop in which I was fortunate enough to have Peter Senge as the primary instructor. The Beer Game was one of the first exercises in the workshop to demonstrate systems thinking.

The Leadership & Mastery course also included a booklet on systems thinking, "Systems 1: An Introduction to Systems Thinking," which is an excellent primer on the subject.[6] Ironically, Dr. Kauffman is also an education major with an Ed.D. from the University of Massachusetts. Even more ironically, early on, systems thinking was probably more widely taught in education schools and in social sciences classes (as I experienced at Notre Dame) than business schools. John Coyle, at Penn State University, was one of the first business professors I met who early on incorporated the subject into his courses on logistics, including the Beer Game.

Kauffman's book has become a kind of folk legend, and his 28 "rules of thumb" about systems thinking are more widely distributed and commented about on the Internet than I could have imagined. I am also happy I saved my two copies of the booklet as when I Googled it; some people were asking $300 to $400 a copy on eBay. Some of the "rules of thumb" are good examples of why systems thinking is important. I will cite some later in this chapter.

When I was at DEC, Michael Goodman and Bill Latshaw from Innovation Associates (IA) and I facilitated many Beer Games for clients around the country. Interestingly enough, IA, at the time, was using it as facilitation for teaching systems thinking as part of their organizational development practice, not really for logistics. Goodman facilitated the game and would lead the OD parts of the game debrief (Latshaw handled the mechanics of executing the game), and I would add the implications for logistics and operations. Supply chain management wasn't even a widely used term then. After a couple of years, I began facilitating the game myself, focusing solely on supply chain implications.

When we engaged IA to conduct the game as part of our internal transformation at DEC, we immediately saw the impact the game could have on teaching internal folks the dynamics of logistics, as well as teaching our customers about the value of information systems in managing logistics. We would often conduct events that brought manufacturing, logistics, and IT executives together to experience the game. We also trained many of our partners about using the Beer Game. Today it's a pretty widely accepted tool for teaching supply chain. It's also a good example of how industry initiatives can impact academia and vice versa.

That said, looking at the market from a systems perspective and how your product will move through it is critical to developing strategies for managing in an ever-changing market. Kauffman's first rule of thumb is, "Everything is connected to everything else" (which he attributes to being a precept of the anthropologist Franz Boas). Remember, supply chain is all about trade-offs. Businesses are complex systems in a complex environment. Changes in one subsystem often result in changes to other subsystems. I can significantly reduce transportation costs by shipping more by boat; however, that may also significantly impact lead times and service levels. I can reduce manufacturing costs with longer production runs; however, that may increase my inventory and holding costs while tying up scarce capital. It's all a system.

Recently, ABC's *Castle* mystery show featured a two-part episode that is a great example of systems thinking.[7] The detectives are involved in a CIA plot based on a former CIA consultant (math professor) who has developed a systems analytic technique called the linchpin theory. He would identify a very small event that would trigger

SIMULATING SUPPLY CHAIN DYNAMICS: "THE BEER GAME"

In 1958, Jay Forrester, the MIT professor, engineer, and data processing pioneer, wrote an article entitled "Industrial Dynamics: A Major Breakthrough for Decision Makers" that he believed would revolutionize business decision making:

> Management is on the verge of a major breakthrough in understanding. The new management concepts will rest in part on recent advances in the data-processing industry. Such strides will far exceed in importance recent steps in using computing machines to execute clerical tasks. . . . This understanding will lead to better usage of information, to improved understanding of advertising effectiveness and the dynamic behavior of the consumer market, and to company policies that keep pace with technological change.

> Reprinted by permission of *Harvard Business Review* (1958). Excerpt from "Industrial Dynamics—A Major Breakthrough for Decision Makers," by Jay Forrester, Volume 36, Issue 4.

The revolution envisioned by Forrester was revealed through a computer model developed to simulate the flow of product through a basic multi-echelon supply chain, including a retailer, wholesaler, distributor, and manufacturer. The product moves from the supply point to the consumer in response to consumer demand and replenishment orders generated at each level in the supply chain. The result of the simulation led to what has become known as the Forrester Effect, or acceleration principle, which states that a 10 percent change in demand at point of final consumption will result in a 40 percent demand change at the point of manufacture.

While Forrester's teachings did not revolutionize management thinking at the time, thousands of business students and professionals over the past six decades have gained an understanding of the impact time delay and amplification have on supply chain behavior through a manufacturing and distribution simulation board game called the Beer Game. Back in the 1960s, there were only mainframe computers, so the Systems Dynamics Lab group at MIT Sloan School of Management constructed a board game versus the original computer simulation. Ask students what product they would like to work with? Of course, you get beer as the answer. The Beer Game simulates sequential information flows and the effects of communication delays. Professor John Sterman at the MIT Sloan School of Management has generally been my contact for board materials and popularizing the use of the game in education.[8]

Four people representing the retailer, wholesaler, distributor, and manufacturer comprise a supply chain, or team. Generally, several teams compete with one another to move "beer" through the channel in response to consumer sales. Weekly consumer sales are represented by a deck of cards revealed only to the retailer. As product is consumed, weekly orders are placed at each level to replenish inventory. A transportation delay is encountered as product moves from the factory through to each level in the channel. At the end of each simulated week of activity, participants record their orders or backorders and inventory. Each team is charged $1 for each case on hand or $2 for every case out of stock. At the end of 52 weeks, the participants calculate their total supply chain cost and graph orders and inventory for the year. The team with the lowest total cost wins.

Having conducted this simulation thousands of times, I have found that the resulting order and inventory patterns are always qualitatively the same for each team (similar to the findings of Forrester's original research) with wild swings in inventory and order quantity curves, which is now commonly referred to as the "bullwhip effect."

The time delays and resulting amplifications create common order and inventory patterns virtually every time the simulation is performed. The inventory is level at the start of the game, but as the weeks progress, order quantities increase and decrease as inventory runs low and is later built up in reaction to and in anticipation of demand. Further, order triggers lag at each level and are amplified. Back at the factory, production lines run at full capacity for a few weeks and then sit idle for a few more. Amazing how similar simulations are to reality.

Another common behavior during the game "debrief," as participants explain the variance in patterns, is the tendency to place blame. At first, everyone blames consumer demand variability. During the debrief, the retailer reveals to everyone's surprise that consumer demand for the length of the game remained virtually unchanged. Naturally, with that revelation, team members immediately turn on one another to place blame. In reality, it is the time-phased delays of information and the reactive manner of trying to predict what demand will be that causes the behavior in the supply chain, not the participants themselves.

Replenishment quantities are determined without knowledge of the actual rate of consumer demand. Demand throughput cycles and replenishment order cycles are "out of sync." The simulation demonstrates how small changes in actual customer demand can create an amplified, whip-like effect on upstream requirements. This bullwhip effect results in bloated inventories and missed deliveries in the simulation and in real supply chains. ■

a series of events leading to a cataclysmic event. In this case, the small event is a botched CIA assassination attempt that results in the "accidental" death of a powerful Chinese diplomat's daughter. The professor determined this event would a trigger a series of retaliatory and interconnected events, like falling dominoes, eventually resulting in World War III and the fall of the United States. The graphic of the system of events in the professor's lab could easily be a supply network simulation.

When you are looking at your company within the context of the ever-changing market, you constantly have to be looking at trends and events, both immediate and causal, that may impact your operations. It's like the P&G example of early recognition that more frequent ordering in smaller quantities by their customers could have a negative impact on their ordering and transportation costs. They developed an organization response that not only prevented significant margin erosion, but also proved to be a lever of competitive advantage in the market.

When I was at Unisys, I was called into a project for a wholesale grocery distributor (privately held) in Kentucky. They wanted someone to come in and help them design a returns processing system. They were having real issues keeping up with the manual processing of returns of damaged products. Well, I was kind of skeptical going in, as you can imagine. Why were they delivering so many damaged products in the first place?

As a course of our overall project approach, we arranged a facility tour (all three shifts) and interviews with everyone involved in processing orders from order entry to collection of payment (order to cash analysis). What we found was that none of the company executives ever stayed for the afternoon and night shifts. We also discovered that their retail customers, as in the P&G experience, were ordering more frequently in smaller quantities. In fact, order volume had quadrupled from customers traditionally placing an order once a month for a 30-day supply to once a week for a 7-day supply. Of course, the order volume didn't impact monthly revenue reports, so it went generally unnoticed by senior management.

When we got to the warehouse for the afternoon and night shifts, it was chaos. The bulk of orders (manual processing at the time) began hitting the floor around 6:00 p.m. for picking and staging so they could be loaded during the night shift. Of course, the warehouse was staffed to handle a fourth of the new volume. Pickers were literally running up and down the aisles, throwing product into totes and cases onto pallets.

The night shift had the same staffing constraints, and when they hit the floor at 11:00 p.m. or so, they were scrambling to get the trucks routed and loaded. Of course, it was a lot more complex because, in the past, there were very few stops per truck. After all, one order was for a 30-day supply of goods. With the change in order frequency, vehicles now had multiple stops and products had to be loaded in stop order. Well, as you can imagine, as the time approached "must ship" by 6:00 a.m., it was helter-skelter and the associates were literally throwing product on the trucks to move them out.

The result, of course, was lots and lots of damaged product that wasn't inspected on the outbound and that the customer either refused to receive or returned with the next shipment. Management never knew what was hitting them because they didn't anticipate the impact the market change would have on their operations. Management didn't go out to the warehouse on the later shifts, and the culture was such that the warehouse supervisors and associates were just doing their job as best they could. They needed a new distribution system, not a returns processing system.

So the Beer Game demonstrates the criticality of taking a holistic view of the market, the business, and the supply chain. Little changes can become overwhelming changes. Variability can result in large swings of inventory levels. Lack of communication can result in blame from "accidental adversaries," as Senge likes to call them.

When the P&G and Wal-Mart operations folks first got together, they did not really warm up to the idea. They were "accidental adversaries." It wasn't until they started mapping their receiving and delivery processes together and identifying what each other's driving performance metrics were that they began to realize they weren't trying to cause each other problems. Until the conflict between ordering practices and processes to support an improved GMROI were mapped to the delivery processes geared to optimizing transportation cost and improving ROIC were made visible, the participants were innocent bystanders.

It's not the strategic intent of anyone in the Beer Game to wreak havoc up- or downstream. It's the structure of the game that determines the strategy and outcome. The structure, with lack of communication, inherent time delays, and resulting amplification of variability upstream, causes the behavior. It is all about managing demand and, in my experience, most people don't extend their view of demand beyond their "silo" within the context of other organization silos let alone the market in general. All of those silos operate independently of one another, creating demand changes and responses that impact the others. After more than 25 years, companies are just now "discovering" sales and operations planning? And most of them still don't get it.

Much of my thinking on supply chain was really crystallized while I was engaged in a consulting project supporting the development of an enterprise system architecture for Colgate US, a division of Colgate-Palmolive Company, in the early 1990s. I had been working on a number of different projects for Colgate as part of my field industry marketing role at DEC. Ed Toben, who would later become CIO and has recently retired, was recommending me to the management team to facilitate a cross-functional initiative that would ultimately define the business requirements for a new enterprise system for the company. Several of the members of the team were concerned about my working for a vendor; however, as I had just accepted a position with Mercer Management Consulting, I was engaged for the project.

What was different about this project from others I had been engaged in over the years was that I was tasked with interviewing and developing requirements across every function in the company. I was invited into every silo. We had to consider the requirements of every aspect of the business from R&D through marketing and sales, through procurement, production, and logistics, through all the aspects of finance.

And it would have to be communicated to executive management. The transformation of the company to the new system would be significant, and I was at the beginning of Colgate's journey. To document and communicate the findings, I developed the methodology that has guided my research and many other transformational projects over the years. I have written many research reports and articles over the years on the methodology and experience stemming from this project, which are cited in the References.

What I had suspected at P&G, was confirmed in the project at Colgate, and is demonstrated in the Beer Game, is that the business can be characterized by three main organizational structures whose strategies determine the organization's capability to respond to, manage, and grow demand profitably. If those Demand Management strategies are transformed to align to and adapt to the changing market, the company will mature in its culture and its capabilities cross functionally, much as P&G has with its demand-oriented culture and Colgate has though their transformation over the years.

The structures and strategies for managing in a changing market, as illustrated in Figure 3.3, are quite simple to understand as they are based on the very basic principles of marketing's 4Ps and the market's 4Cs.

Promotion is its own structure, which I call Demand Creation. This structure really determines and drives the business's product strategy and demand chain. Depending on the product, services, and industry that the company is in, it will determine the functional organization of this structure. However, in general, the functions will be innovating new concepts, scanning the market for new products or needs, researching and developing the concepts into commercial offerings, and marketing and selling them to customers (channels) or consumers.

Product and place are closely aligned into what I call the Demand Fulfillment structure. This structure really determines and drives the business's channel strategy and supply chain. While I have lived in the Demand Creation structure of technology

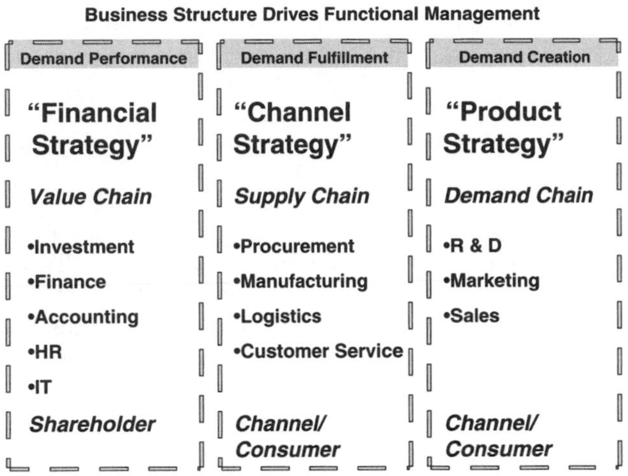

Business Structure Drives Functional Management

Demand Performance	Demand Fulfillment	Demand Creation
"Financial Strategy"	**"Channel Strategy"**	**"Product Strategy"**
Value Chain	*Supply Chain*	*Demand Chain*
•Investment	•Procurement	•R & D
•Finance	•Manufacturing	•Marketing
•Accounting	•Logistics	•Sales
•HR	•Customer Service	
•IT		
Shareholder	*Channel/ Consumer*	*Channel/ Consumer*

FIGURE 3.3 Demand Management Structures and Strategy

companies, Demand Fulfillment is obviously the structure that I operate in the most. But critical to our success in transformation is the alignment with the other structures. After all, the results of our ability to source, make, and deliver to the demand created by the Demand Creation structure drives much of the business's financial performance.

Price is also its own structure, which I call Demand Performance. This structure really drives the business's financial strategy and value chain. Based on the development of a corporate strategy with associated objectives and performance metrics, this structure is really the driver of the Demand Creation and Demand Fulfillment structures to achieve profitable growth through investment and appropriation of capital to fund the business, measuring and guiding the operating performance of the demand creation and demand fulfillment structures, providing overall governance, ensuring compliance with the regulatory environment, recognizing (hopefully) a profit, and managing the return to shareholder value of the business.

Not only communicating the benefits of transformation within the perspective of the business, as we discussed in Chapter 2, but communicating how your supply network impacts and is impacted by the company's vertical structural strategies and changing market conditions are critical to gaining support for any transformation initiatives. Forrester's research and systems thinking is all about supporting management decisions and strategy across the organization to ensure alignment of the five critical horizontal process flow systems within an organization: capital, material, cash, information, and human resources.

What I have learned from systems thinking and working with companies of all sizes and in many different markets is that you cannot control the market or even necessarily your own organization. And you certainly cannot control your competition. As you will learn in more detail in Chapter 4, systems thinking teaches us that the vertical business structures and horizontal process flows are the real levers of organizational change. If you can place your company, one step at a time, one department at a time, on the transformational journey, your company culture will mature to a level of self-esteem and self-actualization that can learn from scanning the market for opportunity and create an organization response that seizes that opportunity and grows . . . profitably!

 ## NOTES

1. Mercer Management Consulting, "New Ways to Take Costs out of the Retail Food Pipeline: Making Replenishment Logistics Happen: A Study," 1993.
2. Martin, Andre, *DRP: Distribution Resource Planning*, Oliver Wight, 1983.
3. Elwin, Toby, "The Cost of Culture: A 50% Turnover of the Fortune 500," blog, 2011, www.tobyelwin.com/the-cost-of-culture-a-50-turnover-of-the-fortune-500.
4. http://money.cnn.com/magazines/fortune/fortune500/2009/full_list.
5. Sherman, Richard. "Look Ahead to Integrated Channels," *Transportation and Distribution*, Penton, March 1989.
6. Draper L. Kauffman, Jr., "Systems One: An Introduction to Systems Thinking" by Future Systems, Inc., 1980.
7. http://beta.abc.go.com/shows/castle/episode-guide.
8. Sterman, John D., "Teaching Takes Off: Flight Simulators for Management Education." *OR/MS Today*, 1992, pp. 40–44.

4

Business Structures Are the Levers of Change

WHILE THE BEER GAME teaches us that structure is a major lever of change, it's important to note that structure has multiple dimensions, or as I like to say, fulcrums . . . boundaries and rules, physical and informational, financial and material, cultural maturity, metrics, functional responsibilities, and other characteristics combine to define structure. How these dimensions or fulcrums are structured will determine how much power the lever has to move the rocks that are thrown on the path as we move along our transformational journey. What I have discovered over the years is that there are dimensions of structure that can be easily changed or, in the case of boundaries, in particular, that are very difficult or even impossible to change.

For example, in the Beer Game, it is not possible to change the physical boundaries of the game as it is structured. But, you say, what if we were to bypass the wholesaler and distributor and go retailer direct? What if we "open" communication among the participants? What if we break the rules? Bingo! Did the electricity light your bulb? Sure, you can change the structure, but when you do, you change the game. Structural changes can be powerful levers and can be game changers. P&G's transformation is a game changer. Wal-Mart's big box, everyday low price strategy is a game changer. Information and communications technology implementations, such as Colgate's, are game changers. Apple's iPhone and iPad are game changers. A look back over the past 10, 15, 25, 50 years yields some fascinating game-changing strategies—strategies that, as we noted earlier, left more than 80 percent of the 1955 Fortune 500 in the dust.

Are you experiencing any changes from the Internet, social networking, location-based services, or mobile communications? Are you planning for the Smart Supply Network? The convergence of cloud computing, software as a service, location-based services (GPS), pervasive wireless networks, smartphones, intelligent telecommunications, real-time analytics, artificial intelligence, transport telematics, intelligent AutoID with sensing and monitoring, and other emerging technologies may just make the next wave of change, a change tsunami. . . . It just kind of sneaks up on you without warning and then envelops you.

Transformation isn't just about *if*. It's all about *when*. The only *if* in transformation is whether you will survive it. Remember that *when* you join only determines whether you realize the rewards or pay the toll, whether you inhabit Leader City or Laggard City, the transformational gap between those at the front of the journey and those bringing up the rear doesn't close. Taking a look at how the major demand management structures in your organization (e.g., Demand Creation, Demand Fulfillment, and Demand Performance) are structured, which dimensions are progressing you forward, and which dimensions are inhibiting your progress is essential to advancing your journey.

Also important, as you will see, is how the structures interact with one another to progress or inhibit growth along the journey to Leader City. My longtime mentor, Bob Sabath, likes to point this out each day that the sun rises. Remember, structure is just a component of the system, and the system as a whole is composed of subsystems or structures that are all interconnected. How many times have you heard presentations on functional silos that say we have to break down the silos? The silos are inhibitors to progress and growth. We have to collaborate! I used to wonder how many years in a row visibility would top the list of major issues or challenges facing managers. Now I wonder how many decades I will be hearing it.

 ## YOU CAN'T BREAK DOWN THE SILOS: COLLABORATION IS THE KEY

As I mentioned earlier, logistics is not going to report to research and development anytime soon and vice versa. But you never know about some organizations. When I left UNISYS to join DEC, I was recruited by my first business mentor, Mike Prusha. Prusha had recruited me into Burroughs in my first real business job after leaving teaching. He mentored me throughout my 10-year career at Burroughs and went over to DEC when we merged with Sperry.

One of the reasons he was recruited into DEC was his experience managing line-of-business or industry solutions sales organizations. As I mentioned, DEC was in the throes of major transformation itself. As he became grounded at DEC, he needed a logistics expert on his consumer goods industry field team. And, because he did not have anyone internally, I became his first choice. It seemed a good move at the time.

So what does this have to do with logistics reporting to R&D? Well, shortly after joining DEC, Prusha took me out to Marlboro, MA (we were based in Chicago), to meet the other managers. DEC was a matrix organization. So while I reported to Prusha, Chief of Staff of the Central Area, and was partially funded by the U.S. Sales organization, I worked for the Director of Consumer Goods Industry Marketing and was partially funded by the Global Industry Marketing organization, and I worked with the Director of the Consumer Goods Application Center for Technology (ACT) and was partially funded by the U.S. Services organization. Of course, all three had different metrics, objectives, and ideas about just what the industry field team was supposed to be doing.

But that's only a background to the heart of the story. When we get to Marlboro, we meet with the industry marketing team. As with any DEC internal meeting, the first thing we have to do is figure out who and why everyone at the meeting is at the meeting. There are always a few people who by virtue of e-mail distribution lists become invited although they were not originally invited. As we are introducing ourselves, I note that all of the marketing people are engineers with backgrounds in product engineering or design or R&D, everything except marketing. When it comes time for Prusha, who is leading the meeting, to introduce himself, he talks about his undergrad and grad degrees in marketing and his 15 years of marketing and sales experience.

He then announces that he is taking a position leading R&D. Well, jaws are dropping and Mike asks why. The people in the room say that he does not have any of the qualifications for R&D. I will never forget Mike's answer. He very calmly points out that everyone in the room, except for me and him, have just said that they are in marketing but none of them had any marketing education, training, or experience. Why were they any more qualified to be in marketing than he or I was to be in R&D? It was then that I figured out that functional silos are silos because of what's required to get a particular job done. You can move people around. You can change reporting structures. You can reorganize a million times. But you can't necessarily change the nature of the work to be done.

Silos are formed around the people responsible for executing the work to be done. The work to be done is defined by the process it is a part of. As in Figure 4.1, everything that gets done gets done through a process. More about process later.

At the end of the day, silos are going to exist; however, if you transform your thinking from functional silos and organizational control and reporting, and start thinking about the organization as a system, you can begin to realize that these functions are not silos, they are *nodes*! They are nodes in the company's business operating system's network.

Note: I am using *system* in an organizational context here, not a technology context. In systems thinking (and in the Lean world), the methodology, culture, processes, people, technology, and other organizational components comprise the

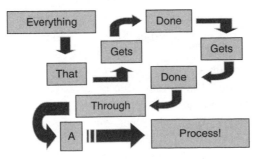

FIGURE 4.1 Process Mapping 101

company's business operating system. For example, the Toyota Production System or the Danaher Business System is not a technology. They are the operating environment of the company. We refer to these transformations as operating systems; they are not technologies.

The nodes of the organization have boundaries as the work moves from one node to the next in the process but they are necessary nodes to execute the company's mission and strategy organizationally.

You can't break them down any more than you can break down any other node in the company network and the supply network the company participates in. It's all a network of systems and subsystems that work independently of one another but whose behavior and outputs can have a major impact on the other nodes, immediately or time delayed. And the consequences can be minor or amplified based on where in the network the affected node is and what the affected process is.

When I was at IRI, we did a road show to evangelize the integration of our POS data and promotional analytics with supply chain planning, DRP at the time. The great thing about working at IRI in the consumer goods industry was that their relationships were with all of the market research and marketing folks and the CEOs generally came out of marketing, so they had great relationships, generally, with the CEOs. It was the first time I was really able to "call high." CEOs, especially at that time, generally didn't make much time available to hear about logistics. It may be changing with the recognition supply chain is getting today; regardless, CEOs don't make much time available to sales people in general. I did, however, meet with and spoke to more CEOs and operating committees during my time with IRI than the rest of my career combined. Keep this in mind . . . Don't waste their time.

So we are presenting at a major cosmetics company in New York City to the CEO and *all* of his direct reports, the company operating committee. The presentation was a demonstration of how as promotions are developed (usually in the quarter prior to the promotion), we provide the marketing analyst with promotional lift factors that will determine the incremental number of cases that the promotion is likely to generate based on a number of causal factor combinations (temporary price reduction (TPR), coupon drop, end aisle display, buy one, get one free (BOGO), two products for the price of one (twofer), etc.).

Based on that forecast, we can determine the number of cases that have to be produced and staged in order to meet the likely incremental demand generated by the promotion (I'll discuss this in more detail in Chapter 5). As we are going through the presentation, I see that the VP of Logistics is becoming increasingly uncomfortable and finally can't take it anymore.

"Time out!" he interrupts. "May I please ask a question?"

"Of course," I respond. "I am happy to answer any questions at any time."

"Not you!" he says emphatically. *"You!"* and he points to the VP of Marketing.

The VP of Marketing is expectedly somewhat surprised. "What?" he says.

"How long have you [marketing department] had this data and been doing promotional analysis?" the VP of Logistics asks.

"About two, maybe three years," the VP of Marketing innocently responds.

With that the VP of Logistics yells, "You son of a b----!" and starts to climb over the table to get at the VP of Marketing (remember, it's the early 1990s, not as PC as today). "Do you realize how much you have been costing me [our operations] by not sharing this information?"

"I didn't think it would matter," said the VP of Marketing. "You don't do the promotions; we do."

As things calmed down, the VP of Marketing learned that in the absence of the promotion plan information it was not unusual for the warehouse managers to come in some days only to find unplanned orders for anywhere from 10,000 to 100,000 cases sitting on their desk. Can you say "firefighting, expediting, premium freight, production changes, ca-ching, ca-ching, ca-ching?"

Is there a familiar ring to this story? Needless to say, let the collaboration begin!

As in the Beer Game, your journey will be impacted by, as well as impact, the other business structures of the organization at the points of process intersection. You can't break the silos down. But, like any network, you can begin to "connect the dots" and set about developing ways for the nodes to communicate and interact cross-functionally, or is that cross-nodally?

It's all about business process and structure. You have to look at the demand management structures of the organization and understand and document the processes they are executing to identify the levers that you have to create or transform to produce the results you want to achieve as you move through your journey. You will also be able to define the fulcrums and assess the power of the levers working for you and against you.

 ## UNDERSTANDING THE BUSINESS STRUCTURES AND PROCESSES THAT GOVERN THE BEHAVIOR OF THE ORGANIZATION

As I mentioned, I primarily developed my concept and methodology for using Demand Management from my experiences observing and working with people from P&G and from the enterprise systems architecture project at Colgate, as well as the "beer" companies. The Colgate experience, in particular, validated the Beer Game and systems thinking as the critical foundation for truly enabling the journey to excellence and Leader City. Of course, systems thinking was pretty institutionalized at P&G through the Leadership & Mastery workshops. I think it's safe to say that they are a learning organization, certainly at the self-actualization level of transformational culture maturity.

Lack of a holistic view, whether systems thinking or just looking at the supply chain as a whole, is probably one of the biggest inhibitors companies have when making the leap and stepping onto the journey. I think it is why so many people get mired in the status quo. They think they can control their environment. They think they can simply make incremental improvements to the operating efficiency of the company. They don't really look at their customers' or suppliers' operations. They don't have a concept of a system, and they consistently think events just happen. They think it will never change or, at least, that the change will never overwhelm them. When you're up to your neck in alligators, it's hard to remember your purpose was to drain the swamp.

I remember when I was with Burroughs and I was helping out one of our newer salespeople with a call on the president/owner (second-generation) of a privately held heating, plumbing, and air conditioning wholesale distribution business in Chicago.

We arrived at his office in time for the appointment. The secretary informed us he was on a call that was running a little late, but he was trying to shut it down and would be with us in a few minutes. Well, a few minutes extended into an hour. As we were waiting, I told the salesperson that he was probably on the phone with Alan Silver, who, along with Gordon Graham, was an industry visionary in developing inventory management principles for distributors. Silver just loved to talk and you could never get him off the phone no matter how hard you tried. I knew Silver and Graham quite well, and Graham and I did several seminars together.

As we walked into the president's office, I said, "Was Alan Silver on the phone with you?"

"Yes, how did you know?" he answered.

"Alan is the only person I know that takes an hour to hang up!" I said, as we both laughed and the ice was broken.

During the call, I explained all of the benefits of a new distribution management system and how the market was changing. We talked about the rapid return on investment and how EDI was going to start changing the way companies processed orders and "turn and earn" as Gordon Graham called GMROI-based inventory management. It was a great call and as we were wrapping up, the president leaned across his desk to ask me a question.

"Are you going to make me buy your system?" he asked.

"Well, as much as I would like to, I don't know if that's possible," I responded.

"Whew!" he sighed.

"Why?" I asked.

"Because I'm happy!" he offered. "I really think—no, I know that your system is great and that we could really use a new system. But it also sounds like it'll be a lot of work to implement it and things are going to change. But I am very, very happy!"

So the great call ended with a thud. Two years later, I saw that his company had been acquired by a competitor. Luckily for him, I am sure he made out quite well on the deal. And, like many second-generation owners of wholesale distribution companies, he was able to take an early retirement. It would not be the last time that I would lose business to the status quo. Getting people to change and managing change are going to be the biggest rocks in your journey.

 ## VERTICAL AND HORIZONTAL BUSINESS STRUCTURES AND DRIVERS

The demand management concept at the time was very new and visionary. And, as Forrester said, we might just have to wait for people to die. My guess is that you are struggling a bit with the fact that you or your organization haven't embraced the concept of demand management let alone begun defining your organization in terms of systems thinking and business process management.

The good news for us is that the P&G demand orientation got picked up by my successors at AMR and they evolved it to their mantra of a Demand Driven Supply Network (DDSN). Today, at least, the concept of "demand-driven" is more widely accepted. Everyone is being "demand-driven." As you'll see, the folks at AMR missed some of the more important tenets of market behavior, and I take a slightly different view, but it's a start to understanding how demand management can work with any methodology or process approach. If you go back to the roadmap I laid out at the end of Chapter 2, it includes define, measure, analyze, improve, and control (DMAIC)—a major tenet of Six Sigma. I also speak to taking waste out of the process and the voice of the customer, which are major tenets of Lean. One size does not fit all; I don't care what size or style shoe you wear. Let's just get them on the journey.

My approach is also simple enough that you can communicate transformational and systems thinking to just about any level of associate or manager that you need to using the building blocks that I am providing you with. At least you probably won't have to move many of the rocks that I have run into over the years. Most people today should have some notion of demand in their business vocabulary.

Let me take you through some more charts that I use to communicate the concepts to people starting their journey. As I mentioned in Chapter 3, it's founded quite simply on organizing around the 4Ps and 4Cs as in Figure 4.2. At the end of the day, all organizations create and fulfill demand in the market for what they bring as an offer to the market, and the results hopefully warrant the continued funding of the organization. I don't care what business you are in, whether you are a nonprofit or not, or

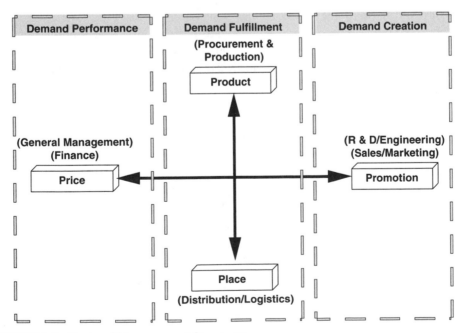

FIGURE 4.2 Demand Management Structures

whether your business involves a product or a service; you have to manage demand for your offer to continue to compete and stay in business.

Pretty straightforward, isn't it? Next, you need to identify the nodes in your company's business operating system network (your functional silos, remember). Here is where we start to make the transition from organizational strategy, reporting, and control and more into a process orientation. So far, I have been defining the business in vertical terms. We organize around activities (the work to be done) that are managed to achieve our objectives. We usually think vertically when we are thinking about developing company strategy and mission, organizational goal setting, span of control, and executing the business strategy that emerges from its business perspective within the context of its market environment (see Chapters 2 and 3).

Figure 4.3 shows the nodes of the business arranged into the demand management structures that are responsible for the activities they perform to meet the company's goals. I am leveraging my experience with consumer goods manufacturers to illustrate the structural analysis. You will have different departments and/or functions depending on the characteristics of your industry and company, but there should not be much confusion about whether the activities are associated with creating demand, fulfilling demand, or the financial management of demand within the organization. Channels and customer facing should also be pretty straightforward.

So here comes the tricky part. When most people look at the supply chain, they look at it horizontally, from point of supply to point of consumption and now disposal, right? Process thinking is horizontal. But, remember, I want you to be a systems thinker. Organizations are *managed* vertically. The nodes in the network are arranged vertically from a management perspective; they *behave* horizontally from a process perspective. As a system, as also illustrated in Figure 4.3, the organization will have to operate both vertically and horizontally to successfully achieve the business goals while simultaneously serving and responding to the demands of its channel/consumer customers. Think of all of the reorganizations and reengineering that has occurred over the years trying to be either vertical or horizontal instead of looking at it as an operating system of horizontal processes managed vertically to achieve the business goals.

Remember the three envelopes story? A manager takes on his new assignment and is handed three envelopes, each to be opened in response to a disaster. The first disaster comes, the first envelope is opened, and it reads, "Blame your predecessor!"

The second disaster comes, the second envelope is opened, and it reads, "Reorganize!"

The third disaster comes, the third envelope is opened, and it reads, "Prepare three envelopes!"

Don't wait for envelope number three. Get on that journey now!

 ## EVERYTHING THAT GETS DONE GETS DONE THROUGH A PROCESS . . . BUSINESS PROCESS MANAGEMENT

Remember Figure 4.1? During the early 1990s, there was a lot of reorganizing, reengineering, rightsizing, and general business disruption. Companies were really just beginning to recognize business process management. The business book writers

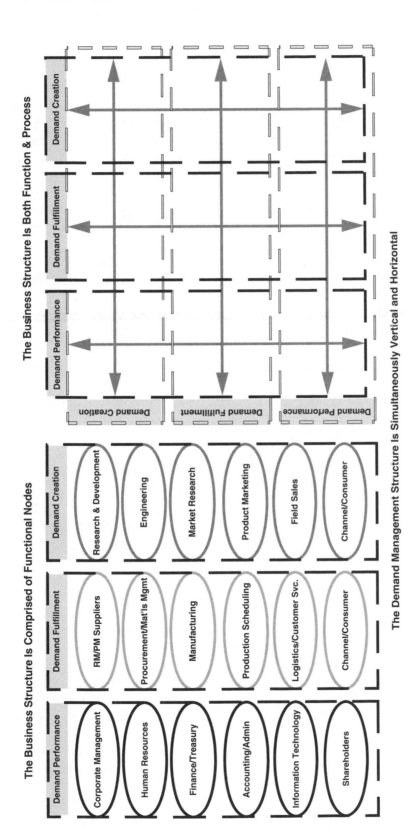

FIGURE 4.3 Organizing the Demand Management Structures

61

were having a field day. Consulting companies were realizing unprecedented levels of utilization. I remember visiting an orange juice manufacturer in Florida when we were on our IRI road show.

We were to meet the senior supply chain team that was working on a process reengineering project. They had leased a couple of floors at a local bank and called it The Bunker. As I began meeting different people, I realized that there were consulting teams from two "Big Eight" firms, one major system integrator, and three leading strategy firms working together on different business process characteristics and leveraging their unique practice capabilities and experience. Some were working technology, some business strategy, some logistics strategy, some production strategy, some were mapping operating processes. And, remember, I said teams of associates. Can you imagine the burn rate on that project?

It was a great time to own stock in 3M. The industry was churning through tens of thousands of Post-it® notes a day mapping all of the activities every major corporation performed. They even came out with different-colored notes so that we could use different colors to represent different process and activity levels and types. Process mapping can take many different forms and methods; however, the essence of process mapping is that like the sentence in Figure 4.1, processes have a beginning and an end with various steps or activities that take you from beginning to end.

It's like diagramming a sentence in elementary school. What does each word (step) in the sentence (process) represent and do? All of the words are subjects, verbs, objects, adjectives, adverbs, prepositions, conjunctions, and so on. Using a visualization technique such as Post-it® notes, index cards, or tools like Visio, SmartDraw, or Value Stream mapping, you simply map out all of the activities you go through to execute the process from beginning to end.

I remember at DEC we used a technique called Top Mapping that created topological process maps with islands and swamps and rivers and seas. It was quite an interesting exercise.

Don't make any judgments. Map the process and activities as is. We are defining the processes at this point. Measure, Analyze, Improve, and Control come later. As you can imagine, in the absence of any guides or standards, you will go through a lot of Post-it® notes during the process mapping exercise.

So, let's go back to 1996. I was at AMR Research. I had just launched the first Supply Chain Advisory Services research practice for AMR.

The problem facing companies and consultants at the time was that there was no standard definition of this new thing, supply chain. And there was certainly no process definition to reference when embarking on a reengineering project . . . kind of like supply chain transformation to a Smart Supply Network and the journey to Leader City right now.

So one of the leading consulting firms in Boston, Pittiglio, Rabin, Todd, & McGrath (PRTM, which is now part of PWC), had an idea to create a reference model that could serve to standardize a significant number of steps in defining supply chain processes. They were very strong in business process and performance management, but not as strong in the technology side and especially the supply chain technology solution landscape. To complement their competency, they approached AMR with a partner proposition to develop the model and we agreed.

When we first got together, PRTM revealed to us that they had conceptually defined supply chain as three major processes: Source, Make, and Deliver. Of course, I argued successfully, but not without a lot of discussion, that we really needed a fourth component: Plan. My argument centered around the fact that there were different types of planning that were utilized in Source, Make, and Deliver that were unique to each, but they had to be integrated into an end-to-end supply chain planning process. So, dragging them kicking and screaming (never suggest to a consultant expanding the scope of a project unless you can bill for it), Plan was added as a fourth process type. At the time, no one was really too concerned about returns; it wasn't until several years later that Return was added as a major process type to the model.

PRTM was very proficient and recognized for their industry benchmarking and wanted to leverage their capabilities as part of the overall metrics component of the model. As a result, the concept of calling the model SCORE was born. Trying to come up with the "E" proved to be arduous; and we couldn't trademark protect it. So, we agreed to go with calling it the Supply Chain Operations Reference (SCOR® is a registered trademark of the Supply Chain Council) model. Figure 4.4 illustrates the model (today, many people want to refer to it as a framework) within the context of the Demand Management business structures. This depiction has Return Source and Return Deliver included as well.

The original project scope was to focus solely on the supply chain (Demand Fulfillment) and not include processes in Demand Creation or Demand Performance.

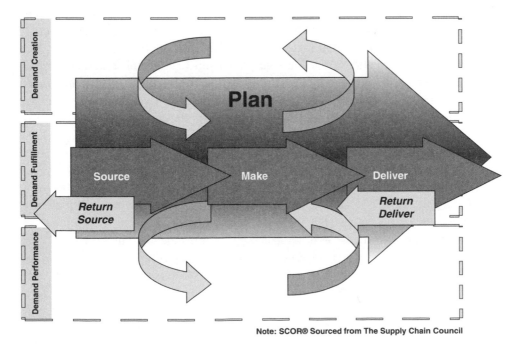

Note: SCOR® Sourced from The Supply Chain Council

FIGURE 4.4 The SCOR® Model or Framework

In fact, in the original project scope and, to this day, the SCOR® model does not include many cost or financial measures. There is a working committee looking into the financial metrics; however, it's still early in the process. The metrics that we focused on were largely process performance metrics and were largely designed around the metrics that PRTM's benchmarking organization, the Performance Management Group (PMG), was using as part of their benchmarking services.

To develop the model, we agreed to invite our mutual clients to participate in what PRTM suggested as the Supply Chain Council. Industry consortia were pretty common at the time as companies were experiencing some real challenges with this thing called supply chain. We obtained a commitment from around 60 companies (it ended up being 69) to send a couple of people to Boston for several working group sessions to develop a cross-industry standard for defining supply chain processes. Bernie Student from PRTM and I led the Deliver team.

So, on April 11, 1996, we were to have our first Supply Chain Council meeting. I will never forget that day. We planned for an 8:00 A.M. meeting at the Boston Hyatt Harborside Hotel as nearly all of the client participants were flying in from around the country. What we didn't plan on was for Boston to get a pretty sizable April snowfall late the night of April 10 that would make ground travel pretty impossible for several hours with significant delays after that. Of course, the snowfall didn't begin until well after our clients had retired for the evening. When they got to the meeting rooms the morning of the 11th, all of the attendees were present and accounted for, but none of the hosts were there. We were all snowed in. So, true to supply chain management, the kickoff of the Supply Chain Council experienced an unexpected, unplanned disruption and delayed start that caused major schedule changes.

Today, the Supply Chain Council is an independent, not-for-profit industry trade association that is focused on developing and maintaining industry standards for supply chain process management and performance improvements and measurement. As a founder, former board and North American Leadership Team member, and director for North America, I will say that I have a bit of a bias toward the SCOR® model. It has been developed and is maintained primarily by practitioners, and its working committees are open to any interested party regardless of membership in the council. It's simply an open industry standard that can get you through the first three levels of process analysis detail with metrics and benchmarking data very rapidly and at a cost of less than three to five days of even the lowest price consulting associate's time. There is no reason any company can't jump start their transformation journey using the SCOR® model to document and assess their supply chain processes. 3M may not appreciate the reduction in demand for Post-it® notes, but there will be some happy trees.

Placing the SCOR® model aside for a moment, Figure 4.4 illustrates how SCOR® fits within the context of the Demand Management structures. However, you can use any process mapping technique or tools that you are comfortable with. As I mentioned earlier, I have seen many companies using value stream mapping to document their supply chain. APQC's Process Classification Framework™ (PCF) can be applied to it. And the enterprise version extends into the Demand Creation and Demand Performance structures very nicely. The CSCMP Process Standards were originally developed around Plan, Source, Make, Deliver, and Return as well. And, while it acknowledged the Supply

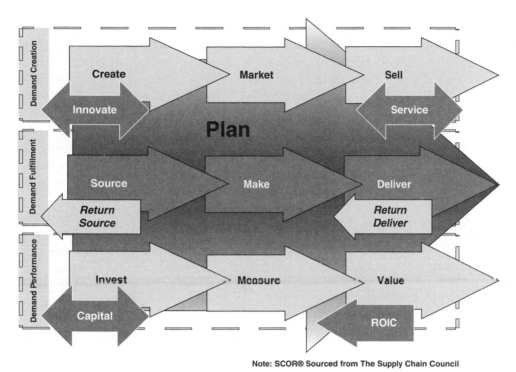

Note: SCOR® Sourced from The Supply Chain Council

FIGURE 4.5 Demand Management Structure Extended Processes

Chain Council in its first edition, in its second iteration, the CSCMP Process Standards aligned more with the APQC PCFs. Both CSCMP and the SCC use APQC as their benchmarking service provider, so they are pretty interchangeable, IMHO.

The Supply Chain Council has introduced two new frameworks, the Design Chain Operations Reference (DCOR) and the Customer Chain Operations Reference (CCOR) frameworks, but they were developed by one of the company members, lack maturity, and lack an industry standard validation. As they are in very early versions that don't tie as well into the Demand Management structures framework, I am suggesting my own extensions for Demand Creation and Demand Performance. As illustrated in Figure 4.5, I have suggested that for a high-level process starting point, similar in context to SCOR®, the major process types for Demand Creation should be Plan, Create, Market, and Sell with extended process types for Innovate and Service. The high-level major process types for Demand Performance are Invest, Measure, and Value with extended process types for capital and return on invested capital (ROIC).

In the Demand Creation structure, Create refers to processes that a company executes to develop new products, services, or offers to market. I include Innovate as an extended process because many companies are extending their development of new concepts for offers to market beyond their own research or product development resources, especially leveraging academic research and private design firms. Create and Innovate are high-level enough to cross industries from a point of process definition.

Market refers to those processes within a company that execute the commercialization of offers coming out of Create and the processes that a company executes to promote its offers to prospective customers, channels, and/or consumers. Market processes are executed as the primary volume driving processes for the company's offers as well as determining the markets both geographic and demographic that the company will promote its offers in and to.

Sell refers to those processes a company executes to convert its offers into orders by the customers, channels, and/or consumers specifically. I consider service to be an extended process as companies may or may not have a significant enough service process component to warrant extended process definition. For example, we included some service in the original SCOR® Deliver process. However, it was not really considered by many to be a process type of supply chain. Return was developed more to deal with the return of physical product than service in a support, maintenance, or installation/implementation context. It wasn't until CCOR was developed that the SCC really began addressing service processes.

There is an old adage that says "Nothing happens until we get an order!" The reality is that if you're not paying attention to all of the "happenings" before the order, in Create/Innovate, Market, and Sell/Service, you will be fighting forest fires more often than you would like. The same can be said for the Demand Performance structure.

The major process types that I have identified within the Demand Performance structure are Invest, Measure, and Value with extended processes for capital and return on invested capital (ROIC). Invest represents those processes, traditionally finance and treasury, that a company executes to attract and appropriate capital to run the business. I have identified capital itself as an extended process as many companies are public and will have extended processes for managing different sources of capital into the company, as well as investments outside the company in the form of joint ventures, mergers and acquisitions, funds management, and so on.

The Measure processes are generally those financial processes that are traditional accounting processes for managing general ledger, accounts payable and receivable, and other processes generally linked to measure and control the financial activities supporting the operating processes in Demand Creation and Demand Fulfillment. It's debatable whether human resources and information technology belong in Invest or Measure; however, I think most people would agree that human resources and information technology are cross-structural assets and flows that are best executed as Demand Performance processes.

The Value process refers to those processes executed to recognize revenue and costs associated with the output of the Measure process type that determines whether the company is profitable and providing a return on invested capital (ROIC) acceptable to the shareholders of the company, private or public. I consider ROIC as an extended process as it is impacted by all of the processes the company executes and is arguably the most important financial metric of company performance, though some may say EBITA or free cash flow is their most important financial metric. I will leave it to the finance people to determine priorities; but, as you are developing your roadmap for transformation, it is critical that you clearly communicate in terms that are important levers to

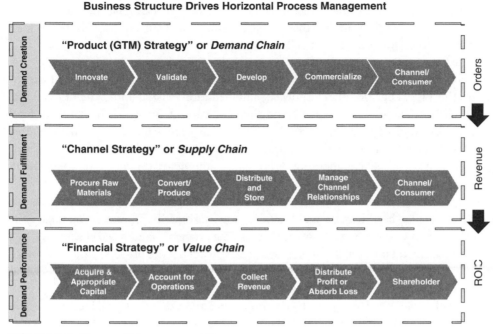

FIGURE 4.6 Demand Management Processes

the senior management and board of directors what the financial benefits and implications are to be realized from making the journey.

Figure 4.6 illustrates a non-SCOR® process perspective of the Demand Management structures to appeal to the SCOR® "bashers" out there. You know who you are! I created the Demand Management structure to be completely agnostic of the various methodologies that can be applied to supply chain transformation. Pick the flavor of the week and use it to move forward. Demand Management is simply a communications tool to frame transformation in a way that considers the business holistically as an operating system and as a part of the larger market ecosystem.

Looking at the business processes from a Demand Management structure perspective enables you to very rapidly and concisely document and define all of the major functions (nodes) in the enterprise and their logical position in the business system network regardless of what methodology, model, framework, or whatever you want to use. The point is, from a visualization point of view, you are able to speak to the interrelationships or intersections among the nodes from a vertical management perspective to implement the company strategy and objectives.

Simultaneously, you can visualize how the nodes take on a horizontal process perspective that identifies external facings and objectives that create value in the market for customers, channel partners, and other participants in the market while generating a sufficient ROIC to meet the requirements of the company's shareholders, public or private.

Defining all of the Demand Management enterprise processes, at least at a high level, enables you to show major inputs and outputs of the different structures' business processes that, as a business operating system, can impact or be impacted by the processes being executed in the other demand management structures. This is especially important in creating a spirit of collaboration and team learning.

Just as the Marketing VP of the cosmetics firm didn't know how not sharing his promotion management information was dramatically impacting the cost of operations, the VP of Logistics didn't know such information existed and couldn't ask for it. And, clearly, senior management and finance weren't aware of how the lack of information sharing was impacting ROIC. Team learning is a characteristic of higher levels of transformational culture maturing; but we often don't know what we don't know. As we will see, collaboration is critical to advancing on your journey. Leaders are part of a team. I don't think an individual "leads" him- or herself.

By focusing on process management and collaboration, you also take the people out of the process. There was no bad intent in not sharing the promotion management information. It was just not part of the process. The process is comprised of activities, not individuals. By taking people out of the process, you can fix the process without blaming the people. Remember the "accidental adversaries" outcome, and blame was generated by the structure and operating processes in the Beer Game.

Another benefit of mapping, documenting, and analyzing processes is capturing the "tribal knowledge" of the company. As companies grow older, so do their employees. Many companies that are now 30 or more years old are facing "gray tsunamis" in that a reasonably high percentage (10 percent or more) of their employees are retiring each year. As those 30-year veterans leave the company, 30 years of experience or tribal knowledge goes with them. And, when many, if not most, of your operations are operated based on that tribal knowledge and a custom spreadsheet that has evolved over the years, that process knowledge documentation may be critical to your future success. Now is the time to start the journey and document the processes. Everything that gets done gets done through a process.

CHAPTER FIVE

If You're Driven by Demand, You're Probably Being Driven Crazy

AS AN OBSERVER OF P&G for many years, I don't think they are demand-driven. In my opinion they *are* consumer-driven and they *are* holistic in their vision of the flow of demand throughout their organization and the channels they operate in. However, their focus is on profitably *responding* to demand. In consumer industries, as I learned at IRI, demand variability is so wide, so unpredictable, and so influenced by any number of dimensions, consumer fickleness among the biggest, that if you are driven by demand, you will be driven crazy.

Remember my good friend Rick Blasgen from Nabisco, now CEO of CSCMP®? When I was at IRI and working with Blasgen at Nabisco on some of our first integrations of POS data analysis and DRP, he called me one night.

"Rich, I finally figured out what we are going to do to improve our forecast accuracy," he told me.

"Wow, Rick, that's great!" I exclaimed. "Did you find a new forecasting methodology? Are you going to implement a POS-based replenishment system?"

"Nope, we are going to put in a call center," he replied firmly.

"What?" was my puzzled response.

"Yeah, we're putting in a call center to phone 200 million consumers every night and ask 'em what they're gonna buy tomorrow," he explained.

Then, after a good laugh, we started to discuss the reality of the unpredictability of what consumers are going to buy every day. My children, when we lived in Chicago, used to love making queso with RO∗TEL diced tomatoes and chiles and Velveeta cheese. When we moved to Boston, the local supermarket did not carry RO∗TEL which was pretty disappointing to the kids. So on my next business trip to Chicago (pre-TSA days), I stopped by a local Jewel and wiped out their shelf stock of RO∗TEL. I probably stuffed two dozen cans in my carryon for the return trip.

While the kids were thrilled, what do you think Jewel did? Do you think they had forecasted the "run" on RO∗TEL that would wipe out the stock at Store 484 that week? Did alerts go off to immediately up the forecast and recalculate shelf allocation of RO∗TEL? Did they see a major demand trend for RO∗TEL in the Chicago market? I doubt it. Probably, there were a few consumers who found an empty shelf the rest of that week for RO∗TEL at Store 484 but, if they really needed it, they went across the street to Dominick's and picked it up. And was that really lost revenue to Jewel? Didn't Jewel run out sooner than expected due to an unusual increase in its *rate of sale* for RO∗TEL? Wasn't my bonus sale worth the couple of lost cans to Dominick's (assuming the consumers didn't just wait until their next trip to Jewel)? Of course, you may say that the forecasting system would just consider it to be an outlier. But the reality, at least in consumer industries, is that outliers are more common than you think and that consumer demand is highly unpredictable.

Keep in mind the term *rate of sale (ROS)* versus *point of sale (POS)*. I will be talking about it from time to time in Chapters 6 and 7. It's one of those little tweaks to perception that lead people to make "blunder assumptions." If, for example, you are doing lost sales analysis based on out-of-stocks (OOS) at the shelf level, do you calculate whether the OOS was due to an increase in the item's rate of sales? If you sold more unexpectedly faster, there may be a temporary loss of opportunity during the period of the OOS to restock. But does it really represent a "loss" in sales? And did you consider if the OOS is temporary or represented a pattern of increased volume? If it is temporary and you recalculate the shelf set quantity, you may risk cost increases due to excess inventory. The devil is always in the details. It's a system of interconnected causes and effects and cost trade-offs. Systems thinking is critical to business analytics.

At the first Systems Thinking in Action Conference in Boston there was an exhibit area with companies demonstrating applications of systems thinking. I met with a young gentleman, Michael Saylor, who was laboring with a mobile connection to demonstrate his application. No one seemed to be paying much attention to his exhibit area, which was quite Spartan. We got to talking and he explained to me that he was an MIT grad (knew Senge and Goodman) who had developed systems dynamics models for simulating the potential product life cycles for a joint venture between Merck and DuPont using what he termed Relational On-Line Analytic Processing (ROLAP) while he was with DuPont.

Of course, I was familiar with OLAP (On-Line Analytic Processing), but ROLAP was really fascinating and took business analytics to a new level of simulation. He suggested to DuPont that it might be a good business in and of itself. But, as I would learn is DuPont's way, they determined that the technology was not a core DuPont business. With their blessing, they engaged him as a consultant to seed his new venture, provided him with an office in Wilmington, and the business intelligence (BI) and analytics company MicroStrategy was born. No one at the conference seemed to pay much attention, but Michael's was probably the most successful application of systems dynamics in attendance. Years later, Mike Goodman was surprised when I told him "Little Michael" was the head of a major BI company. Today, Michael is a legend in business and technology and an example of the impact systems thinking can have on business analytics.

It doesn't matter whether you're operating in the Demand Creation structure or the Demand Fulfillment structure. The process behaviors of one will have consequence in the other at the points where the processes intersect, as in the example of the cosmetics company in Chapter 4.

As I intimated, one of my pet peeves is how many industry pundits that make blunder assumptions evangelize them as new "industry trends or strategies" without considering the details, the reality, or the practicality. As I alluded to earlier, investors, for example, should really bone up on operations, supply chain management, and, for that matter, sales and marketing. Think of how many millions have been invested in "hype" over the past decade. I would recommend that investors use my demand management structure template in every due diligence they conduct to understand how and why a company's processes generate the financial results they do. Instead, they pick up some trendy article or do some Googling and all of a sudden everybody is an expert. How hard can this be? It's very hard, if you are not thinking systems dynamics. In supply chain, holistic thinking is critical.

Just the other day, I was in a "community" discussion about POS-driven replenishment and an executive (CEO) of a company said that if the retailer has a good ERP system, data capture and sharing shouldn't be an issue. It should just be simple demand planning. Hear that, all you forecasters out there? It should be simple demand planning, right?

Look at the Internet-based home delivery bubble hype and burst that I mentioned earlier. Was I the only person who did the math? Was I the only person to think you should build in multiple engines and brakes changes cost into the depreciation schedule of equipment in the financial model? How can you use "off the lot" vehicles when they have to have different temperature zones to keep products from spoiling? Where will all of the drivers come from? In fact, if home delivery was going to be so profitable, Schwan's Foods would be the largest food retailer, not Wal-Mart.

Direct Store Delivery (DSD) was a really hot strategy until someone, like me, did the math on that. A retail store typically carries hundreds to thousands of suppliers' products. If they all delivered their products direct to the store as in our Visioneering exercise, there would be no room in the parking lot, let alone the store, for the consumers. Try shopping during a *consolidated* restocking of a grocery store.

Here is one of my favorite blunder assumptions. It's the early 1990s and we, at DEC, are popularizing the Beer Game across all industries, but heavily in consumer (it was my assigned industry, after all). Soon after we stopped marketing the Digital Logistics Architecture and using the Beer Game as a promotional tool. By this time, though, I had written some articles, Senge was becoming a business rock star, and a number of the advanced planning and scheduling (APS) vendors were growing their marketing and picked up the Beer Game as a natural. But they never spent much time actually looking at POS data. They did not understand the underlying principles of what the Beer Game was designed to demonstrate. They just wanted to sell systems based on the inability of the people playing the game to control the bullwhip effect.

The main tenet of the game is that there is only one slight fluctuation in consumer demand in the early part of the game. For the most part, demand is constant or flat through the year simulated. That isn't reality. Forrester added only one slight change to show that the assumption that demand variability was the reason for the bullwhip effect was flawed. While Forrester probably had no idea what real retail demand variability was, he developed the rules to demonstrate systems dynamics' behavioral impact, not what really happens in a retail supply chain.

But the APS vendors at the time were pitching statistical forecasting and planning tools, primarily targeted to consumer goods manufacturers. And, after all, the Beer Game depicted a multi-echelon consumer goods supply chain. It's MIT; it must be real, right? So what do they do? They go out evangelizing that retail demand is actually relatively flat, and the manufacturers, at least the residents of Laggard City, *believed* them. Most of the supply chain planning software companies didn't pick up on causal factors and event-based planning. They did, however, sell millions of dollars in software.

You can't imagine how far behind that put collaboration and operations improvement initiatives. I think it's why sales and operations planning (S&OP) has taken 25 years, probably 35 years, to become relevant again. It's probably why so many people, like my CEO buddy on the community discussion, think it is just "simple demand planning." It's also why so many people want to be "demand-driven" instead of being "demand-responsive." My purchase of RO∗TEL should have immediately triggered either an alert to order RO∗TEL on the next store replenishment or automatically added it to the store replenishment order. The store would profitably respond to the demand variability and not be "driven" by it. Semantics, maybe; but the subtle difference is causing companies to spend millions on low-impact fulcrums and levers.

Why not give the day-to-day planners and schedulers the tools they need to support the daily million-dollar working capital decisions they make correcting the forecast, planning, and scheduling errors being generated by the gazillion-dollar ERP system?

So, let me dispel the flat demand at POS myth. Figure 5.1 is a chart for the forecasted sales rate (ROS), actual store sales rate (ROS), which is based on the POS data, fair share allocation based on availability, shelf pack-out quantity replenishment, and store

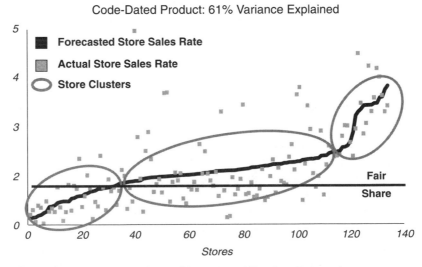

FIGURE 5.1 A Retail Chain Analysis of Store-Level Product Demand

clustering (stores with similar sales) for a code-dated product (orange juice, not beer) at a regional retail chain of about 140 stores. In my experience, its behavior is more common than not for most products. It was certainly that way when we were doing analysis of retailer-shared store by store demand data early on at Colgate. It's what we did for a living at IRI. It's what many people in the Demand Creation structure do for a living; only many do it often without thinking through the impact on Demand Fulfillment. The Leaders do. The Laggards? They probably don't know.

Do you see much variation in demand from store to store? The orange juice supply chain team in "The Bunker" certainly thought so. What was really interesting was that this was the demand analysis for the "premium" brand product. The demand for the "regular" brand product was almost the opposite on a store-by-store basis, but, more important, it was definitely opposite in the clusters of stores in the upper and lower demand clusters of each.

What we figured out was that the demographics for the high-demand stores for premium was upper income and the demographics for the low-demand stores for premium was lower income and exactly the opposite for the regular brand (surprise?). As you can see, the demand at the largest cluster was reasonably close to the fair share, but the product overall had a 61 percent variance. So the behavior at the high- and low-demand stores was that they would be out of the product in demand and dumping (code dated) the other product down the sewer or leaving it for the reclamation center to pick it up. All with additional labor and back room cost, by the way.

The solution was to replenish to the shelf set at the large cluster stores and let the store managers at the high-demand and low-demand store clusters adjust the product shelf sets manually to reflect the demographics and actual demand at their stores. This is what merchandising managers, category managers, and brand managers do for a living. In the absence of collaboration and sharing the information between Demand Creation and Demand Fulfillment structures, chaos reigns in Laggard City.

In the absence of integrated business planning, operations runs their monthly or weekly statistical, historic shipments-based forecast—in consumer goods, at least, forecasts based on historical data produce hysterical results—and turns it over to the planners and schedulers to apply their tribal knowledge and custom spreadsheets to fight the fires of variability of actual from plan. At DEC, we referred to it as Actual Delta (difference from) Plan, A∆P. Remember, the main driver of the Demand Creation structure is to change history, hopefully, by creating new demand. The Leaders are extending well beyond S&OP and some, beyond integrated business planning. The Laggards think it is a fad that won't last out the year.

WHAT ARE THE DEMAND CREATION STRUCTURE PROCESS TYPES?

While my "day job" over the years has largely been in sales and marketing with technology companies, I took "consultative selling" so seriously that I actually have been a consultant as long as I have been a sales and marketing professional. And, of course, I have been an industry analyst as well. I have worked on projects and with firms in wholesale and retail distribution for industrial, electrical, vehicles, electronics, food, drugs, convenience, and just about everything in between.

I have worked with manufacturers in automotive, food and beverage, grocery, all types of consumer goods, chemical, high tech and electronics, pharmaceutical . . . job shops, assembly, process, discrete, high and low volume, and just about everything in between. Remember, supply chain is relatively new. When I started, logistics was new. . . . There weren't a lot of business or engineering programs focused on supply chain. So, in the early days, if you knew how stuff moved and why, just about every industry had a need for your skills. It's not too different today, there are just a lot more of us. And, much to my chagrin, more educated. Sometimes you need to learn things the old-fashioned way . . . on the job. Brilliance, in the absence of the wisdom of experience, can be problematic to the management of the organization. And vice versa!

So, as we look at the Demand Creation structure, I have experience both working in and with the processes for demand creation, especially from a high-tech perspective. Of course, I am also going to leverage my experience in consumer goods a little more than other industries and probably share another beer story or two. Over the years, I have found two things: (1) People across industries can relate to the consumer experience and (2) the techniques, issues, and process learning from consumer can be applied to most other industries. My consumer Demand Creation process experience has led to some pretty innovative recommendations to nonconsumer clients.

That's not to say, however, that I won't be drawing on my experiences outside consumer from time to time as they have led to some pretty interesting approaches to consumer challenges. Best practices, I have found, evolve from the unique problems people experience across industries. You can learn a lot working for a fish broker, as I did in Chicago. Ben Kozloff Foods was a seafood distributorship and I was invited to conduct a distribution audit.

Ben would jump on the road buying fish, usually in Asia. He would phone in the amounts he purchased. Whoever took the call would jump up and yell, "Sell it or smell it!" And the office would mobilize into a frenzy, selling the catch, pound by pound, starting with large restaurant chains and working their way down to the corner store in their sales network. That was one nimble supply chain and it taught me about lead time and profitable response. If a small office in Chicago can distribute time-sensitive product from Asia to points located throughout the United States, with only the basic technology of the 1980s, why can't you do it today? It's time to get on the journey.

I think you will be able to relate to many of the techniques and approaches that I will identify in the Demand Creation structure as important to influencing behavior in Demand Fulfillment/supply chain management. The elements of Demand Creation will be important fulcrums and levers to your supply chain transformation. It has also been my experience that demand uncertainty is not limited to consumer industries, and I have leveraged my consumer industry experience across many industry segments both process and discrete and vice versa. Managing uncertainty is just a way of life in the supply chain, regardless of the industry you operate in.

As mentioned in Chapter 4, there are six major process types in the Demand Creation structure as illustrated in Figure 5.2. Planning is common to all Demand Management structures. You have to plan the Demand Chain and you have to plan

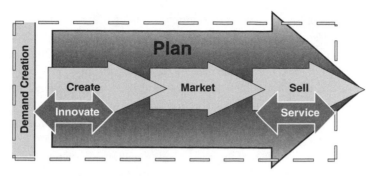

FIGURE 5.2 The Demand Creation Structure

each of the process types, Create, Market, and Sell, as well as plan Innovate and Plan service. The overall objective of the Demand Creation structure is to increase market share and volume while creating a competitive advantage for the company.

The Create process type is composed of those process categories and elements that are required to develop new products, services, or offers to the market that will generate business for the company. I identify Innovate as a subprocess type of Create, as I believe that there are innovators and there are followers. Some companies invest heavily in research and being the first to market; others invest heavily in development of like products and don't take as much risk. I attended a conference of the Healthcare Distribution Management Association in May 2012. Doug Long, vice president of industry relations from IMS Health, Inc., postulated that many pharmaceutical companies are evolving from research and development to "search and develop." They are looking for new products discovered by outside sources, buying them, and developing them for commercial release. As a result, the innovate process is subtly different from the Create process in that it often extends outside the organization through academic sponsored research or open bids to design firms and other sources of innovation including suppliers. One of my tennis friends in Austin, Mike Durrett, is a physicist who works for an independent research and development firm, Nanohmics, that is a contract innovation and engineering company.

Regardless of the company's investment strategy, companies will perform research to determine the products, services, and offers they *can bring* to the market. While distributors and retailers generally don't make products, they do execute a Create process for research into the various brands, product lines, and items they will bring to market, often in the form of a merchandising or marketing department. Many retailers are also manufacturers with either owned or outsourced assets producing private-label products to be carried by their stores. TOPCO Associates LLC is an example of a retail co-operative that develops private label products for its members, contracts for the production, and manages the distribution of product throughout the retail member network (for private label and, often, redistributed branded products). The members, often regional competitors, benefit significantly from this collaboration, or, should we say, "co-opetition." Collaboration is the key to Leader City.

The Market process begins with the *validation* analysis of the products, services, or offers coming from the Create process. Market research will determine the market segments most attractive for the company's offers and the size and competitive landscape of the segments to *develop* the company's offer to be a *commercial* success. If the offer can be *validated* and *commercialized* in the market the company competes in, the Market process *develops* the "go-to-market" (GTM) strategy and recommends competitive pricing for the offer. Another component of the GTM is the product launch and promotion plans for creating sufficient volume and revenue to achieve market share and product profitability objectives for the product.

Once the GTM strategy is completed and the offer is launched into the market, the Sell process takes over. Depending on the company's industry and offer, the Sell process may be direct or indirect . . . selling directly to the buyer or selling through channels of trading partners, such as distributors, brokers, retailers, manufacturer's representatives, and so on. The Sell process categories and elements will be defined by the company's sales model.

Some of the categories of the Sell process type may be to validate the GTM, develop the sales model, relate to the customers or channels, and maintain the relationship over time. Of course, all of the process elements in the Sell process type are driven by AFTO ("ask for the order") and CTO ("close the order.") I have also included Service as a process type as many industries have to install or implement the company's offer as well as provide support, maintenance, and repair to the customers. There can also be a warranty component that has to be considered, which can be a Service process type as much as a category.

While my purpose is not to develop a complete demand creation operations reference model (I will let the Supply Chain Council continue in that vein), I do want to emphasize that the processes being executed in the Demand Creation structure are every bit as complex and specialized as the processes in Demand Fulfillment. That's why they are considered separate structures and why R&D won't report to logistics and vice versa anytime soon.

As we learned in Chapter 4, it is critical that you identify the nodes and then the players in the Demand Creation structure. Your supply chain transformation will largely be based and driven by establishing collaboration with those nodes and players and an implementation of an integrated business planning (call it sales and operation planning [S&OP], if you want) process between the Demand Fulfillment and Demand Creation structures. It will also have to include integration with the product lifecycle management (PLM) process that, like S&OP, is finally becoming relevant again. These integrations generally comprise the difference between Leader City and Laggard City as the activities and results from successful execution of Demand Creation are what drive Demand Fulfillment. At the highest level of transformational culture maturity, collaboration is institutionalized and assumed. The Leaders have even systemized it. Collaboration is the key to Leader City.

 ## DEMAND CREATION PROCESSES IMPACT DEMAND FULFILLMENT BEHAVIOR DRAMATICALLY

Remember my story about the "beam me a Bud" analogy that I use at virtually all of the presentations I give? It's been a source of some fun and learning for me and, hopefully, my audiences over the years. When presenting at a CLM conference one year, as I was getting ready to begin the presentation, I saw, sitting in the first row, one of my clients from Anheuser-Busch, and we chatted a bit. Naturally, when it came time for the beer story, I said, "Beam me a Bud," so as not to annoy him.

After the presentation, another one of my clients, Howard Stone, from Bass Brewery, came up to me a bit agitated.

"So why didn't you beam yerself a Bass, then, Rich," Howard said in his English accent.

I can understand Howard's agitation as we had spent a few times scouring London for a pub with Bass on tap (Bass is more their export brand), and Stone also knew that Bass was the first beer I ever had. And, of course, I had used Bass as the object of my beaming when I knew he was in the room. But I hadn't known he was in attendance at this meeting.

"Howard, I am so sorry," I sincerely responded. "I didn't know you were here and, well, you know I have other clients, and one of the gents from A-B was in the front row. But, tell you what, I'm doing a repeat of the presentation tomorrow; and, I promise to 'beam me a Bass,' okay?"

Well, he definitely understood but I could tell he was still a bit snorkeled.

The following day, I presented the session a second time and when I got to the beer story, I exclaimed, "Beam me a Bass Ale, Scotty!" Sure enough, from the back of the room, Stone runs up to the stage and places a nice cold Bass Ale in my hands. (Unfortunately for me it was unopened.) The audience was in an uproar. So what's the point? Let me generate a little electricity to the lightbulbs as I did for the audience that day. It turned out to be a perfect transition.

In the first session, Stone had forecasted that I would beam a Bass Ale to my hand without consulting me. His forecast was wrong, and he had to bear the cost of carrying excess inventory for that day. To support his forecast the second day, he not only consulted me, but we *collaborated,* and the result was a 100 percent accurate forecast.

Think back to the example of the company and the suntan lotion launch in Chapter 3. Marketing developed its GTM strategy without collaborating with operations, resulting in the late order for the end aisle displays. Operations did not collaborate with marketing, resulting in higher priced displays, expediting costs, and negotiating under pressure a 10-year supplier agreement with a supplier they had rarely done much business with in the past. In both cases, if the players in the two structures/nodes had collaborated, the result would have been synced-up plans and much lower cost. It all adds up. If you want to close the gap and reside in Leader City, collaboration is the key to the city.

It extends beyond what traditional processes and most of the S&OP or SI&OP (sales, inventory, and operations planning) processes that I have seen propose. When my good friend Nari Viswanathan was the VP of supply chain research at Aberdeen Group, we would speak about this all the time. I am on the board of directors for a small company, Lead Time Technology (LTT), based in Wilmington, Delaware. It was founded by some DuPont engineers (not unlike Michael Saylor) who were in an internal consulting group conducting process improvement projects. To make a long story short, they developed a suite of software tools to support the day-to-day decisions of those planners and schedulers I speak about who make the million-dollar working capital decisions daily.

Their processes and tools extend beyond traditional S&OP and APS, so I was brainstorming with Nari about what to call it.

Knowing that we were treading on a term that already had a life of its own, we decided that instead of jumping on the S&OP bandwagon, we would speak to Integrated Business Planning (IBP) processes versus S&OP. The reasoning, as I will explain, is that the collaboration between the Demand Creation and Demand Fulfillment structures by necessity must extend beyond traditional notions about S&OP and include elements of product lifecycle management (PLM) that S&OP processes don't necessarily take into consideration.

The Create process type, as I first learned when I met with Lou Boudreau at P&G, is from a product development perspective going to entail some sort of packaging. At a minimum, the Demand Fulfillment processes should be involved in packaging decisions. In some companies, packaging engineering is in the Demand Fulfillment structure. From a supply chain perspective, packaging will impact conveyance, could introduce changes to production lines and/or equipment, and may include both outer pack and inner packs, palletization, warehousing, and transportation, to name a few elements and costs impacted.

Development people need to be aware of plant layout and production methods and equipment as they are developing product. This is applicable to nearly all industries that sell products. And collaboration must extend beyond the four walls. I remember a story about a cereal manufacturer that tried to engineer their product for top shelf display (preferred placement). They made the box just a few inches taller than most retail "between" shelf spaces, thinking the only place the retailer would be able to place them was a top shelf facing. The retail category manager saw through the ploy immediately. Instead of top shelf, the cereal brand was allocated to the bottom shelf, stacked on its side (virtually no facing). Needless to say, the manufacturer's salesperson was punished mercilessly for the next several months by the buyer.

Anyone who has had to sell to retail buyers knows what tough negotiators they can be. They know what I mean about being punished.

It's often a pretty good idea to bring in some customers to review your new product and packaging to assess whether the design will cause any operational or merchandising issues on their end. As in the previous example, with margins as tight as they are in retail, any discomfort or cost you bring to them will be met with punishment or, worse, delisting of your product. By collaborating with supply chain colleagues, development people can get some immediate feedback on any operational cost or merchandising activity issues with the design.

It's just as important to collaborate with suppliers on new product design. I was the very proud owner of a 1998 Chrysler Sebring convertible (Limited Edition) and I wish there had been some collaboration in its design for placement of a standard battery size. Unknown to me, until the first time I had to replace the battery, the engineers designed the battery placement in such a way that the left front fender had to be removed to change it. The labor cost more than the battery!

Think that's bad? The engineers at Renault in the late 1960s were worse. I had an R4 with a pushbutton electric automatic transmission. (My electrical engineer father insisted that anything we bought had to use as much electric power or components as possible. I had to endure the laughter of my friends whenever I cut the lawn with a 100-foot electric cord strapped to and dragging from my belt). So, the R4 transmission was great . . . until the carbon brushes wore down, without warning, and I had to be towed to the dealer (at my cost). Does it get worse? Of course; they had to pull the engine out to replace the brushes. Yeah, you guessed it! The brushes cost about $10 and the tow and labor about $150. And it wasn't easy explaining to my date's father why I was so late bringing her home.

Needless to say, I am a real proponent of collaborative design and design from usage back, not product forward. Working with supply chain personnel and suppliers can provide a significant amount of innovation to product design. This is not meant to be a treatise on the Create process; however, there is a lot of material and operational cost reduction opportunity, customer satisfaction, and revenue opportunity that can be gained from collaboration between Demand Creation and Demand Fulfillment personnel from both sides. The Leaders know it. That's why they are on the transformation journey and why they enjoy a 50 percent cost advantage. Ready to take the step? Collaboration is the key to Leader City!

In the business operating system, the create process can impact the behavior of a lot of nodes, internal and external. It's usually, in my experience, more than many people consider. It's also why I like to speak to Integrated Business Planning. If you're going to expend the energy in your transformation (you eventually will) to implement S&OP best practices, it is worth the effort to include PLM best practices in the process. It can make life a lot easier and more productive on the journey.

GUESS WHAT? THE FORECAST IS *WRONG*, DEAL WITH IT

Earlier I dispelled the flat sales rate at retail myth, now let me dispel the one-number myth for you. Many people think S&OP processes and software result in a one-number forecast. I can't tell you how many times I have heard it spoken about at conferences . . . but no one can tell me what the one number is. Is it units, dollars, euros, pesos, yen, lire, cases, loads, production runs, raw materials, market share, pounds, metric tons, barrels, hundred weight, or any other of the forecast quantities that I need to plan the business? For what region, country, or continent is the one number forecast? What product line is it? Color, size, or style? Is it the forecast to the point of sale, customer distribution center, my warehouse, my manufacturing location, or which location? Everybody in the organization is forecasting what they are responsible for and everyone uses different numbers . . . and their timing requirements are different . . . is the forecast for the day the product is sold or delivered or shipped or produced or packed? What and when are we forecasting?

Let me share what I have observed at many companies where I have worked or consulted for as illustrated in Figure 5.3, The One-Number Forecast Myth. In the beginning of the year, the CEO and the board come to an agreement on what the financial picture for the year needs to be, and the CEO forecasts that the company will need earnings growth of about 10 percent per quarter to achieve the objectives of the board.

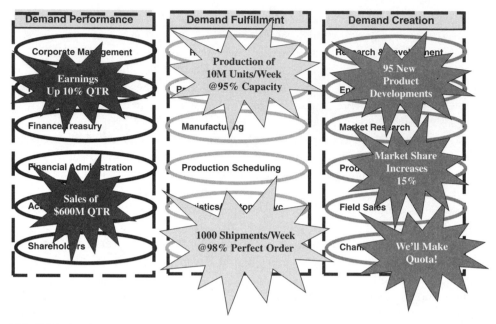

FIGURE 5.3   The One-Number Forecast Myth

The CEO turns to the finance team to forecast the level of sales the company will need to achieve the earnings forecast. The finance team determines what the company will need in sales to achieve the board's objectives and divides by 12 (customers always purchase in equal months quantities, right?) to set monthly targets to achieve sales, in this case, of $600 million per quarter to achieve the quarterly earnings forecast and meet the board's overall financial goals. Finance in turn goes to marketing and says that the company will need $600 million sales per quarter to achieve the earnings forecast.

Marketing takes the $600 million in sales and forecasts that it will have to develop marketing programs to generate an increase in forecasted market share of 15 percent to generate the incremental sales required to achieve $600 million per quarter, which will have to be supported by R&D, who, in turn, forecasts that to increase market share, they will have to release at least 95 new products and/or line extensions.

In the meantime, over in the Demand Fulfillment structure, manufacturing is forecasting that in order to hit a forecast of $600 million in sales with 10 percent earnings growth, they will have to produce at least 10 million units per week with at least 95 percent capacity utilization. That is, unless someone would like to allocate an increase to the capital budget for new flexible production lines, retooling, upgrading the presses, and making overall facilities improvements? We didn't think so.

Logistics looks over the production numbers and the $600 million in sales. . . . Yes, that sales number has just become a revenue number to the head of logistics, which means we have to deliver on $600 million sales per quarter. Remember, if you can't ship it, you can't bill it. To do so, logistics forecasts at least 1,000 shipments per week while maintaining at least a 98 percent perfect order fill rate. That is, unless someone would like to allocate an increase to the capital budget for a new distributed order management system; an increase in DC space, dock doors, and conveyance; and a new inventory optimization software package? We didn't think so.

Finally, we ask sales for their forecast, to which sales responds, "We'll make the $600 million per quarter sales quota that has been given to us by finance." You see, sales never forecasts more than quota because they'll be asked to bring it in faster and risk a quota increase. And they never forecast below quota because then people will question their ability to sell and risk being fired. So, sales can be counted on to generally forecast quota. . . . Gee, maybe there really is a one-number forecast. It's called quota. Does this sound familiar?

Of course, every month or so, we all get together in an S&OP meeting to figure out how we are doing, reconcile what went wrong, and see what we have to do to achieve quota. Then we go back to our respective departments and systems and input the newly agreed to targets in our operations planning system. The plans are updated and distributed, generally on a weekly basis, either Sunday night or Monday morning. By noon, the plans are now all wrong and the firefighting begins. But, of course, point of sale–driven forecasting will fix all of that . . . Really? One thing I can say with 100 percent accuracy, in most businesses, the only thing accurate about a forecast is that it is wrong, deal with it.

Years ago I developed Sherman's Law of Forecast Accuracy: *Forecast accuracy improves in direct correlation to its distance from usefulness.* I have found that aggregate forecasts are generally pretty accurate. Most of the breweries I worked with knew total consumption was pretty flat. They knew what their market shares were and what initiatives they would be taking to increase them. They could forecast the number of barrels of beer that they were going to have to produce and the dollars that they would sell annually pretty accurately.

The problem is that, with the exception of myself and a few other people I have met, most people don't buy beer in barrels! They buy six-packs, twelve-packs, 18s, 40s, cans, bottles, cans that are shaped like bottles, glass, plastic, aluminum, steel, quarter barrels, quarts, and they buy thousands of different types and labels. Can you imagine the havoc that was wrought in beer forecasting with the introduction of microbreweries?

They buy more beer at events like baseball games than at the theater. They buy more beer when it's hot than snowing. And they have different tastes regionally. Holidays are for green bottles, working days are brown bottle days, and, well, I can only imagine what will drive consumption of beer in blue bottles. And that's just the USA . . . try forecasting globally. It is the same across all industries. . . . We are great at forecasting the aggregates, but we don't ship or receive in aggregate. The most useful forecasts are at the level where the work is done, by stock-keeping unit by location (SKUL); and they are horribly inaccurate . . . 50 to 60 percent at best, once in a while.

When I was at Burroughs, I first met the late Dr. Don Bowersox at Michigan State University, who was heralded as the "father of integrated logistics." Don became a good friend, and when I was at DEC, I was able to work closely with Don and his team on a couple of sponsored research projects leading to the publication of at least two of Don's books on logistics. I was also able to meet Dr. Patricia Daugherty and Dr. Dale Rogers when they were graduate assistants under Don and working on their PhD. Pat is now back at MSU and Dale is now at Rutgers University. Both have been good friends over the years and we have shared many brainstorms about logistics and supply chain management. The great thing about the field of supply chain and logistics is the close relationship between academics and their research and the practitioners and their needs.

Don provided me with the "Bowersox Corollary" to Sherman's Law of Forecast Accuracy. He often asked me and his audiences, "Why do people waste so much time and money trying to forecast something that someone else already knows?" As I have said, collaboration is the key to Leader City. The Leaders collaborate internally and externally to gather as much information as possible to support their planning processes. For me, it really all started to come together at Colgate; and, ironically, it was from looking at POS data.

FORECASTING IS AS MUCH ABOUT ART AS IT IS ABOUT SCIENCE

Colgate was among the first group of companies to which Wal-Mart began releasing its store sales data via an Internet portal. As part of our account relationship with them when I was at DEC, they asked me to work with one of their analysts, Maurice Mora, on reviewing the data and trying to find out what we could learn from it.

This was before I was at IRI; it was my first experience working with POS data. The first discovery was the end of flat sales at retail assumptions. The data for each item were all over the map. They were impossible to predict. Lots of peaks and valleys and no real pattern that was obvious to us at first. While I can't show actual data, I can draw an overly simplified representation of what we were looking at as illustrated in Figure 5.4, Retail Store Sales Data.

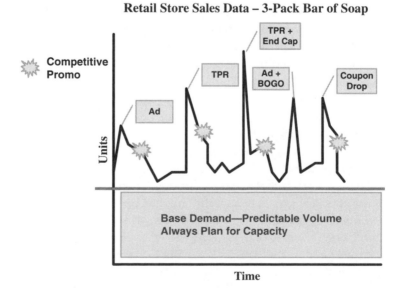

FIGURE 5.4　Retail Store Sales Data

After a lot of staring at the graphic display of the data, I had a revelation. I drew a line just below the bottom of the lowest valley on the chart. This line represented the consistent sales of Colgate product into Wal-Mart. As Wal-Mart represented a substantial percentage of shipment volume, we should make sure that our production and distribution capacity plans included this "base" volume. It was consistent and predictable. I remember saying that the base represented the brand-loyal Colgate customers and the rest of the demand was probably the price shoppers. It turned out to not be far from the truth. We started by trying to *explain* the highly erratic variability of the incremental peaks and valleys of demand above the baseline.

After some investigation, we found that the volume peaks were generally associated with promotions; after the peak, demand would begin to tail off. We also figured out that some of the valleys occurred or were accelerated by competitive promotions. So I recommended that we begin looking at all of the forecasts based on planned promotions and that marketing and operations should be working together on refining the statistical forecasts being generated by their Manugistics (now a part of JDA) supply chain planning tools. Nick LaIIowchic was director of logistics for Colgate at the time and was excited about the breakthrough. (Nick became a good friend and later went on to a great career with Becton-Dickinson and then headed up all of distribution for The Limited. He is one of the most strategic logistics thinkers I have met.)

Not only were we able to begin considering the promotional plans from marketing as part of the forecast, but by comparing shipments in and store sales out, we were able to build the Wal-Mart Distribution Centers into the Distribution Requirements Plan (DRP) SKUL planning capabilities of Manugistics to improve the accuracy of Colgate's logistics, production, and procurement plans. We were able to forecast to the ship-to location reasonably accurately. Remember, I said "reasonably"; the forecast was still wrong.

Regardless of the industry you are in, capturing customer usage and any promotional activity or event that can cause a demand change and adding it into your planning process will produce some astonishing results. But it is not an IT systems–only solution, as we later found. The math and timing that the different processes required made integration into a single statistics-based system like Manugistics difficult. It became as much a synchronization issue as a forecasting issue.

Of course, when I joined IRI, I discovered that Magid M. Abraham (IRI) and Leonard M. Lodish (Wharton) had written an article on analyzing baseline and incremental volume from promotions entitled "Promoter: An Automated Promotion Evaluation System."[1] Not only was IRI using the techniques as part of their services, but leading-edge marketing people across all industries were beginning to use event-based forecasting and causal factor analysis fairly routinely. Unfortunately, it was mostly in the marketing department and wasn't making its way into operations. As my story about the cosmetics company demonstrated and my experience later at AMR Research revealed, the concepts were not and still are not broadly applied to supply chain and operations planning.

At IRI, we partnered with Think Systems, later acquired by i2 Technologies and now also part of JDA, to attempt to create a POS data-driven DRP, but there were major issues with scale. Needless to say, there are terabytes of POS data. I argued unsuccessfully that we should focus on delivering the promotion analysis results to operations and not try to develop software. But that's a story for another day. Needless to say, IRI Logistics was later acquired by Manugistics (they knew how to develop software).

As you begin collaborating with your colleagues in the Demand Creation structure, you will understand that Create, Market, and Sell process types are composed of many elements whose output manifests itself in most of the variability that impacts Demand Fulfillment. It is often the hand that wields the bullwhip that is mercilessly inflicting pain on operations. The reason collaboration is necessary is that the perspectives and tools employed, in particular, by Market and Sell processes are set in very different time and analytic buckets; but, if you take them into consideration, you will significantly improve your forecast accuracy. You will able to put out more fires when they are matches versus burning down the forest. The forecast will still be wrong, but not as wrong. And it won't be as wrong for as long or as frequently wrong.

EVENT-DRIVEN FORECASTING IS A BEST PRACTICE IMPERATIVE

Event-driven forecasting, as illustrated in Figure 5.5, is not as widely used in operations as it is in marketing. And as we learned at the cosmetics company, marketing uses it primarily to analyze and evaluate the planned promotion's effectiveness. They really don't do it for forecasting operations requirements. It is a best practice that must be shared. It is a key to collaboration and the integration of the actions taken in the Demand Creation structure that can impact the performance of the Demand Fulfillment structure systemically.

Marketing is tasked with the development of products and programs to increase market share and volume to drive increased sales. While promotional events such as

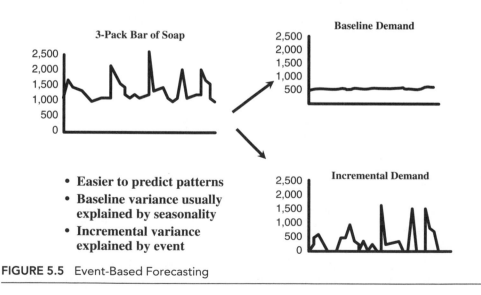

FIGURE 5.5 Event-Based Forecasting

coupons, advertising, displays, and so on are easily recognized in consumer goods, the marketing departments in most companies and industries are employing similar techniques and promotional events to drive share and volume. Check out the pricing strategies in the automotive industry. "Demand shaping" through use of various promotion techniques is becoming common in high tech. Volume discounting is a long-time practice across many industries. Monty Hall could easily be the VP of sales in nearly any industry. If these events are not tightly integrated into your operations forecasts and plans . . . well, you heard me, forecasts based solely on historical data produce hysterical results.

Integrated Business Planning incorporates event-based forecasting techniques by taking into consideration marketing's promotional event plan. If you separate demand into baseline demand and incremental demand, your forecasting efforts will be less daunting. In my experience, statistical forecasts of historic baseline shipments data will provide operations with a fairly accurate forecast of *unpromoted, predictable* baseline volume regardless of the industry you are in.

As I did at Colgate, draw a line just below the lowest valley in the statistical forecast. If you have any seasonality to your product or offer, you can account for that in variations to the shape of your baseline. Most statistical forecasting engines are pretty good with seasonality. The key is to identify the base level of demand that is consistent and predictable throughout the year for all products. This becomes the basis for your minimum capacity plan. You must be able to meet this demand consistently throughout the year and accurately. For many industries whose demand is not highly impacted by price and promotion, it can be a fairly sizable percent of annual volume. Unfortunately, there aren't many industries that don't have erratic and frequent variability.

Once you have established the baseline of unpromoted demand, you can begin to explain the peaks and valleys in the historic data-based incremental demand forecast. Do it first based on the past shipment data, as this is where the timing and often quantity issues between the two planning processes (and often, IT applications) become apparent. If marketing is using syndicated or retailer-provided POS data, for example, the event that causes the incremental lift is evident at the *time* the product was scanned. The product had to be sourced, produced, and delivered well before the demand generated by the promotional event occurs or is planned to occur (remember the suntan lotion). It's one of the complications arising from the use of POS data.

For any industry, the timings when product is promoted, sold, delivered, produced, and sourced are all different. Therefore, the forecasts coming from and going to the processes responsible for these activities will all have to be different. These "time delays," as we discovered in the Beer Game, can have some dramatic impacts on the plans and flow of goods throughout the supply network. It is the bullwhip effect manifested simultaneously across many interconnected, but often independent, nodes in the supply network. We can't break down the silos. They do different things but they are interconnected and have to collaborate to improve the performance of the components and the whole. The whole is the sum of its parts. This is why it is important to focus on the *rate of sale* of product at each node. Rate of sale analysis is the basis of synchronization, which I will speak more of in Chapter 6.

Generally, historical data will provide insight into the time delays and amplification associated with the operations plans and the impact that a particular promotional event can have on demand; but it all has happened in the past. Chances are that the marketing and sales departments' plans are constantly changing based on economic conditions and the market dynamics and drivers we evaluated in Chapter 3. If marketing and sales have no impact on volume in your market, great. But chances are good that the Demand Creation structure processes are operating with great haste to change history and the results of the historic data analysis. Increasing share and volume, changing the demand of the past are what they do for a living.

Implementing Integrated Business Planning as a best practice component of your transformation provides the organization with the motivation for the collaboration that is needed to improve the *financial* results of the company. You can be made aware of events that are being planned that cause your forecast error. Are marketing and/or sales planning any pricing actions in the future? A price reduction, temporary or permanent, is not an exclusively consumer goods demand-shaping tactic. Price reductions may *cause* demand to vary, usually upward. Are they planning any trade show activity to increase demand? Advertising? Are they aware of any upcoming competitive initiatives that may impact demand? Are any new products or line extensions planned? Are any product innovations or features coming? Are there options or accessories that will change product configuration or demand?

Many companies are leveraging different components of product and pricing to shape demand. For example, if Dell has too much stock on a particular accessory, it will offer a "special" on the accessory to drive demand and reduce the level of inventory. Conversely, if supply for a particular commodity chemical is constrained, the producer may raise the price to increase profitability of the product during the period of constrained supply.

EXTEND COLLABORATIVE PROCESSES TO THE CUSTOMER (AND SUPPLIER)

So, hopefully, you're going to start speaking with and collaborating with your colleagues over in the "ivory tower." But, before you do, let me share the thinking about collaborating one step further . . . with your customers (not to mention suppliers)! Remember the Bowersox Corollary: "Why do people waste so much time and money trying to forecast something that someone else already knows?" We've already figured out that there are any number of strategies and tactics that the Market and Sell processes execute that will cause demand to vary. Do you think that the customers may be doing things in their Demand Structure that may be causing demand variability? After all, customers generally behave exactly as we plan, right? Take time to have a hearty laugh, followed by the tears from painful reality.

I always challenge my clients with the question, "If you want to know what your customers are going to buy, why don't you ask them?" Maybe, just maybe, we are accidental adversaries. Maybe we are Pogo: "We have met the enemy and it is us." Ron Johnson at J.C. Penney certainly did.

Ted Rybeck, who founded Benchmarking Partners after leaving AMR Research, was one of the more visionary analysts that I met in the industry. When I left Numetrix, Rybeck tried to bring me to Benchmarking Partners as a supply chain research director. Unfortunately, I had an enforceable noncompete with AMR that would not expire for another six or so months. As luck would have it, Rybeck was in the process of working with Yossi Sheffi, certainly one of the most influential academics in supply chain and a professor at MIT, to commercialize some technology Benchmarking Partners had developed to support their Collaborative Forecasting and Replenishment (CFAR) initiative, not unlike what we had done at AMR/PRTM and the SCOR® Supply Chain Council initiative.

Not to get into the details, but, like the SCC, the CFAR participating companies decided to keep it as an industry initiative, formed the Collaborative Planning, Forecasting, and Replenishment (CPFR®) committee, and found it a home in the Voluntary Inter-Industry Commerce Solutions (VICS) association. CPFR® is a registered trademark of VICS. VICS is now headed by Joe Andraski, former head of supply chain at Nabisco and mentor to many current supply chain leaders in the industry. Rick Blasgen at CSCMP, Rick Jackson at The Limited, and Nick Lahowchic are a few examples. Andraski pioneered CPFR® and is a recipient of CSCMP's Distinguished Service Award. He has influenced my thinking and supply chain thinking across industries over the years.

Since I couldn't join Benchmarking Partners, would I be interested in joining the Newco that Ted and Yossi were starting along with Chris Sellers, who had worked at IRI (ironically) and Accenture, and Matt Johnson, who led the Benchmarking Partners technology team that developed the software to support a CFAR pilot between Warner Lambert and Wal-Mart? Of course, being the bleeding-edge advocate I am, I accepted and became heavily involved in the CPFR® initiative and committee. Before I share my learning about external collaboration, we ended up branding the company Syncra Software and then Syncra Systems, largely based on my affinity for synchronizing supply chain business cycles.

While CPFR® was composed primarily of consumer goods companies, both retailers and manufacturers, there was fair representation from the high-tech and electronics industry, and we did a fair amount of collaboration, at least early on, with the Automotive Industry Action Group (AIAG). Over the years since then, I have evangelized the principles of CPFR® across the many different industries I have been working with. This is not meant to be a CPFR® primer, but it is important to note that supply chain transformation evolves into a trading partner–focused initiative as P&G has so effectively done over the years.

If you read any of the articles I have written on CPFR®, you will also discover that I am much more an advocate of CFAR than CPFR®. In my experience, sourcing encompasses many different suppliers and dimensions. When you do the math, as you now know I like to do, scale becomes an issue with many of the initiatives and causes people, especially the purists, like to advocate. As a realist, I did the math. Purchasing folks simply have a hard time finding the time to engage in substantial joint planning with the numbers of suppliers they have to engage. If you are a strategic source to your customer, you will be able to engage in the "P" in CPFR®. If you're not, then I recommend that you embrace CPFR® and implement it with customers and suppliers that consider you strategic; but focus on CFAR for the rest. Just make sure you collaborate; don't let any rocks stop you from collaborating. . . . It is no longer an optional path on the journey.

During the CPFR® period of my career, I was involved in a dozen or more pilots and scores of meetings between retailers and manufacturers. While I had met Marty Hanaka when he was running operations at Staples, it was his foresight as CEO of The Sports Authority to the benefits of CPFR® that led to a pioneering pilot with New Balance. Later, as my career progressed, I engaged with suppliers and customers in other industries. The key takeaway is that just as in the Demand Creation structure, your customers' Demand Management structures are business operating systems as well. The events and activities of their structures within the dynamics of their markets provide them with unique perspectives and strategies that will create behaviors that you certainly can't forecast, but that will certainly impact your forecast and subsequently your organization and its performance. They are the matches that light the fires you fight on a daily basis.

Incorporating their plans into your business structure will be the basis of profitable response to the uncertainty that results from not knowing what they are planning to do. Collaboration, like transformation, is a journey, and they are journeys that are not optional in Leader City. Customers, in most industries, will not, and often legally cannot, share with you *why* they are planning to buy the product quantities from you, but they can share *what* the quantities are and *when* they are planning to place the order. The *why* may be competitive or economic actions that they simply cannot share, but it's my bet that they are more likely to behave according to their plan than yours. So why not ask them?

In nearly all of the discussions that I have participated in, the level of joint planning was commensurate with the level of strategic importance that the customer placed on the supplier. And in most product types or categories, there were very few strategic sources among the many sources the customer did business with. I also found that nearly all of the companies that I participated with had a forecast or plan of what they intended to buy. It may have been generated by a suggested purchase order, merchandising, MRP application, or an Excel spreadsheet. But there was a buy plan.

And in every discussion that I had with the buyer or category manager or purchasing agent or other sourcing professional, they were willing to share the plan with the supplier as long as it could be done effortlessly and without a significant time investment. The supplier could not question *why* it was unless the buyer volunteered the information. Just as collaborating with marketing and sales provided major revelations to improving operations forecasts and subsequent execution, collaborating with customers provided similar results. Seems the customers really are not trying to disrupt our operations. They are just trying to execute *their* plans. My guess is that your suppliers feel the same way about you. Collaborate with them. Collaboration is the key to Leader City.

So, there are any number of strategies and tactics in which the market and sell processes and our customers and suppliers engage that will cause demand to vary. If you are not aware of them within the time necessary to profitably respond to the variability, well, welcome to Laggard City. The leaders collaborate. They already have the key. They aren't demand-driven. They are demand-responsive. And they aren't being driven crazy.

 NOTE

1. Abraham, Magid M., and Leonard M. Lodish, "Promoter: An Automated Promotion Evaluation System," *Marketing Science*, Spring 1987, vol. 6, no. 2, pp. 101–123.

CHAPTER SIX

Supply Chain Management: A Pipeline of Opportunity

W HENEVER I AM INVITED to speak at universities, either as part of an executive in residence program or at the invitation of my many academic colleagues, I like to talk about why a career in supply chain can be rewarding and secure. In fact, Glenn Richey and Alex Ellinger, both Pat Daugherty doctoral students and now professors at the University of Alabama, routinely invite me to speak to all of the undergraduate and graduate business students considering what to major in. They claim I have an outstanding conversion rate as more students declare supply chain as their major after my presentation than anyone else's.

Of course, I include my "Beam me a Bud, Scotty" story whenever I present. And then I talk to them about the fact that over the years, I have only identified a few professions who truly offer the security of lifetime employment. I use the example of swordsmen and typing pools as examples of careers wiped out by change. Then I tell the story of how, when I was at Burroughs early in my career, I became a little disillusioned. I applied to a blind ad for a director of marketing position in Chicago. It was a game-changing interview for me.

What company? Rosehill Cemetery was seeking a new marketing director and had a hired an Austrian M.D. in psychiatry to hire someone. As I entered the suite at the Drake Hotel for the interview, I noticed a tabletop of pamphlets and articles, authored by the interviewer, about cemetery marketing and sales. My first question was, why would they be interested in a computer sales professional for the position? He explained that cemetery marketing was not what most people expect. They don't want to sell you a plot and services to your family at the time you pass away. They want to sell you when you are young. Not to give a treatise on cemetery marketing, but people can make better, more economically reasonable decisions when they aren't grieving, and they can pay for the cost over time. They even had a shared network of cemeteries so that if you moved, you could have your choice of where you would be interred. And they wanted sales and marketing people from a business-to-business background. They wanted professionals to sell to professionals, as he explained it.

He explained further that it's a career that's very secure. Everyone is going to die and there will always be a market for burial/cremation services. But, he cautioned me, death knows no holidays or time schedules. You are always on call. And it's not necessarily the most popular job to discuss at cocktail parties. So why was this a game changer?

While I wasn't interested in the position by this point, I was interested in how such an acknowledged psychiatrist got into cemetery marketing. He explained that during his doctoral studies in Vienna, he asked his mentor which field of psychiatry he should specialize in. His mentor told him to *"specialize in something unique"* as it would offer more career opportunities and less competition. He decided to specialize in death.

He also could have specialized in health care, since people are always going to get sick; but he chose the end of the line . . . less pain to deal with. He was a pretty entertaining guy.

As I like to tell the students, death wasn't a career I was particularly interested in. And it was too late for me to embark on the education and training for a career in health care. So, I started thinking, we can't beam beer to consumers; we can't beam anything to anybody. But everyone, consumer or commercial, needs stuff. Someone has to source, make, and deliver the stuff people and businesses need . . . distribution does that! Specializing in distribution, now supply chain, will offer a "pipeline of opportunity" for a lifetime career, at least until someone develops a source of energy many times that of the sun.

As I said, it was a game changer for me and, if my professorial colleagues are telling me the truth, it is a game changer for many young people entering the field. So let's take a deeper look at this process of supply chain management and what drives the world's engine of commerce.

UNDERSTANDING THE DEMAND FULFILLMENT STRUCTURE

The Demand Fulfillment structure, as illustrated in Figure 6.1, consists of Plan, Source, Make, and Deliver. Some pundits like to use Buy, Make, and Move. Personally, I thought of using Procure, Convert, and Fulfill with Synchronize replacing Plan, but why reinvent the wheel? Years have gone into the development of the SCOR® model. As it is supported by practitioners and regularly maintained, it is a de facto industry standard, although I do think that my naming conventions can be more applicable to a broader set of industries.

APQC developed a Process Classification Framework (PCF) that is designed to encompass enterprise processes rather than just supply chain operations per se, and, as a result, procurement, manufacturing, and logistics are not as seamlessly linked as in the SCOR® model. CSCMP has adapted both the SCOR® model and APQC's PCF in different versions of its process standards. And APQC has also linked its open standards research to the SCOR® model and CSCMP's process standard making them all the more

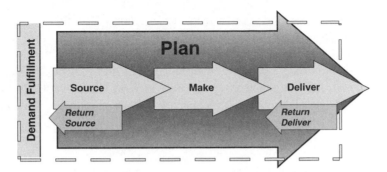

FIGURE 6.1 The Demand Fulfillment Structure
Source of Process Types: The Supply Chain Council

interchangeable. There are also models developed by academia and consulting firms. Having been a founding team member of the Supply Chain Council and co leading the Deliver team, and not wishing to reinvent the wheel, I will focus primarily on SCOR® as my model of choice. Being HTML based, it is also the framework most easily adapted to your company and easy to work with.

The SCOR® model, while widely published in the public domain, is available, in detail, from the Supply Chain Council at www.supply-chain.org. It is maintained by any interested party that wants to participate on a technical development team and includes many practitioners, technology and service providers, academics, and consultants from all industries and geographies. As such, I consider it to be the global open industry standard for supply chain process definition as there is no proprietary interest per se in its development. You don't have to be a member to participate, so it's truly open. Also, anyone can purchase a copy of a version of the model. It truly amazes me that some people continue to criticize its relevance and validity. It is a source of process definition, performance metrics, human resource requirements, environmental and risk processes, and best practices constantly reviewed and updated by the industry.

Using the model as a baseline analytic tool to define your demand fulfillment processes will save a lot of time and Post-it® notes. It will serve as your navigation guide on the journey to transformation. Sure, you will have to fill in the details of your specific industry and operational requirements, but it will get you off the ground and align people to the process a lot faster than a whiteboard. Of course, there are any number of computer-assisted process graphics tools available that will also save the forests and time. The major objectives of the Demand Fulfillment structure are to fulfill customer requirements while reducing operating costs based on the company's strategic goals. Remember, if you can't ship it, you can't bill it!

Aligning to the company's strategic goals is critical to balancing the trade-offs that occur in demand fulfillment operations. Does the company want to be the lowest cost provider or highest service provider? I won't say it's impossible, but it is very difficult to be both. Best in class companies, the Leaders, approach optimal balance. But you have to meet with senior management to align. It's a great way to open the dialogue to gaining executive support for your transformation efforts. Whether your business is driven primarily by cost or service as your competitive differentiator, the lack of transformation to a continuous improvement, self-actualization culture will result in poor financial performance, regardless of your focus. The numbers show it. Laggard City is inhabited by underperformers in cost regardless of service level. And, believe me, it is no easier to be a Laggard than a Leader. Laggards, in my experience, often work harder and under more pressure than the Leaders.

MAJOR OPERATING FUNCTIONS OF THE DEMAND FULFILLMENT STRUCTURE: PROCUREMENT, PRODUCTION, AND LOGISTICS

Once you have gained understanding and agreement on the strategic goals of the company (see Chapters 2 and 3), you can begin looking at your demand fulfillment processes (Source, Make, and Deliver) and the corresponding functions that they represent: procurement, production, and logistics. It is the traditional notion of supply chain management.

The Source process type is composed of those process categories and elements that are required to procure/purchase the materials necessary to produce the offer (products or services) that you bring to market in the Demand Creation structure, driven by planned and actual customer orders.

It has always been interesting to me that the SCOR® model does not really address thoroughly the process of strategic sourcing and negotiation. I am not going to take it down to three levels of detail; however, supplier relationship management is critical to the effective operation of the company. Material cost generally represents a high percentage of cost of goods sold. In wholesale and retail distribution it's just about everything. If there is one thing every company should understand about their customers; it is that their price of sale relative to the customer's price of sale of the products purchased represents the margin and return on invested capital of the customer. It's why retail buyers make the salespeople sweat for every hundredth of a percent of price.

For distributors, wholesale and retail, in particular, gross margin return on investment (GMROI) is critical to sourcing success. GMROI is calculated by dividing gross margin dollars by average inventory dollars. So, for example, if I have a product that generates $500,000 gross profit with an average inventory value of $400,000, my GMROI is 1.25 or for every dollar of inventory investment, I make $1.25 in gross profit. Some distributors also calculate a "turn and earn" (T&E) index by multiplying gross margin (GM) percentage by inventory turns. For example, if I have an item with 10 percent GM and 10 turns, my T&E is a break-even 100. Most distributors want to have a T&E of around 130 to 140 or more.

GMROI drives distributor buying and behavior. One of the least understood distributor buying behaviors caused by T&E is investment buying. Manufacturers don't like it because it creates variability in demand, and it can also result in the dreaded diversion word. But it's another "Pogo" in the supply chain. The manufacturer creates the economic opportunity for investment buying and the undesired outcomes by offering volume-based discounts (bracket pricing) and/or promotional pricing to drive volume. However, pricing incentives can produce unintended results.

In its simplest form, if you are offered two tubes of toothpaste for the price of one, do you brush your teeth twice as much? Probably not. What does happen is that it will take you twice as long to rebuy toothpaste thereby disrupting the predictability of the replenishment plan. And, when you get home, if your neighbor offered to buy the extra tube of toothpaste for 75 percent of the price paid, you will made a little profit on the transaction. Now, not only does your neighbor not buy into the promotion, the demand is spread over two consumers and, well, see why being demand-driven can drive you crazy?

Commercially, if I am buying an item regularly from a manufacturer that has a GM of 10 percent with an average turn of 24 (15 days of supply), my T&E index is 240. If the manufacturer offers me a buy-on-get-one (BOGO) free with 5 percent in promo allowance, my GM jumps to 25 percent with a T&E index of 600. Even though my rate of sale (ROS) is 15 days, if I buy an extra 15 days of supply, my turn may drop to 12, but my T&E index is 300 or 60 points higher. So, I'll take the hit in inventory turns to improve GM performance. I know these are *way oversimplified* examples; and there are other considerations.

Simply put, an investment buy is one that a buyer makes to improve GMROI as opposed to purchasing to replenish to demand. I can take a hit in inventory turns if I can improve gross margin enough to cover the carrying cost, and if I have the cash flow to cover the inventory "investment"; hence the term *investment buy*. Investment buys screw up every forecasting algorithm in the manufacturer's system. They can lead to diversion of the product by the distributor selling excess inventory from the investment buy to another distributor that may not have the cash to cover their opportunity for an investment buy.

I remember a case during my Collaborative, Planning, Forecasting, and Replenishment (CPFR®) committee days to illustrate how, at least I believe, manufacturers create diversion opportunity by making it economically attractive based on bracket pricing. (I also think bracket pricing is the root cause of why the promise of Efficient Consumer Response was never realized; but that's another story for another day.)

I was working with a CPG company on establishing a CPFR® pilot with a regional grocery chain. We were in the meeting with the retail category manager and the CPG company's sales and operations account team. As we were setting the goals, the operations manager wanted to set an inventory goal of 15 days of supply (DOS) for the pilot product. His sales manager said it couldn't be done, which outraged (to put it mildly) the operations manager.

Upon further explanation, the sales manager pointed out that at the chain's current rate of sale, 15 DOS would put them below bracket one pricing and into bracket two pricing, which would kill the GMROI. And, as the GMROI was already low, it might result in the delisting of the product. The chain had to carry 30 DOS to maintain bracket one margins.

Later, at dinner, I also pointed out to the operations manager that there was a high degree of likelihood that there were some smaller independent stores in the area that would be more than happy to purchase the excess 15 DOS of the product from the chain and split the difference between the bracket one and bracket two pricing. This would allow the chain to maintain turn while enjoying the additional bracket one margin plus some margin on the sale of the excess inventory. It was a win-win for both distributors.

Well, the operations manager was still unhinged until the sales manager brought up that it was also a win for them because they were making their numbers without the imminent threat of delisting. At the end of the day, the GMROI with a little diversion was more than acceptable to the category manager and the sales manager. In the absence of the diversion, the sales manager said the volume would be at high risk . . . and profitable volume trumps operations. It was a win for everyone, the manufacturer, the chain, and the independent store owners.

The only losers are the planners back at the plant. However, with an industry best practice like CPFR®, the retailer could *share* the forecasted purchase plan with the manufacturer. The planners would have visibility of the demand the retailer was planning to place on the manufacturer in the future and adjust their plans accordingly. It's a pretty safe bet that the retailer will behave according to their plan, not yours. They won't or can't necessarily share *why* the demand will be what it is, but they can share *what* it is.

Why not share why? Well, they may be planning to buy more or less because of competitive activity in the category. They can't share another supplier's business strategy. They won't share with you investment buys, sells, or diverted product purchases for obvious reasons. So don't get hung up on the whys! Remember the Bowersox Corollary: Don't spend time and money trying to figure out what someone else already knows.

Speaking of win-win-win, I remember another project I was working on for a major tire producer. We were conducting an inventory management audit and part of the analysis was tracking shipments from production to final consumer sale. One of the containers we were tracking was shipped from the manufacturing plant in France to their East Coast port. It was offloaded and shipped by rail and truck to the customer, a tire distributor in California. The distributor had made a volume (investment) purchase of several containers of the product due to a promotion the manufacturer was offering.

The distributor, ironically, sold the tires as a full container to a distributor in Europe at a better price than could be obtained from the manufacturer's rep in Europe. They then shipped it from a California port, through the Suez Canal, into the Mediterranean, and it was offloaded in Marseilles. The container of tires was then trucked to the distributorship, which was located about 50 kilometers from the plant that originally produced and shipped them. The container had literally traveled around the world and everybody involved, the manufacturer, the distributors, and all of the transport providers made money or at least thought they did.

We were working on another project, this time a warehouse operations evaluation, for a wholesale grocery distributor. As part of the evaluation, we were reviewing receiving procedures. As a pallet of goods was being pulled from the truck, what do you think we discovered? If you guessed that it was diverted product, you were right. It also still had the wholesaler's shipper labeling on it. You probably didn't guess that the wholesaler had bought the product as an investment buy, then sold it over the diversion wire for a profit, and then bought it back at a profit because the prices had returned to normal. As Paul Harvey, the legendary news commentator, said, "Now you know the *rest of the story.*" And you don't think there is excess cost in the system? Supply chain transformation can unlock the hidden treasure as in Figure 6.2 and the key is collaboration.

Again, the numbers aren't as important as the gaps between Leader City and Laggard City. The numbers will change slightly from year to year but the gap has remained consistent over the years. The overall Demand Fulfillment structure metric for measuring the performance for supply chain asset management is cash to cash cycle time. If you're looking for opportunity from supply chain transformation, you won't have to dig deep. The Leaders, as in overall cost, have a significant advantage over their median competitors and an overwhelming advantage over the residents of Laggard City.

The Source process type is more complex than most people think. I also want to mention that with my logistics orientation, I have long been a member of CSCMP®. However, for the procurement professional, the association that focuses on Source is the Institute for Supply Management (ISM, www.ism.ws). Source complexity is probably the reason that the Supply Chain Council has limited the scope of process definition. I know when we first started working on the model the most challenging issue we faced was limiting the scope.

However, Source represents the critical intersection with the Demand Creation structure on both ends. On the supply end Source intersects with its suppliers' Sell process type. On the demand end, its Sell process type intersects with its customers' Source process type. Let the games begin. You have two process types with often

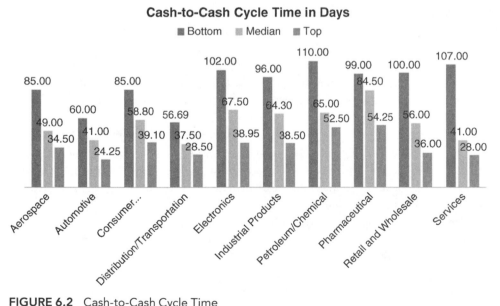

FIGURE 6.2 Cash-to-Cash Cycle Time

completely different drivers, metrics, behaviors that are at the end of one organizational structure and at the beginning of the other.

Interestingly enough, Source process elements, as we saw in Chapter 5, can also impact the create process type and vice versa. It's the Beer Game on steroids! And accidentally adversarial relationships abound. It's also, as CPFR® bears out, a huge collaborative opportunity. By aligning your Source process elements and metrics with your suppliers' Sell and Deliver process elements and metrics, you can truly unlock the gates to Leader City as P&G and Wal-Mart have clearly proven over the years. On the Sell side, it is critical to understand the economics of your customers' Source process elements (business). As we'll explore in more detail, aligning your Deliver processes with the customer Source processes will unlock more opportunity as well.

From a Source perspective, complexity is being driven by globalization, economics, the competitive landscape, and all of the variability of costs that have to be considered in assessing the "landed cost" of the materials to be procured. The landed cost is the *total* cost of the goods as received at the buyer's door. For the manufacturing enterprise, it gets very complex, very fast. It includes every cost component associated with the procurement and receipt of the product including the price of the purchase, transportation and handling, customs, taxes, tariffs, brokerage, insurance, currency conversion, and so on. In Chapter 5, we discussed the need for Source and Create to collaborate. It's equally important for Source to collaborate extensively with Make and Deliver.

A few years back when I was at Mercer Management Consulting, I was working on a transportation department reengineering project for a major consumer goods manufacturer. Incredibly, as we first started mapping out the processes, we discovered that the transportation people (Deliver) were neither responsible for nor involved with inbound transportation. The buyers simply negotiated with the suppliers for a "delivery" charge to be associated with the purchase.

The inbound transportation spend, as we began a landed cost calculation, was almost as large as the outbound transportation spend. And as the buyers had no transportation management training, the suppliers were treating delivery charges as almost as big a profit center as the product they were selling. By breaking up the cost into its components, we were able to identify the inbound transportation-related costs and compare them to our outbound costs. We found back-haul pickup opportunities, volume consolidations with carriers on the same lanes, optimized capacity, and a myriad of other transportation savings opportunities. The treasure chest was opened. Collaboration was the key that unlocked it.

On the production side of the Source process type, Make is critically dependent upon procurement to determine the best sources for the materials or components that comprise the bill of material, recipe, or formula of the product the company produces for sale. I remember the quote by America's first man in space, Astronaut Alan Shepard, "It's a very sobering feeling to be up in space and realize that one's safety factor was determined by the lowest bidder on a government contract." There has to be a close collaboration among procurement, production, and development on the quality of material being purchased for producing the product. If your strategy is to sell drills, for example, to the typical home handyperson, your sourcing specifications will be for a very different set of components than if you are selling to a professional craftsperson.

LEAN SIX SIGMA IS NOT AN OPTION—IT'S A REQUIREMENT

The Make process type is composed of those process categories and elements that are required to actually *produce* the products or services that comprise your offer to the market. Just as CSCMP is associated with logistics and ISM with procurement, the professional association most know for serving the needs of production professionals is APICS®, The Association for Operations Management (www.apics.org). The Make process type will not generally be applicable to retailers and distributors; however, in today's market, more and more retailers and distributors are manufacturing or co-packing to offer private-label product. As they build their brands into trusted commodities, their customers will often purchase the store brand over the manufacturers' brands. In Europe, for example, the retailers have built such a strong brand franchise over the years that manufacturers' brands are allocated to the shelf spaces that private-label goods occupy here. In any case, I also think it's important for distributors to understand the role of production as I equally believe it's important for manufacturers to understand distributor roles and economics.

Obviously, there are as many different production methods as there are industries and products. Companies often create competitive advantage based on developing proprietary production methods and even equipment. I remember being at a P&G manufacturing plant and noticing that security was out front with binoculars and writing down the registration of a small plane flying around the plant. It turned out to be a charter by a competitive company that was taking pictures of the storage tanks, silos, and piping of the facility to try to analyze the production methods and even the recipe P&G was using at the plant. Amazing, huh?

I always like to joke that one of the reasons I chose to specialize in distribution was that when I was at Burroughs, we had to decide which line of business (LOB) solutions we were going to sell. Since I had been placed in the commercial business division, my decision was to be between manufacturing or distribution. When I asked what the difference was, they told me that the manufacturing LOB track required production and inventory management certification by APICS®. The certification process required significant classroom time, reading, and taking an exam.

I said, "What do I have to do to go into the distribution LOB?"

The response was "Show up." Distribution looked very attractive again to this English and education major even though I had worked for several years during college at Union Carbide's Films and Packaging Division (chemical products) and Inland Steel's Coke (as in carbon residue from processed coal) Plant.

While I did dabble some in the manufacturing space supporting sales of the distribution functionality required in many manufacturing applications, it wasn't until I joined Pelion Systems, a small startup for lean manufacturing apps, that I really had to understand the "inside the four walls" manufacturing processes and challenges.

Of course, being on the board of Lead Time Technology has continued my exposure to the Make process type, categories, and elements and the inherent challenges of the manufacturing industry.

In manufacturing, maybe even more so than logistics, many things must be done specifically right to succeed and only one thing done wrong can be very costly. Manufacturing also has very different challenges, again based on product, industry, and technology. Discrete industries typically make stuff with edges. There is a bill of materials, which contains all of the components that will go into making the product, accompanied by the routings, which are the instructions for actually making the product, usually requiring the product to flow (hopefully) through any number of workstations or areas through the steps or stages of production. In process industries where gooey or liquid stuff is made, they use recipes and formulas.

Manufacturing can be very technical and complex, and my intent is not to write a book on the topic; APICS® does that very well thank you. However, manufacturing costs are typically highly variable and susceptible to inefficiencies in processes. Having been around manufacturing for the past few years, I have drawn the conclusion that the supply chain transformation requires end-to-end visibility and collaboration and that Lean Six Sigma best practice is simply not an option; it is a *requirement*. It may have its roots in the discrete industries and in manufacturing, but it is applicable and adaptable to all Demand Management structures.

Lean Six Sigma is the combination of the principles of Lean Manufacturing and Six Sigma Process Quality. It's also not all that different from the concepts I heard Charlie Eberle present at Bretton Woods on high performance work systems. I admit that I am not a manufacturing process or Lean Six Sigma black belt, or any color belt or any kind of an expert. And, as such, I am not going to write a treatise on the topic. But, in my experience, the transformation to Lean Six Sigma principles, formally or informally, for an organization is a critical component of supply chain transformation. When I say informally, I mean it's like systems thinking. You don't need to get a degree or implement it dogmatically. You need to think Lean—eliminate waste and inefficiency. And apply DMAIC to every process in your supply chain . . . define, measure, analyze, improve, and control; and/or plan, do, check, and act (PDCA). Just these simple principles will get you started on your journey and provide visibility into the performance and cost improvement opportunities in your organization.

One of my first Lean Six Sigma transformation experiences was with a large axle manufacturer and tier-one supplier in the automotive industry. Like many suppliers in automotive around 2005, they were being squeezed by the original equipment manufacturers (OEMs), particularly in Detroit, to provide significant price cuts while delivering on superior service. The particular plant we were introduced to was running around an 85 to 88 percent on-time ship rate. Not bad, you think? Think again . . . suppliers could miss their on-time ship date all they wanted; however, late deliveries in a just-in-time (JIT) production environment could shut an assembly plant down. Believe me, you don't want to be the supplier that shuts a plant down. And, as a result, the on-time compliance penalties for late delivery, especially resulting in a shutdown, could be enormous. You had to have 100 percent on-time delivery within your appointment window.

So, how do you think the supplier was coping with 88 percent on-time ship to make a 100 percent on-time delivery? Premium freight? Correct. So now you're thinking that because of the stringent compliance penalties, most plants are located within a reasonable driving distance to the assembly plant, so air freight probably won't work. And, after all, axles are pretty heavy for air shipping. Wrong . . . they were using air freight, but not cargo planes. They were using *helicopters.* Yep, when it positively has to be there . . . they chartered helicopters to pick up the pallets of axles and fly them to the assembly plant. What do you think their freight bill and profitable response to demand variability was? We won't go there. Suffice to say, we not only had a burning platform; we had a patient that was arterial bleeding. Transformation to lean manufacturing best practices was not a hard sell. The opportunity was painfully obvious.

What was interesting, though, was some of the root causes and unintended consequences that we found. Not to mention some interesting union responses to the changes. For some reason the forklifts initially were out of control any time they came close to a scheduling board. That said, as we designed the material flow through the operation, we realized that there could be any number of bottlenecks as material flowed through dozens of different work centers, almost all of which were pretty manually intensive. And, in order for them all to be working, they all had to be fully staffed.

So here is one of those unintended consequences and chicken and egg stories. Overtime was a major issue. The plant, not unlike many union operations we later discovered, was running at about 38 percent absenteeism. Yes, that's a lot . . . and, to keep all of the departments running . . . you got it, 38 percent of the personnel from the previous shift had to be recruited to work a double. Well, if you have ever worked in manufacturing operations, you'll discover that most of the personnel are required by their "significant others" to bring home a 40-hour weekly paycheck or there will be severe "compliance penalties."

If I am a laborer, and I work two doubles and a single shift on day three . . . 8 hours' shift one, time and half or 12 hours' pay shift two for 20 hours of pay times 2 the following day . . . that's 40; home is happy! An 8-hour shift on day three for the bonus . . . and I'm going fishin'! Three-day work with a bonus and four days of fishing . . . that's living! And I am senior union personnel that can't get fired for missing some days each week. Detroit, we have a problem.

By implementing a flow manufacturing plan based on lean principles, we are able to identify just what work orders in what work centers *need* to be working on to meet that day's requirements. By implementing a finished goods "supermarket" at final assembly, we are able to establish a buffer against variability and increase on-time ship to 99 percent, more than manageable. By assigning personnel *only* at those work centers that are required for the required output for that shift, we reduce the need for more than half of the overtime personnel we required before implementation.

Forklifts knocking down scheduling boards? Well, the union personnel were not particularly happy about having to work five days now to make their 40 hours of pay; however, when they started to see the numbers and the pizza and beer parties for hitting goals, and realized that the plant was getting closer to profitability (there was still a lot of bleeding; we slowed it, but didn't stop it) and would not be closed, they got on board. People want to survive. They want to do what's right. You have to give them the opportunity to seize the opportunity. Lean Six Sigma is not an option; it's a requirement.

When you think about it, the Make transformation was driven by a Deliver problem—on-time ship. The relationship between Deliver processes and Make processes are key drivers toward transformational success. The Deliver process type is comprised of those process categories and elements that are required to fulfill the customer order in full, on time, damage free, with the right documentation . . . the "perfect order" metric. While we will be looking at performance measurement in more detail in Chapter 7, delivering the perfect order requires excellence in order management, demand management, deployment management, inventory management, warehouse management, and transportation management. As illustrated in Figure 6.3, Deliver processes are generally referred to as logistics management. As we have seen throughout our discussion, logistics operations excellence requires collaboration with all of the process types across the enterprise Demand Management structures as well as collaboration across the channel for effective overall supply chain management excellence.

There are any numbers of pundits today who speak about orchestration as the peak level of maturity in supply chain management. When I was with Mercer Management Consulting, Bob Sabath (who headed supply chain consulting and was my mentor) and I would have many discussions using the orchestra analogy. You have many different instruments, each with its own tone and musical characteristics. Each on its own is capable of performing beautiful music. If you put them together, you need a conductor and sheet music for each instrument's part in the production. The conductor sets the tempo (takt time) and directs the different instruments to perform together. Certainly it has some play (pun intended) . . . lots of different instruments all playing to the same SCORe (another pun intended) that have to be in tune, on tempo, and in harmony to be music and not just noise. There is a lot of noise in supply chain management.

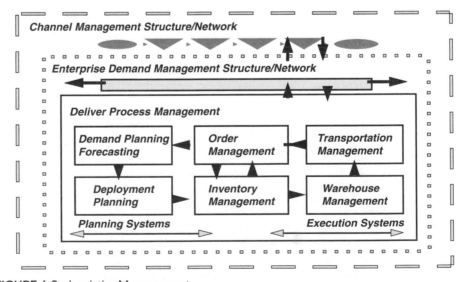

FIGURE 6.3 Logistics Management

LEVERAGING SUPPLY CHAIN CAPABILITY FOR SYNCHRONIZATION: STRATEGY, PLANNING, AND EXECUTION

Here's my problem with orchestration and why I never really went with it beyond my discussions with Sabath. Orchestration implies a conductor and as far as I am concerned, I don't see any supply chains with a single conductor. At best, there are as many conductors as there are different instruments. In the consumer industry, Wal-Mart may get a lot of companies to sing to its tune, but they aren't going to let Wal-Mart conduct their symphony.

For me, it really started to happened in the DEC days, gained validation when I was at Mercer and managing the Colgate project, and really took hold at IRI when I was able to experience the depth of information on market and consumer behavior on demand variability that was available. Kind of like my revelation about being demand and market responsive versus driven. For me, the highest level of supply chain maturity is *synchronization*. It's really what the Beer Game teaches us.

For many years, probably since I first heard George Stalk speak about his book that he wrote with Thomas Hout, *Competing Against Time*,[1] at a DEC seminar in Chicago, my research has been guided by the concept of synchronizing the various cycle times and managing the demand variability that results from time delay and amplification as material and information moves from one cycle to the next as in the real beer company supply chain in Figure 6.4.

It's why the *rate of sale* in each supply chain cycle is more important than point of sale quantity. The economic order quantity for each cycle will be the forecast of *what* will

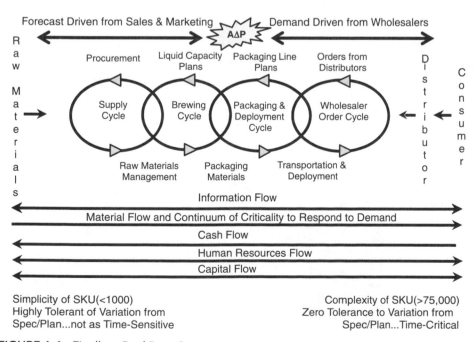

FIGURE 6.4 Finally, a Real Beer Company

be ordered. It's the *when* that is the root cause of supply chain problems. Synchronizing your operations to when product is needed versus what quantity of product is needed will eliminate the waste from uncertainty in the supply chain.

The breakthrough is understanding how to manage the *continuum of criticality* of material flow and the *periods of risk* (as my friends at Lead Time Technology refer to buffer stock coverage) that result when cycles intersect. Another good friend and fellow AMR Researcher and ND alum, Kevin Doyle, referred to these points of intersection as *process gates*. They are *critical action triggers* at the point when process control moves from one controlling interest to another. As I suggested earlier, supply chain management is all about managing across boundaries. And collaboration is the key to opening the gate.

You can't, in reality, conduct multiple supply chains beyond your organizational control, which is what you actually have to manage to. However, you can synchronize your cycles to customer and supplier cycles by understanding the cycle dynamics of the different supply chains your Demand Fulfillment structure interacts with and by adopting a collaborative strategy. It's removing the speed limits on your transformation journey. I am hoping the following explanation will not be "death by PowerPoint," but a picture can be worth a thousand words (see Figure 6.5). In my experience, a picture or visualization is really the only way to effectively communicate complex holistic, systems thinking concepts.

Figure 6.5 is about as simple as I can portray it. For the sake of simplicity, this is only the front end of a supply chain. The problem is always those darn customers. They just never behave as we plan. Solving the extended enterprise problem and synchronizing your business cycles to your customers' business cycles is the best of the best practice in supply chain management. Transforming your organization to be more demand responsive and become a Leader City resident requires the key to the city and the treasure chest. Collaboration (CPFR®) is the key to unlocking the hidden pipeline of opportunities in your operations and in becoming a strategic supplier to your customers. Doing so will result in sustainable best in class performance. And, if you can extend

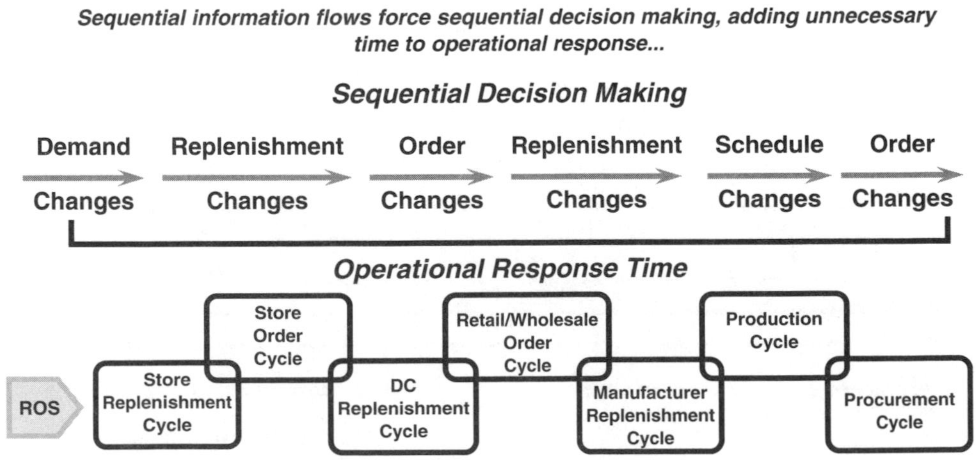

Sequential information flows force sequential decision making, adding unnecessary time to operational response...

Sequential Decision Making

Demand	Replenishment	Order	Replenishment	Schedule	Order
Changes	Changes	Changes	Changes	Changes	Changes

Operational Response Time

FIGURE 6.5 The Extended Enterprise Problem

collaboration to your supplier network, more opportunity awaits. Think of what you will harness as your journey continues. . . . Remember, the journey is the reward.

How do we start? Just like eating the elephant, we have to take it one step at a time. As I have inferred throughout our discussion, you have to understand your customers and the challenges of managing their business cycles. I am going to my roots—the consumer world—to explain synchronization. Remember Figure 5.1, A Retail Chain Analysis of Store Level Product Demand? If you are a retailer, you have my sympathy and I hope you will appreciate the following (see Figure 6.6). If you're shipping to a retailer, how would you like to be managing this much variability across your stock-keeping locations? You probably don't even have the number of locations (within your controllable network) to replenish that your customers have to manage. The variety, velocity, and variability of flows for the tens of thousands of products stocked in a retail outlet are staggering. Yet you want to beat them up for running out of *your* product in Store 494? And, keep in mind, their margins may be a tenth of yours.

I have always said that I can generally forecast *what* a supermarket will order with nearly 100 percent accuracy. For the most part, the store will order whatever the pack-out shippable unit is . . . a case. The quantity of items in the pack-out case will be determined by the retailer, often in conjunction with the manufacturer, when determining shelf space allocation or facing and depth. Using plan-o-gram software tools, most retailers will determine store product assortment and shelf space allocation. Based on product size and packaging, the number of units required to fill the shelf space allocated to the product will be the "case" outer pack size (e.g., 6, 8, 10, 12, 24 units). We like to work with even numbers to balance the next level of shippable unit, a pallet or skid.

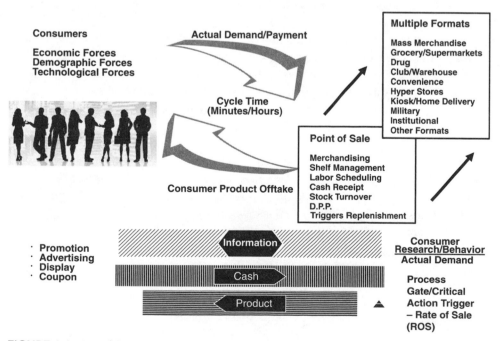

FIGURE 6.6 Retail Store Business Cycle

Stores don't like broken case lots as they are prone to shrinkage (i.e., theft). Therefore, they will generally reorder the item in the outer pack quantity . . . a case. *Voilà!* Nearly all stores' reorder quantity will be a case. Very easy to predict, right? Well, remember I said to pay attention to *rate of sale* more than *point of sale*? While it is pretty easy to predict *what* a store will reorder, it's not so easy to predict *when* it will reorder it. And all of the products in the store (thousands) have different rates of sale and reorder times than the others and they also vary by store as in Figure 5.1.

You see, retailers have a Demand Creation structure as well. Their merchandising department is all about increasing same-store sales volume and velocity (rate of sale). There are any numbers of ways they can do it. That's why the "P" in CPFR® (Collaborative Planning Forecasting and Replenishment) is so important to some brands and unattainable to others. Joint planning is great for both parties, especially the brand company. Unfortunately, category managers don't have the time to invest in joint planning with the dozens or more brands in each category. They generally plan with the "category captain" or lead brand in bringing consumers to the category and maybe the number two. The rest are pretty much at the mercy of the merchandising tools that the retailer uses and will be relegated to dealing with the "rebuyer" and not the category manager.

Let's think about the two learnings we just experienced. First, *the rate of sale of a product at the point of sale will be the lead determinant of forecast accuracy.* This is why point of sale (POS) is difficult for the manufacturer to manage. It is not enough to know what and when a product sold at POS. You really need to know the rate of sale of the product to determine the reorder time. POS systems were developed to improve the speed and accuracy of checkout, not to determine inventory levels and reorder points and triggers (while this is changing with new POS systems, it is a slow process based on the cost of replacing POS systems).

Retail stores come in many different formats and with different strategies depending on your product and industry. Mass merchandisers and big box retailers are increasingly carrying a wide assortment of product categories, from bags of dirt to bags of pet food, from apparel to foods, from appliances to home improvement, and the list goes on. Supermarkets are moving from just grocery to electronics, variety, lawn and garden, and the list goes on. You have to deal with clubs and drugs, convenience and fuel, and all things in between including Internet sales and military. It's an awful lot of data; it's not the cleanest or most accurate data; the product codes are not always in sync with the manufacturer's identification codes; the demand, as we have seen, is highly variable from store to store; and it's in sale units, not shippable units (e.g., each versus case).

That leads to the second learning: *Packaging has a lot more to do with product flow and forecasting than most people think, especially the developers of forecasting algorithms.* While I think that economic, demographic, and technological factors are hard to statistically account for, I think that packaging is the factor most overlooked and more easily statistically accounted for. Your packaging strategy can often be a lever to increasing demand and/or direct product profitability (DPP). It can also be a loser, if you proliferate SKUs by adding new packaging options. As a best practice, leveraging packaging for consumer convenience, different sizes for different demographics, can increase pricing options; however, it is important to realize the impact on the merchandising strategy of your customers. Big box retailers, for example, don't want a lot of variety in size SKUs. Shelf space is gold and they are more interested in variety of brand offerings at an extreme consumer value point than variety of size and choice for the consumer. Their consumers are value and price driven.

If you're not in the consumer industry, what's important here? Regardless of the industry or offering to the market, your demand will be determined by the rate of sale at the end of your "true" supply chain. You can determine the end point of sale/consumption (POS) in your supply chain by identifying the point at which the next flow of your product will not be a sale; it will be, for the most part, scrap or induction into a "used" resupply chain.

For any industry, this is the POS. For example, in the automotive industry, the end of the chain is the dealer sale. However, preowned vehicle sales will impact new-vehicle sales. The aftermarket is a different supply chain than the primary market and will have to be planned and considered altogether differently. We will examine supply chain definition more in Chapter 9, but it's important to note that you probably don't have one supply chain; you have many. It's increasingly becoming a multichannel world. That's why they pay us the big bucks.

My friend and another mentor over the years, Andre Martin, really got it right. If you can forecast what's selling at the end point of your supply chain, all of the other requirements can be calculated. He now calls that "flowcasting." It's just that for most companies, POS-driven forecasting is very difficult, if not impossible, unless it's your point of sale. The lack of understanding of POS dynamics and variability causes many companies to spend too much time and capital on chasing the Holy Grail. That does not mean that some companies with a high concentration of volume into a few high-volume customers can't improve flow and forecast accuracy for those lanes and ship to locations. It's that you won't be able to do it with the bulk of your customers. There are, however, best practices that can improve your visibility and forecasting.

Invoke the Bowersox Corollary: Ask your customers what they are planning to buy. And take the time to understand and consider the factors in their purchase decision. You know my issue with the "P" in CPFR®. The category manager simply can't invest the time to do joint planning with all of the brands in the category. This became painfully obvious to me during the CPFR® days and we were trying to recruit retailers into the pilots. I was working with a secondary brand in a category and the operations manager was getting shot down in the meetings almost before we were getting started. He would lead with the joint planning and the category manager would leave the meeting in the hands of the rebuyer. One thing was for sure: If you are not the category captain, and you use all your "chits" to get the rebuyer to convince the category manager to meet with you, don't waste their time. It's often harder to keep a category manager interested than a CEO.

The next meeting we had scheduled, I asked to lead the meeting and, I think largely due to the onset of depression, I was granted the task. I started the meeting with the benefits that the retail customer would receive from the manufacturer's increased forecast accuracy from visibility to what the retailer was planning to buy focusing primarily on increased GMROI. I then asked the category manager if they received a suggested purchase recommendation from their ERP system. Yes, and would they share the next four weeks' planned purchases for the manufacturer's products? That's all we would like to see.

The category manager leaned forward and says, "That's all you want?"

I replied, "Yes, if we can get a rolling four-week plan of what you are planning to buy, we can compare that with our forecast and reconcile the quantities ensuring improved service and GMROI."

The category manager affirmed that they could do that and I said that he could leave, if he wanted to, and we would work out the details with the rebuyer. As the category manager was leaving the room, he turned to the manufacturer's sales manager and said, "Kelly, you know that up-sell plan you've been wanting to present to me? Call me Monday and let's get it scheduled."

And the bonus! Waste their time and you will be punished. Optimize their time and you will be rewarded.

The customer plans, too. The customer has the data and analytics to forecast more accurately than you do what they are going to order from you. Just ask them. If you transform your supply chain to look from consumption/usage backward, you will unlock a treasure chest of opportunity. Your customers' sales cycles are very different from yours. In the case of consumer goods, demand is changing by the minute and they are analyzing it by, minimally, the shift. They have visibility of not only the *rate of sale* of all of the products they carry; but also of most of the causal factors (e.g., upcoming competitive initiatives that you won't have). At the end of the day, the POS owner is in the best position to forecast and plan based on what's actually being sold/consumed, regardless of industry or offering.

Collaboration is the key to managing your product flow within the context of the POS demand cycle. It determines the process gate or critical action trigger—the store order. The quantity will be in store shippable units, usually cases or totes in the case of smaller than outer pack item quantities. Note that the sales unit will generally be each's, replenishment order in cases. Your order will be cases shipped in pallets. Are you beginning to see the synchronization issues? Sales cycle time (ROS) will be in minutes, hours, and shifts by day, while the reorder cycle time will be day multiples and vary widely by product/store (SKU by location) with hundreds or thousands of locations resulting in millions of SKUs by location combinations. It gets complex fast.

The store order or POS replenishment order (Kanban or purchase order?) is the induction point from the retail store/POS replenishment cycle to the store/POS replenishment order cycle in Figure 6.7. Kanban is the lean production term that is used for reorder point. When the inventory at the shelf reaches a predetermined level, a reorder or purchase order is created based upon the lead time for the replenishment quantity to arrive coincidental with the last item being consumed or sold.

We were doing a distribution analysis for McDonald's and were speaking with a store manager. I asked him what the reorder point was. He pointed to lines drawn on the wall. When the stack of cases of products reached the point that the line became exposed, it was time to place a replenishment order. I call that McKanban.

The challenge in managing the demand generated at the final point of sale is the variability of demand being generated at so many different locations. Remember Sherman's Law of Forecasting: Forecasting improves in direct correlation to its distance

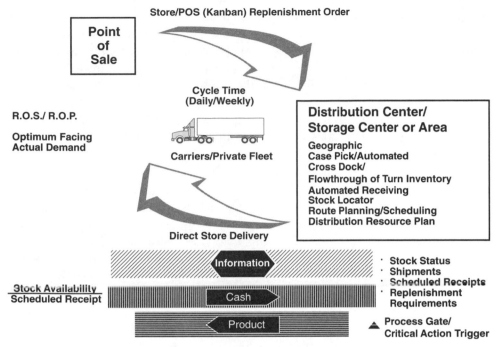

FIGURE 6.7   The Retail Store/POS Replenishment Cycle

from usefulness. The first company I saw to really get this was STSC, which became Manugistics and is now JDA. Their planning strategy was one of the first to be based on SKU by location or, as they called it, a demand forecast unit (DFU). It's the most useful operations forecast as you're loading the trucks with SKUs for a particular location. If your DFU matches what Lenny can load on the truck, Wall Street will be happy.

Colgate was the first customer that I worked with that we actually planned to the customer ship to location level, and the best practice dramatically improved our forecast accuracy. The early CPFR® pilots, notably the pilot between Warner-Lambert and Wal-Mart, really demonstrated the power of collaboration in improving SKU by location forecasts. The more you can understand the drivers of variability (e.g., demand-changing events and seasonality), the better you can plan and manage inventory levels at your distribution locations.

Most companies will have a distribution center of some type located within their customer replenishment lead time. Some industries such as build to order or engineer to order manufacturing strategies have the luxury of determining lead time . . . until a competitor does it faster. But most industries are at the mercy of the customer when it comes to replenishment lead time. In Chapter 2, I discussed the change in the wholesale distribution industry. We used to have this wonderful channel that sat between the manufacturing facilities and the customers' selling locations that would assume all inventory and sales risk and manage all of the distribution activities for us. Then some accountant or pundit decided that these "middlemen" were robbing margin from us, so we either built or contracted for facilities with 3PLs to replace them, paid for all of the activities they absorbed on a transactional basis, and we assumed all inventory and sales risk and the associated working capital required to do so. There has never been a case that I have seen that demonstrated to me that the manufacturing companies (using 3PLs and financing retail inventories) or self-distributing retailers (who own most of their facilities) gained significant economic benefit from the disintermediation of the wholesalers. We just replaced them with the third-party logistics (3PL) industry and associated cost.

If you are replenishing to the POS/consumption, *rate of sale analysis* is a best practice that will move you forward on your journey. For each of your SKUs by ship to location you have to calculate the reorder point (ROP) and frequency (ROS) by which an order will be placed to replenish the shelf or work center in commercial industry. Generally, the ROP will be the "facing" unit level that keeps the shelf looking stocked (e.g., 2, 3, or 4 units wide). No one likes to take the last one. If the pack-out quantity matches space, there should be adequate on-shelf storage to hold excess allocation. Too technical? Next time you go shopping, look at the very top shelf or very lowest shelf and you'll find the "extra" stock. Best practice retailers will have their associates walking the aisles throughout the day to optimize facings so that shelf display is stocked and looks in order. Retailers don't like backroom stock anymore because it is also subject to shrink.

If you are selling to other manufacturers, this can be in the form of the bill of materials, routings, and production schedule. As components or raw materials are consumed in the production routings, a replenishment order, sometimes referred to as kanban, is issued and before the work center runs out the component storage is replenished. As the facility consumes its stock, a replenishment order is generated and sent to the supplier (supplier kanban) to release a replenishment order that will arrive just prior to the stockroom running out.

Whether you are replenishing to production or a store, product is being consumed, and the *rate* at which product is consumed, ROS, will trigger the replenishment order in the pack-out quantity or the most economic shipping quantity from the supplier to the location being replenished. Most of the time, you can easily predict what quantity will be ordered; the best practice is determining *when* it will be placed. My friends at Lead Time Technology recalculate on a daily basis to set control limits for peak, cycle, and safety stock levels that planners can use to keep all of the locations and cycles in synch in response to highly variable demand. They are like the lines on the wall of the McDonald's store. We will discuss the technology aspects of transformation in more detail in Chapter 8.

Depending on your industry and/or product mix, the distribution center may or may not be automated. In general, when the DC is replenishing to a POS/consumption location, the DC will be receiving in pallets or skids and picking and shipping in cases. The retail leader and best practices pioneer that I observed executing this earliest and to near perfection is Meijer, the Grand Rapids, MI-based retailer that is privately held and regional. But they are every bit as advanced and sophisticated as any retailer I have observed. They are very private and very competitive and very controlled in their quality and growth. However, in my observations, working with their people in various industry initiatives and working with their suppliers, they have strong values with a self-actualization transformational culture.

It was Meijer that was one of the first companies to combine the IT function with the distribution function, which created competitive advantage from advanced analytical capabilities. They took their store ordering analytics to the point of implementing the first true cross-docking facilities in the industry. Cross docking combines all of the store replenish plans and combines them with supplier consolidation plans considering the rate of sale, the rate of store replenishment, the supplier-required order and lead time necessary to synchronize the receipt of goods from the suppliers in bulk, break the bulk into individual store orders, match the store orders to the route and truck schedule to deliver the stores, convey the product to the dock doors with the right store delivery truck, load the truck in store-stop order, and ship the same day within different shift windows. That's what we're talking about, true cross-docking flow-through of product and near-zero latency.

Another Grand Rapids, MI-based distributor, Gordon Food Service (GFS®), implemented similar programs and best practices in the institutional foods distribution industry. Notre Dame was a customer at the time I was working the distribution LOB at Burroughs. The foodservice manager would determine the number of students to be fed in the dining halls and the menu to be served the next day and enter it into GFS®'s system. GFS® maintained the recipes and each night would explode the menu into the individual meal recipes, create a replenishment order with all of the ingredients necessary for the ND food services to prepare the meals, and deliver the order to ND the following day in time for breakfast preparation. They provide service that is seamless, synchronized, and at a competitive level of quality and value. Like Meijer, family-owned, and quietly going about the business of industry leadership and controlled, profitable growth. This how self-actualization and transformation stuff works.

And don't forget competitive advantage. Here is another Paul Harvey "rest of the story" about GFS®. I had been trying to convince Notre Dame's long-time local institutional distributor (ND was their largest customer) that they needed to implement new technology and a distribution management system (GFS® used Burroughs' systems). Notre Dame was very committed to supporting local businesses as the economy of South Bend, Indiana, was fragile to say the least. Doing business in Michigan was like off-shoring. However, the day after the GFS® salesperson delivered the proposal to Notre Dame with all of the cost and time savings associated with the GFS® electronic menu and order system, the local distributor was out; and, I got the call for a new distribution system. GFS® leveraged its supply chain capabilities for competitive advantage. And now you know the "rest of the story."

The retail store order replenishment cycle is driven in response to the requirements of the store business cycle to respond to consumer demand. The cycle time is generally measured in delivery days or times per week. Some stores may see a delivery every day; others may only see a delivery once a week. The rate of sale, pack-out quantity, and reorder point drives its demand and, in turn, will consolidate store demand into economic order quantities placed on its suppliers. Of course, all of those Demand Creation structure elements and events add to the complexity; but, if you focus first on the basics, transform your perspective to the point of consumption or usage, and design your processes back, you will discover the opportunities that can be unlocked by collaborative best practices (CPFR®).

In nonconsumer industries, you also have to design your processes from usage back. The store business cycle is the production facility work center consumption cycle. The rate of sale is the rate of production. The reorder point is the kanban signal. The retail store/POS replenishment cycle is the stockroom, raw material storage, or other production inventory storage area that is replenished by the supplier kanban signal. The processes, at least at the type, category, and element level, are remarkably similar. It's why SCOR® remains relevant and a transformational lever.

In fact, CPFR® is not just for consumer goods. I can guarantee that whatever industry you are in, your customers are forecasting, planning, and scheduling their operations. They are producing planned purchase orders and material requirements. They have material release schedules. Invoke the Bowersox Corollary . . . *ask them to share*. Go to www.vics.org and you'll find information and case studies that support CPFR® adoption across many different industries. Collaboration is the key to unlocking the value of transformation.

The DC replenishment order to the supplier/manufacturer is the induction point from the store/POS replenishment order cycle to the Customer Replenishment Order Cycle in Figure 6.8.

Unfortunately for most manufacturing companies, this is where their perception of the supply chain begins. The retailers generally don't understand this cycle and the constraints associated with it. I asked the manufacturers to pay attention to the first two cycles; retailers and customers of manufacturers, it's your turn to pay attention. There is

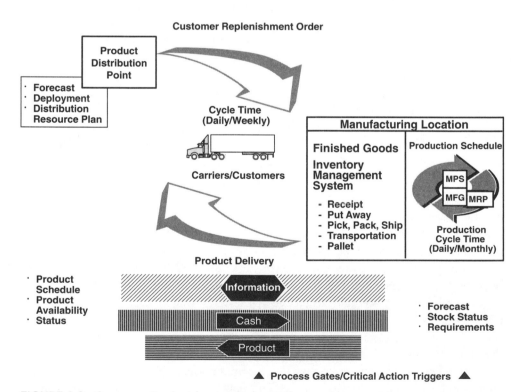

FIGURE 6.8   Customer Replenishment Order Cycle

margin to be made here, but you have to look for the opportunity. P&G and Wal-Mart found a lot of opportunity when P&G's consolidated shipments savings were visible to them, and they worked together to create a best practice process that enabled Wal-Mart to maintain GMROI and increase their T&E index while enabling P&G to optimize their transportation costs—win-win.

In my experience, if you took out all of the gamesmanship and eliminated the adversarial relationships that we are discovering are purely accidental, we would have more productive, profitable commerce. In fact, Kate Vitasek, founder of Supply Chain Visions, whom I have known since she was a grad student at the University of Tennessee and who now teaches executive education there, has written a book on what she has termed *Vested Outsourcing* to improve the value and strategic relationship between third parties and their customers.[2] Maybe she and I should collaborate on a book for all of business and call it *Vested Commerce*. That's what we probably should have called CPFR® . . . everybody wins.

Transforming your supply chain to a Smart Supply Network and pursuing the journey from your new home in Leader City requires you to think outside the box. Both customers and suppliers have to understand the drivers of their Demand Fulfillment cycles and take action to synchronize the cycles. Traditional supply chain management will have you whipped by uncertainty, variability, stock-outs, excesses, and other costly miscalculations. Ed Fogarty, head of Colgate US at the time I was managing their ERP transformation requirements definition, coined the phrase SLOB inventory for "SLow moving and Obsolete" inventory. (I found out later that he had actually coined it at a previous company, and it was a trademark of his management approach to distribution.)

We spent a lot of time on integrated business planning and forecasting in Chapter 5. Here is where the rubber meets the road, and why it's so important to document the processes and standardize on the tools the daily operations planning and execution personnel use to make their decisions . . . decisions that comprise millions of dollars in working capital and the capabilities as to whether you can "ship it and bill it" or not.

The complexity in most manufacturing operations lies in the management of several cycles within one as, the "real" beer company in Figure 6.4 illustrates in more detail than Figure 6.8, which is a more simplified version.

The process gate and trigger point that intersects with the customer's replenishment cycle is finished goods inventory replenishment and deployment cycles, which place demand on the production cycles in the form of work orders, which in turn will place demand on the next cycle, supply replenishment. Of course, like the real beer company, many manufacturers have multistage production cycles. Discrete manufacturers, such as our axle manufacturer, have many steps with many work centers, each with its own cycle that needs to be synchronized, which in Lean Six Sigma is called *takt time* . . . the rhythm of production.

The process gate between finished goods and the critical action triggering a work order is also the intersection that represents the "push-pull" boundary in many manufacturing companies. If you are not in some variation of a "make to order" industry, unless you have found a way to beam product, you probably can't be 100 percent "pull." Because customer order lead times are generally shorter than the production and/or sourcing lead times, most companies have to "push" finished goods, at least in some state, into inventory in anticipation of the customer's actual order. Think of the supermarket inventory we created for the axle manufacturer to ensure on-time shipment of the customer's order.

Here again is some pundit frustration. A concept was put forth that everyone should strive to design their manufacturing processes to build to an efficient lot size of one. Mass customization was an evolution of the process. There is another one out there to make every product every day. Great ideas, but they are not for everyone. If you have any significant cost or time in changing over from one product to another, building every product every day can be a killer.

I remember doing a process review for TRW Nelson Stud division. They produced precision fasteners for a variety of industries. The division president read some article or book on the importance of inventory turns. He mandated that every product turn 10 times per year. To make a long story short, manufacturing implemented the policy and costs went through the roof! Why? The setup costs for many of their products, due to extremely tight specification tolerances and low initial yield, mandated longer runs to keep costs down. The carrying cost of inventory was extremely low (you could store a year's supply in a tote). It was more cost effective to run those products once a year to maintain a high gross margin. I guess the article didn't talk about GMROI or the T&E index.

Think about P&G and producing Pampers® diapers. Diapers sell as fast as babies poop. Why would you want to design a process to produce to an efficient lot size of one? Why would you want to build to a pull system? Those babies are going to be pulling diapers faster than you can push them out. In fact, at many high-volume manufacturing facilities, outbound dock capacity is their biggest constraint. They can't deploy product out to their 3PL network fast enough to keep up with production.

This is why the exercises in Chapters 2 and 3 are critical. If you don't have the business perspective and market strategy right, you can transform yourself to a loss. It's also why you better track what the CEO is reading and read it first.

Managing the push-pull boundary in light of an inaccurate forecast and high levels of variability is what keeps most supply chain managers up at night. It is also why, as many of them are, if they are reasonably good at it, stuck in transformational maturity somewhere around social and self-esteem. Sitting at the truck stop instead of moving forward on the journey is your biggest barrier to true transformation to self-actualization. Don't let it happen to you.

The challenge to managing the push-pull boundary is the capability to determine the frequency to run product. How many times should I place a product into production? Once I determine *what* products to run *when*, I need to determine what sequence I should run them in to minimize changeover costs. The classic example is that I don't want to run vanilla after chocolate. Vanilla requires less cleanout time than chocolate does. After determining the run sequence, I determine the optimum run length considering yield and my period of risk, as Lead Time Technology refers to it. The period of risk is the time between when I produce a product and the next time the product is scheduled to run. I want to have just enough finished goods inventory (remember the finished goods supermarkets at the axle manufacturer) to cover the period of risk.

Of course, this sounds pretty simple. There should be the math to do this, and there is. The problem lies in the fact that the market is highly volatile, variable, and dynamic over time. It's not something you can do once and then go away. It has to be done as variability occurs . . . daily! This is the reason for the continuum of criticality that we discovered at the real beer company. Demand variability hits you on a shift-by-shift basis. The longer you wait to respond, the greater the time delay; the greater the time delay, the larger the amplification; and, well, you're getting bullwhipped.

Let me share another Paul Harvey's "the rest of the story." This is why the daily operations folks have all of those custom spreadsheets. They have to reconcile inventory to demand variation on a daily, often shift-by-shift, basis. They have to fight fires and place change orders or expedite orders on production and warehousing. They're the ones getting bullwhipped and their decisions are either costing you or making you millions. Now you know the "rest of the story."

In the absence of collaboration, the lack of visibility to customer orders becomes maddening, and many SKU by location forecasts are less than 60 percent (I am being generous) accurate on any given day. Transformation to a demand-responsive, customer-driven operation from a forecast-driven operation is mandated to achieve best practice leadership. Effective *daily* management of the push-pull boundary to respond profitably to daily demand variation is the critical best practice to unlocking waste and working capital . . . and, of course, collaboration is the key, both internally and externally.

At the tail of the bullwhip and trying to figure out if the tail is wagging the dog are the raw material/packaging material and other suppliers of the fuel that drives the supply network and its cycles. The supply purchase order to the supplier is the induction point from the customer replenishment order cycle to the supply purchase order cycle in Figure 6.9.

Depending on the material required, this may or may not be the ending cycle type of your supply chain but it is the beginning of your cash-to-cash cycle (Figure 6.2). We invest cash in materials for production, sale, distribution, invoicing, collection, and return cash into the bank. You will be tasked with synchronizing your supply purchase order cycle to your suppliers' customer replenishment cycle. And, if your suppliers have suppliers, they will be replicating the process until the final final supplier. It's a system of networked nodes each operating a different series of cycles. Are you getting more interested in systems dynamics and thinking? Remember the old saying: If builders built buildings the way programmers developed systems, the first woodpecker to come around would destroy civilization. Supply chain is a system of systems.

The easiest way for me to explain supplier relationship is the golden rule: Treat your suppliers as you would have your customers treat you. The same information and process integration that you need from your customers to synch up and optimize your business cycles are, more than likely, the same information and process integration that your suppliers need from you. And any adversarial relationship that you have with them is probably as accidental as the adversarial relationship you had with your customers before your transformation.

It all starts with the production schedule. The production schedule will provide the material requirements, which, in turn, are converted into supply purchase orders to be fulfilled by the supplier. Sounds easy enough . . . *if* we are fully integrated with our

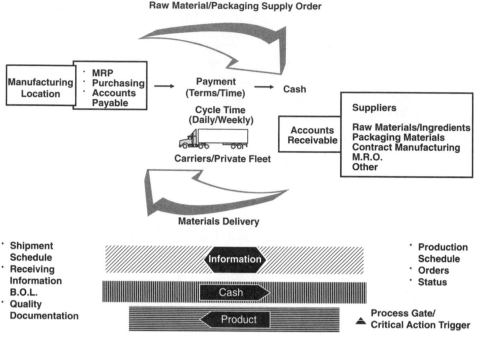

FIGURE 6.9 The Supply Purchase Order Cycle

suppliers. The reality is that supplier variability can be as volatile as customer variability. Sure, if we have enough clout with our suppliers, we can develop requirements that suppliers have to comply with, maintain supplier scorecards, and impose penalties on suppliers for noncompliance. Like the axle manufacturer, we can hope that our suppliers transform their supply chain and raise their performance before they go out of business (as the axle manufacturer was about to do).

Or, as a best practice leader, you can move along on your transformation journey to implement supplier integration, cycle synchronization, and a strategic relationship. CPFR® works as effectively on the back end of your supply chain as it does on the front. Don't wait for your suppliers to ask you. They fear asking you as much as you feared asking your customers. What are you waiting for?

Supplier collaboration based on partnership and a strategic versus transactional relationship, as experienced on the front end, can yield significant benefits if we identify the opportunity in best practice processes that can result. Start with supply inventory. How much working capital do you have tied up in raw materials?

When I was with Burroughs, I had the opportunity to manage the Skyline Corporation account. My first discussion with the IT director was pretty interesting. Back in the early 1950s, well before Michael Dell was born, Art Decio founded the company to build mobile homes. Having very little capital, he negotiated with suppliers to provide the materials he needed to manufacture each individual unit as it entered production . . . just in time, matching the unit's bill of material. Their win? Immediate payment terms. Working through a network of dealers, Skyline would build the units to order, receiving payment with one-third down, one-third upon shipping, and one-third upon delivery. The down payment covered the cost of the materials, allowing Skyline to pay upon receipt. The second payment covered the cost of manufacturing, and the final payment was profit. Skyline Corporation is now traded on the NYSE, but it still follows a process of maintaining only work-in-process inventory with little or no raw material or finished goods inventory and with the agility to flex up or down with low risk. Just-in-time delivery makes sense, as Dell has well proven over the years.

Sure, there are risks with just-in-time delivery. Supply lines can be broken through many different risks; and, with no inventory in reserve, you are vulnerable. And not many suppliers really want to bear the risk of deploying their inventory within the proximity that a Dell, Skyline, or any of the major automotive assembly plants require. That's why vendor-managed inventory (VMI) can be an effective synchronization strategy. While retailers may, based on T&E indexes, not be as economically motivated for VMI, most manufacturers can have a significant amount of working capital tied up in raw material, packaging, material, tooling, and so on.

So let's get back to the golden rule. When I was talking about CPFR®, I talked about asking the category manager for his suggested purchase schedule for my products. You probably have a master production schedule (MPS) that is input to material requirements planning (MRP) that generates your purchase orders. Why not share with your suppliers your production schedule of when you are planning to consume the supplier's product and your beginning and ending inventory of the supplier's products? Also, share with the supplier the MRP for their product, which will be a time-phased schedule of planned purchase orders and due dates. If the supplier has this information, they can sync it up with their forecasts and internal plans. The supplier, with this new visibility, can look for transportation consolidations, inventory efficiencies, capacity utilization, and so on, not unlike what Wal-Mart and P&G did. After evaluating the opportunities, the supplier can propose a relationship based on cost sharing . . . a vested relationship, as Kate Vitasek would call it. It may or may not include VMI or other supply relationship best practices, but it will be transparent based on value, not on gamesmanship.

Synchronizing your supply order cycle with your supplier cycle will unlock many economic opportunities for you. Supply consistency cannot be underestimated. Earlier in this chapter I talked about outbound dock capacity at P&G's Pampers facility as an issue. Well, what do you think the implication is to receiving dock capacity? Visibility of scheduled shipments from suppliers and advanced shipping notices (ASN) can provide you the opportunity to optimize receipts and schedule appointments with supplier carriers. Positive receiving can eliminate the need for the three-way match: invoice, receiver, and purchase order. This transformation journey is proving that the yellow brick road just may be paved with gold. The journey is becoming more rewarding.

Guess what? You just ate an elephant! Sure, I know there is a lot of detail to go through and a lot of work. But transformation doesn't have to be that scary. It's a continuous journey that will provide continuous reward. You just have to pick a place to start eating one piece at a time. Remember: Leaders and Laggards are both working as hard. If you're going to work hard, work hard on the right things and you'll be a Leader before you know it. Figure 6.10 illustrates the journey you just completed, starting with the retail store or point of sale cycle.

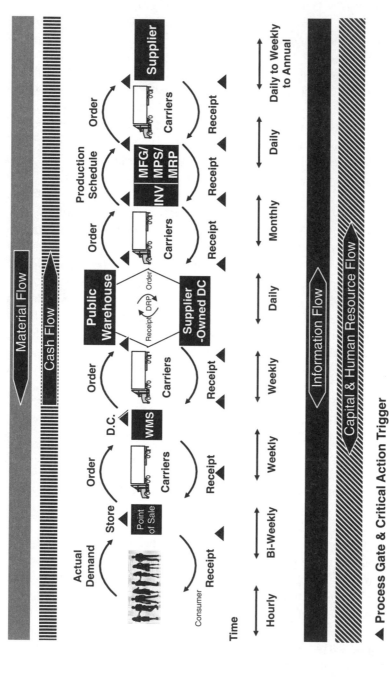

▲ **Process Gate & Critical Action Trigger**

FIGURE 6.10 Supply Chain Cycle Time

118

Unlike Figure 6.5, The Extended Enterprise Problem, this one is a bit more complex, don't you think? It's probably not what you want to display at the front end of your presentation. However, it does convey the complexity and systemic nature of supply chain management. If any one of these cycles goes haywire, it can have the rippling effect of a bullwhip cutting through the other cycles. *Sequential information flows force sequential decision making adding unnecessary time to operational response.* . . . It's the beer game!

And this is the nature of supply chain management . . . singular. You probably have many products, product groups, customers, global locations, and suppliers that comprise your *supply network*. Each is a node in the network driven by a different cycle time operating at different speeds with different characteristics and performance requirements. It's a herd of elephants! If you're not careful, they can stampede. But this is why they pay us the big bucks. Supply management is a pipeline of opportunity to liberate working capital, increase revenue, optimize cost, increase margin, and improve return on invested capital . . . but by now I think you realize why in all of those transformation case studies, the one constant is *management commitment and/or executive support.* I know you can start the journey without it. If you're not already on the journey, you will have to be the one to start it. Continuing on the journey, transforming the culture, and sustaining the journey *will require* management commitment. So let me show you how to get it.

 NOTES

1. Stalk, George, and Thomas M. Hout, *Competing Against Time: How Time-Based Competition Is Reshaping Global Markets*, Free Press, 2003.
2. Vitasek, Kate, *Vested Outsourcing: Five Rules That Will Transform Outsourcing*, Palgrave Macmillan, 2010.

CHAPTER SEVEN

Okay, We Need Management Commitment; So, How Do We Get It?

ID YOU SKIP TO this chapter early? If you did, go back and read the other chapters. There really aren't any shortcuts to transformation. It's a journey that you will have to be prepared for. The Demand Performance structure simultaneously fuels the Demand Creation and Demand Fulfillment structures and is driven by them. It's more than finance and accounting. It's the executive office, human resources, and information technology. It's the enterprise enablement and accountability structure that's responsible for the strategic direction of the company and, ultimately, its financial performance and health.

So, here's a common scenario. The supply chain vice president (SCVP) presents to the chief executive officer (CEO) and chief financial officer (CFO) that he believes he can reduce inventory by 30 percent.

"Wow, that's great!" says the CFO. "How are you going to do it?"

The SCVP responds, "We can implement a new software application for inventory optimization. It will only cost $100,000 and the ROI is less than nine months."

"Really?" counters the CFO. (The CEO has stepped out to take a call.) "We don't have $100,000 in capital at this time. And there are at least four other projects already in the capital appropriation process that will take priority over you doing your job, which is to reduce inventory.

"And, by the way," the CFO adds, "one of those projects will also reduce inventory."

"Really?"

"Yeah, the VP of manufacturing needs a new filling machine for $400,000 or he won't be able to meet production. No filling machine, no product, and no inventory . . . *capiche*? Go do your job!"

Sound familiar? Let's replay the scenario. Only this time, I will be the SCVP. In the same meeting with the CEO and CFO, I kick it off by saying, "I think I found a way to get $41 million in capital." (Inventory is $136.9 million; 30 percent is around $41 million.)

The CEO, leaning forward, says, "When?" Turning away from me for a moment, "Excuse me, tell them I am in a meeting and will call them back." Turning back to me, "Okay, when?"

"I am confident we can get it all in about 9 to 10 months, definitely by Q4," I respond.

The CFO chimes in, "Okay, sounds good, but what is going to take?"

"We'll only need about 2 percent of it. I figure somewhere south of $800,000 should do it," I respond. (Hey, I am giving them $41 million cash. Why should I only ask for a measly $100,000? I have a transformation to fund here. If I asked you, right now, for $10 and guaranteed you by year end that I would hand you $450 in return, would you do it?)

"Bingo! You got it!" says the CEO, seconded by the CFO.

"By the way, is this part of that transformation project you've been noodling?" the CEO adds.

"Yep, just an early phase," I respond.

The CEO pulls the CFO aside for a moment, then comes back at me. "Tell you what, Rich, why don't you pull together a plan for the whole enchilada, run it by me and the finance guys, and we'll put it on the board agenda for Q3, after we see the results of the working capital project. Count on me and the CFO for any support you need. Wow, an unplanned $41 million in the bucket this year? That's going to make the shareholder meeting fun again."

Do you think you'd like to learn a little more about what goes on in the Demand Performance structure? Do you want to learn about more ways to get projects funded? Do you want to know what you need to know to justify fueling the transformation journey? Replay the same scenario with you talking the talk. Sounds good, doesn't it? The journey is sounding more and more doable, don't you think?

 ## UNDERSTANDING THE DEMAND PERFORMANCE STRUCTURE

If the Demand Creation structure manages the demand chain and the Demand Fulfillment structure manages the supply chain, then the Demand Performance structure manages the *value chain* and determines the *financial strategy* for the enterprise that the other structures must align to. So, what are the critical success factors, as illustrated in Figure 7.1, that we need to focus on to achieve profitable growth?

Of course, the senior management team is responsible for the overall strategy, governance, and performance of the company. To execute on the company's strategy the management team must align the organization for effective response to changing market conditions. They must ensure that the resources within each management structure are capable of developing the demand, supply, and value chain strategies to execute on the corporate strategy and achieve the company's financial objectives. Human resources' chief human capital officer (CHC) and information technology's chief information officer (CIO), usually under the direction of the CEO and CFO, as heads of the

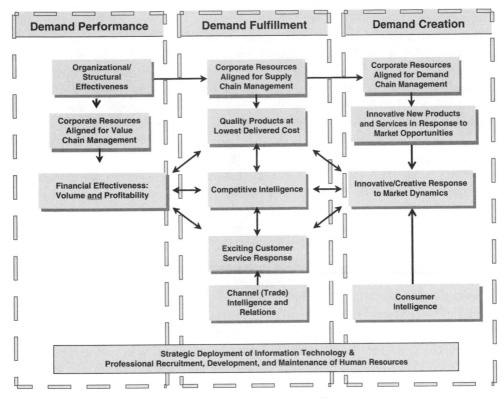

FIGURE 7.1 Critical Success Factors for Profitable Growth

Demand Performance structure, provide the enabling support infrastructure to meet the HR and IT needs of the Demand Creation and Demand Fulfillment structures. Critical to the success of the company is the strategic deployment of information technology and the professional recruitment, development, and maintenance of its human resources. Both of these will be discussed in more detail in Chapters 8 and 9.

The heads of the Demand Creation structure are usually the head of R&D and the head of sales and marketing. Depending on the industry, R&D governing titles may be chief research officer, chief technology officer, chief scientist, chief engineer, and so on. Many organizations are resisting the anointing of "chiefs" and staying with director or classes of vice president, senior vice president, executive vice president, and president. By industry, we are seeing the chief marketing officer (CMO) heading marketing and sometimes R&D and sales. Sales have been slow to move to a "chief," but often the CMO will report to the SVP or EVP of sales. If there is a chief, it is more often the chief customer officer (CCO) than the chief sales officer (CSO).

Similarly, the Demand Fulfillment structure is typically governed by the chief operating officer, but we are seeing the emergence of the chief supply chain officer (CSCO), as well as staying with director or classes of vice president, senior vice president, executive vice president, and president. Some organizations, like The Limited, have spun off Demand Fulfillment or the logistics component as a wholly owned business unit. Generally, if there is a CSCO, they will be responsible for procurement and logistics (often real estate and facilities), but not manufacturing. I have seen chief manufacturing officer, another CMO, but, for that reason, more often a COO or VP class.

As we discussed in Chapter 4, organizational structure is more about *alignment and collaboration* as critical success factors than it is hierarchical structure. The organization will operate simultaneously vertically and horizontally regardless of how you structure it. I developed the Demand Management structure so that I could apply it to any organizational hierarchy and industry. For purposes of this discussion, let's just say that the CFO heads Demand Performance, the CSCO heads Demand Fulfillment, and the chief marketing officer (CMO) heads Demand Creation.

The CFO has the responsibility to ensure that the resources are in place to measure, manage, and control the critical success factor of the financial effectiveness of the company placing equal attention on volume and profitability. Of the five "capital flows" within a company, the CFO is most responsible for cash, capital, information, and human capital flow governance. While the other executives contribute significantly, contrary to popular belief, the CFO exerts the controlling pressure on these flows in support of the CEO's overall strategy. I will define the Demand Performance structure processes in more detail later in this chapter.

The CMO has the responsibility to ensure that the Demand Performance structure has adequately funded (capitalized) the Demand Creation structure to execute a demand chain strategy to research, bring forth, and develop innovative products, services, or market offers in response to changing market conditions and the windows of opportunity the changing conditions open. In addition, the CMO will be responsible for the commercialization of the offers in the marketplace and the effective promotion and profitable sale of those offers based on customer, consumer, and competitive intelligence. The company's ability to respond to market dynamics, competitive initiatives, and economic conditions are critical success factors for the Demand Creation structure.

The CSCO has the responsibility to ensure that the Demand Performance structure has adequately funded (capitalized) the Demand Fulfillment structure to execute a supply chain strategy that will delight its trading partners, customers, and the ultimate consumer profitably. The CSCO is most responsible for managing and controlling the remaining capital flow, material.

Critical to the success of the Demand Fulfillment structure is the capability to produce and deliver to the company's target market segments quality products (offers) at the lowest delivered competitive cost in alignment with the corporate strategy and financial objectives. Simultaneously, it is also critical that the Demand Fulfillment structure understand customer needs and requirements to provide exciting competitive customer service also in alignment with the corporate strategy and financial objectives. To be successful, the Demand Fulfillment structure must maintain intelligence on customer and trading partner behaviors, requirements, and market conditions.

Critical to the success of the organization, as a whole, is the maintenance of any competitive activities, strategies, best practices, press relations, and other intelligence that may be relevant to the capability of the company to compete or to gain competitive advantage.

YOU CAN'T MANAGE WHAT YOU CAN'T MEASURE

Peter Drucker, the world-renowned writer, management consultant, and university professor, is supposed to have said, "If you can't measure it, you can't manage it." Whether you are trying to get management buy-in, start your transformation journey, or just manage your operations, it's critical to be able to measure the performance of the operations. Before we get into the Demand Performance structure processes, I think it's important to look at what we measure in supply chain management so that we can effectively translate our performance and transformation initiatives to the financial performance of the organization. (I am intentionally not going to get into Demand Creation measurement and metrics. I'll leave that for my colleague, Laura Patterson, at VisionEdge Marketing.)

Speaking of colleagues, I mentioned earlier that I first met Kate Vitasek, founder of Supply Chain Visions, a management consulting firm, when she was a graduate student at the University of Tennessee. Professor Ray Mundy, now at the University of Missouri, had developed what I considered to be the best executive-in-residence program in the academic world. I include this here for two reasons. First, I want to acknowledge the contribution and collaboration of Supply Chain Visions in developing the performance management model that I am going to discuss. And, second, in the hope that many students and academics will read this and develop more classes like Mundy's.

A MODEL FOR AN EXECUTIVE-IN-RESIDENCE CLASS

The Executive-in-Residence class at UT was a formal three-credit class. Dr. Ray Mundy invited a different executive each week to reside at the university for a couple of days. Mundy would assign several students to research the background of the executive that would be visiting that week and his or her company. On the Tuesday before the executive was scheduled to speak during the Thursday class, these students would present their findings and analysis of the executive's company and market.

Another couple of students would be assigned to meet the executive at the airport on Wednesday and take the executive to the hotel. They would also host breakfast the following morning for the executive, which would provide time for the students to ask questions and discuss areas of interest with the executive.

On Wednesday evening, Mundy would host a dinner with the executive and three or four other faculty members to engage in industry talk and discuss current and pending research.

Thursday morning, following breakfast, the executive would deliver a relevant presentation to the class followed by Q&A. For lunch, the class would host a private luncheon with another group of students and faculty for further open discussion.

Following lunch, we would return to the department offices and 5 or 6 students would be selected to have a closed-door, "no holds barred" discussion. With no faculty present, the students could ask any question on any topic related to the business or professional career of the executive.

At end of the day, the original students assigned to the executive would return the executive to the airport.

The students were then required to submit a paper on their specific experiences with the executive and their learning from the experiences and presentations, which were read and graded. Unlike many of the informal executive-in-residence programs I have been invited to over the years, the Tennessee program, in my humble opinion, was probably the best experience and learning for both the students and the executive. ■

So, as part of my work at CSCMP, I developed a performance management workshop with Vitasek's company, Supply Chain Visions, and specifically with Mike Ledyard, one of her senior consultants. Ledyard, in fact, when he was at CSC Consulting, had co-authored a CLM (now CSCMP) book on supply chain performance measurement. During the course of developing the workshop, I really liked one of Supply Chain Visions' slides depicting "Building Blocks of Successful Performance Management."

Knowing that performance measurement and metrics are critical components of a supply chain transformation, especially when it comes to integration with the Demand Performance structure and gaining executive and financial management confidence, I decided to adapt it for purposes of this book. Obviously, I have my own cut on the topic, and, with my background with SCOR® and technology, I felt I needed to develop a simple way to communicate why transformation is critical to the profitable growth of the company. If you're going to be a resident of Leader City, you're going to have to have a place to live.

Taking the base graphical context of "Building Blocks of Successful Performance Management," I adapted it and developed "The House of Excellence," as illustrated in Figure 7.2, which you can use with your team to architect a performance management operating system in the business context. To a large extent this book is about transforming your organization to build the House of Excellence as your residence in Leader City.

When we developed SCOR®, it was our intent to have a set of practitioner-maintained, industry-standard performance metrics available to anyone in the industry. We wanted the enabling technology providers to build them into their offerings. Both Oracle and SAP use SCOR® metrics as a basis for performance management functionality in their applications. So, why reinvent the wheel?

The key, though, is not just the metrics. There are over 550 metrics defined in SCOR®. The key is which of them to implement and how you go about implementing them. That's why the foundation for your House of Excellence is performance management aligned to your strategy. I don't think you want to implement all 550 metrics. It would probably drive you and your organization batty. Aligning your performance management operating system strategy and implementation to the corporate business strategy will enable you to select and implement only those metrics that you need to achieve success.

We've already talked a bit about business strategy in the past chapters. If your strategy is volume growth based on being the lowest cost provider, Wal-Mart comes to mind. Your metrics will be focused on the performance attributes of asset management and cost-reducing processes, such as the overall cost of supply chain management at

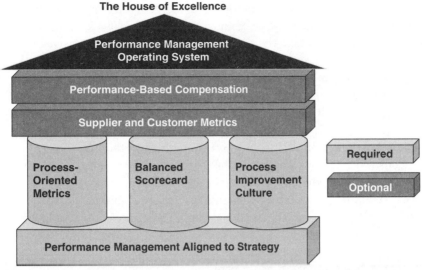

FIGURE 7.2 The House of Excellence
Adapted from Supply Chain Visions PowerPoint: "Building Blocks for Successful Performance Management"

the highest level. You would then measure the cost of the supply chain types comprising the next level of supply chain costs, such as costs to Plan, Source, Make, Deliver, and Return. You would then break these metrics down further to the category and element level. Cost is critical to meeting your strategy, so you would align your supply chain performance metrics accordingly. You would, at a high level, develop process type metrics for the other performance attributes, but you would probably not dive too deep. Metrics drive behavior, and you want your performance measures to align supply chain behavior with the company's business strategy.

I remember a past client's director of logistics as being a brilliant strategist; he was very customer focused and a long-term thinker. He was transforming the supply chain organization based on doing the right things. However, the CEO was concerned with short-term profitable growth and pushing the revenue envelope at the lowest possible cost. He was a turnaround executive brought in to drive financial stability and grow the business. Remember that if you can't bill it, you can't ship it. The strategies of logistics and the business were out of line . . . and it came time for my colleague to find new employment. During the debrief, the director of logistics was devastated, but, in the long run, it was the best thing that ever happened to him. Both he and the CEO were right . . . it was their strategies that were misaligned. And CEO trumps director. It was the best thing that ever happened to the director of logistics who went on to a long and great career as a president in an industry driven by meeting customer expectations.

If your strategy is profitable growth through superior customer service, another example of aligning supply chain strategy is Neiman Marcus. You may consider cost an important metric, but your focus and your performance measurement will be much more driven by reliability and responsiveness attribute metrics. Perfect Order

Fulfillment would be a critical metric—100 percent customer satisfaction, 100 percent of the time. You may set your strategy around cycle times and in-stock performance. You would take the metrics for reliability and responsiveness from the type level one, through to category and element levels two and three, and maybe even to the activity and workflow level.

The attributes of supply chain performance, according to the Supply Chain Council (and, a large community of users) are:

- Reliability—how well do I meet my customer's expectations?
- Responsiveness—how long does it take to meet my customer's expectations?
- Agility—how quickly can I scale up or down?
- Costs—what does it cost me to operate my supply chain?
- Asset management—what are the capital requirements for me to operate my supply chain?

If you set your performance management objectives and measurements along these attributes to align with the business strategy (Demand Performance structure), then I don't think senior management is going to have an issue. And presenting your supply chain strategy with the understanding that you are driving performance to achieve the business strategy and objectives, who can argue? Laying the foundation of your transformation's House of Excellence to meet the business strategy, financial objectives, and board/executive management expectations is the first step toward obtaining management commitment and a great ongoing communication and progress monitor.

The first pillar of the House of Excellence is to base your performance on process-oriented metrics. As we discussed in detail in Chapter 4, excellence in process execution drives results. Do you know the definition of an auditor? They are the people that come in after the battle to kill the wounded. Process-oriented metrics, such as perfect order fulfillment, order cycle time, delivery to customer commit date, package cycle time, upside production flexibility, finished goods inventory turns, and cash-to-cash cycle time drive behaviors; behavior drives results. The great quality guru, Joseph M. Juran, said, "Goal setting has traditionally been based on past performance. This practice has tended to perpetuate the sins of the past." Focusing on process performance aligned with strategy will keep metrics current and relevant to achieve results.

Using SCOR® metrics as the foundation of your development will accelerate your journey. Why do I constantly refer to SCOR®? It's an open industry standard, regularly reviewed and validated in the market by practitioners; it is user friendly because it is in electronic form and more easily accessed and searched. However, I will also refer you to CSCMP's Process Standards and APQC's Process Classification Framework (PCF) as well.[1] All, including SCOR®, are also tied into APQC's Open Standards Research database for ease in benchmarking, which we will discuss in more detail in Chapter 9. Regardless of your choice, using industry-standard resources and benchmarks accelerates your transformation development and journey. They are simply hard to dispute, and it is easier to sell industry standards to senior managers.

The second pillar of the House of Excellence is to develop a balanced scorecard. Robert S. Kaplan and David P. Norton wrote the book *The Balanced Scorecard:*

Translating Strategy into Action.[2] As you develop and organize your metrics, you should develop your scorecard minimally around both internal and external metrics as shown in Figure 7.3. It is also a great example of how the SCOR® Level One metrics align to supply chain performance attributes.

External or customer-facing metrics and perspectives will be those measuring the reliability, responsiveness, and agility attributes. Internal business process metrics and perspectives will measure performance in cost and asset management. From Kaplan and Norton's perspective, we would also want a dimension to track the financial results from our process performance. And, very importantly, we would also want to include a dimension measuring performance objectives for innovation, learning, and growth, which are topics to be covered in more detail in Chapter 9.

The third pillar of our House of Excellence is to create a process improvement culture, which is self-actualizing and, to a large extent, the objective of this book. But your culture needs a house to live in. Because transformation is a journey, you need to decorate and remodel the house with all the learning you experience along that journey. It is also a communications tool when presenting to your senior management team, associates, and colleagues in other Demand Management structures, customers, and suppliers. The House of Excellence is your supply chain operating system for driving performance improvement. I include it here as it must be aligned to the business strategy and overall performance objectives of the company as set in the Demand Performance structure.

Within the conversation of performance measurement, the driving force of self-actualization and a process improvement culture is process orientation and systems thinking. As we discussed in Chapter 4, when you focus on process, you generally take people out of the equation. The people execute the process, but the metrics are process metrics and not necessarily people metrics. When you focus on process, you also often take the gaming out of the development of the metrics. Process metrics are generally cross-departmental and require collaboration. Process performance metrics should be visible and successes should be celebrated. Bring on the pizza and beer!

SCOR® Standard Strategic (Level 1) Metrics

	Attribute	Metric (Strategic)
Customer	Reliability	Perfect Order Fulfillment
	Responsiveness	Order Fulfillment Cycle Time
	Agility	Supply Chain Flexibility †
		Supply Chain Adaptability †
Internal	Cost	Supply Chain Management Cost
		Cost of Goods Sold
	Assets	Cash-to-Cash Cycle Time
		Return on Supply Chain Fixed Assets
		Return on Working Capital

† upside and downside adaptability and flexibility metrics

FIGURE 7.3 SCOR® Balanced Scorecard
Source: The Supply Chain Council

Once you have your "house" in order, you should optionally extend your process definition and metrics to include suppliers and customers. As you begin to *synchronize and collaborate* with customers and suppliers, you will also be mapping your processes to the processes of your customers and suppliers as we discussed in Chapter 6. As you determine responsibilities for managing the *process gates and the critical action triggers*, you and your partners will also be defining the performance attributes associated with the processes based on the collaboration. You can then identify the process metrics required to successfully execute across those boundaries.

The second option in the House of Excellence is performance-based compensation. On the one hand, I have always been a proponent of performance-based compensation. One of my colleagues at Burroughs, Mike Pajakowski, used to say, "Money talks, BS walks." Money, reward power, is always a motivator. One of my colleagues, Dave Simbari, when he was at IMI implemented a compensation plan that included a component that was directly tied to the revenue of the company. Even administrative assistants and the receptionist received a percentage of monthly revenue generated. It certainly focused everyone's attention on their role in growing revenue. When you called IMI, you received the warmest welcome and most professional handling of your call than anywhere else.

On the other hand, performance-based compensation isn't for everyone. The criteria for the compensation have to be clearly defined and communicated, and the employee has to have a role in achieving the performance driving the compensation. If you have a union shop, it's going to be really difficult, but it will be well defined.

Clearly, the success of your performance management operating system will be driven by your leadership on the transformation journey. Peter Drucker said, "Management is doing things right; leadership is doing the right things." Taking that quote along with his "you can't manage what you can't measure" quote and your performance management operating system will drive your operations to build a value-based and sustainable House of Excellence that any senior manager will support. But that's only a part of the process for gaining senior management support. Before we get into the other drivers of executive commitment, let's look at the processes that comprise the Demand Performance structure.

 ## PROCESS TYPES THAT DRIVE THE DEMAND PERFORMANCE STRUCTURE

Let's take a look at the Demand Performance Structure process types in Figure 7.4. From Chapter 4, you know that there are six major process types in the Demand Performance structure. Planning is common to all Demand Management structures. You have to Plan the value chain and input the financial plan as a component of the Integrated Business Planning process. And you have to plan each of the process types, Invest, Measure, and Value, as well as Plan capital and Plan return on invested capital (ROIC). The overall objective of the Demand Performance structure is to grow profitably while generating increased shareholder value for the company.

Remember the two stories I told to open this chapter about how to present your capital request? The Invest process type is typically where this story gets played out. And

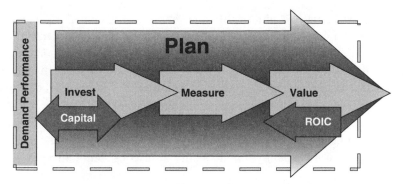

FIGURE 7.4 The Demand Performance Structure

the "subtype," capital, is what it's all about. This discussion is going to be less on the Demand Performance process categories and elements themselves and more on the key types, and how you will integrate and leverage them to gain executive commitment.

The most important thing about capital is that for most companies it's scarce, highly competitive to get, and there are several different sources of capital that can be leveraged. As in my first example, any time you convert any assets to cash, you are liberating working capital. The supply chain can be a money-printing machine. Joe Francis, who formerly led some of the highest return SCOR® projects on record while he was at Compaq and then Hewlett-Packard, and who is now the executive director at the Supply Chain Council, uses one of the greatest metaphors that I have heard on supply chain capital opportunity.

He likes to ask, "Why should we focus on supply chain?" He then refers to the famous bank robber, Slick Willy. "When Slick Willy was asked why he robbed banks," Joe relates, "Willy responded with 'because that's where the money is.'"

Supply chain *is* where the money is, and, as we shall see, liberating working capital in the supply chain is often easier than reducing cost. As my story illustrates, it is a major lever in obtaining executive support . . . you are financing your own project. You are handing the company cash and just asking to use a small portion of it to do so. The bulk of working capital projects I have worked on and observed as case studies at conferences can be guaranteed to return the investment in the same amount of time to execute them with virtually no risk. If you want to kick off a transformation project with a bang, start with raw material, work-in-progress, or finished goods inventory, particularly SLOB (slow moving, obsolete or excess). You will nearly always find 10 to 30 percent of inventory cost reduction or resulting working capital that can be liberated.

 WHAT KEEPS THE CEO AND CFO UP AT NIGHT?

I thought I would drop that little attention getter in here so that I can point out some potential points in the Demand Performance structure that cause insomnia for the chief financial officer (CFO) and chief executive officer (CEO). You may think

I am going to start with capital right now. Wrong! The one thing keeping your executives up at night is the fear of surprises. Executives like predictability and consistency . . . finance likes everything in monthly and quarterly buckets, and the CEO puts his job on the line with guidance every quarter. Surprises both good and bad are punished by Wall Street. So, for sure if you are with a publicly traded company, surprises are not welcome. It is also one of the harder concepts for operations folks to understand, because our life is surprises. The plan is always wrong, it's bullwhipping us, and we never know what to expect one day to the next. Presenting your plans as a means to achieve more visibility, predictability, and consistency in your operations will be well received.

So, back to capital; it is the start of the Invest process type. Access and appropriation of capital are certainly sleep inhibitors in both public and private companies. Capital is the fuel the company runs on. Without it and without the company's ability to generate a return each year to increase it, the company eventually will run out of gas. Generally, there will be a process category in Invest for treasury management. In addition to generating profit and liberating working capital, treasury processes manage the capital and cash of the company to generate capital from money management and investment in the liquid capital funds of the company. Examples would be leveraging the cash position of the company in money markets, investments, currencies, bond trading, and so on. Not particularly relevant to operations, but good to know that they aren't just counting beans over there.

At some point each year, the executive committee commissions finance to develop a capital requirements plan. The Invest process category is very relevant. As I related in the automotive engineer story in Chapter 3, the capital appropriation process at many companies can be very complex. More importantly, it can also be political and emotional, as I alluded to in this chapter's opening story. You will have to justify everything, and nine times out of ten, it will have to be justified financially . . . based on any number of methods, such as internal rate of return (IRR), net present value (NPV), economic value added (EVA), economic profit (EP), return on invested capital (ROIC), rate-adjusted return on capital (RAROC), and/or other methods.

Do you know what the difference is between MIT's Sloan business school and Notre Dame's Mendoza business school? At Notre Dame, if you win the business-plan contest, you get an A. At MIT, if you win the business-plan contest, you get $40 million in venture capital funding.

Competing for capital appropriations is not all that different at most companies. The capital appropriation request is highly competitive and the capital sources are scarce. You have to gain a real understanding of the process and what, in your company, are the key drivers for approving capital requests. It is not always for the best project, and, more often than not, not for funding future benefits. Remember the CEO's first response to my pitch at the beginning of this chapter? *"When?"* He didn't even ask how!

Capital investments are made to support the company's business objectives and strategy to achieve them. And that means the CEO's objectives and budget. The key term for you to consider is *investment.* At this moment, open your vocabulary, find *spend,* and replace it with *invest.* You will no longer ever spend the company's money; you will invest it. From now going forward, you will be investing in your vision, strategy, tactics, processes, and human resources to create value aligned to the company's business strategy. Your thinking should be to ask: Why would the CEO or CFO invest in this? *This* being anything you apply company funds to. If you speak in terms of investments in the corporate business strategy by your organization to achieve the company's business objectives, you may gain a seat at the table.

Are you beginning to see how the Demand Performance structure works? Everything is an investment in the strategic direction of the company. Every company will have slightly different takes on the Invest process categories and elements, but, just like the Demand Creation structure, I will leave it to the finance folks to convene and develop their operations reference model. I do like Invest, Measure, and Value, though.

Speaking of Measure, it's the second process flow type that I envision for the Demand Performance structure, and it is composed of process categories and elements for measuring the performance of the Demand Management structure or enterprise as a whole. Measure creates and maintains all of the financial records for the enterprise. Functionally, these processes will support management of day-to-day accounting of the business, including the general ledger/financials, accounts payables, accounts receiv ables, invoicing, and purchase order management.

They are important to understand as the Demand Creation and Demand Fulfillment structures are largely responsible for the contents of those records. While the Measure process type records the performance, supply chain, in the context of Demand Fulfillment, is accountable for the performance. Do you remember Figure 2.2, The Ultimate Goal of Transformation? Supply chain initiatives will have significant impact on the income statement and balance sheet . . . and the financial health of the company. Working closely with the Measure process management team will provide insight to communicating your investment plan to management and gaining not only executive support but financial team support of your initiatives. Garnering the support of the finance team for your initiatives cannot be understated. They can make life better or worse for you and your team.

The third process type is Value. I also considered calling this process type Return, but settled on Value. The Value process is composed of the process categories and elements that manage the creation of wealth for the company. Value is the process type that I would also see treasury management in, for example. The Value type, from an operations perspective, is where I would see information technology's process categories and elements, human resources' process categories and elements, and probably risk management, including corporate security. Managing the Value and creation of wealth crosses financial lines and should include corporate social responsibility, corporate brand, legal, IT, and HR as nonfinancial wealth-creating processes. Again, I am not going to pretend to know exactly how these processes would be mapped; however, I do know that supply chain, if not already, will be called as a major contributor to the performance of the corporation in these process categories.

I included ROIC as a subtype to support an operations view of the Value process type. From an operations point of view, the impact that supply chain has on generating and improving return on invested capital is the main intersection with the Value process that will be the basis for the next discussion on how to obtain executive support for your initiatives.

HOW DOES OPERATIONS (SUPPLY CHAIN) EXCELLENCE IMPACT THE INCOME STATEMENT AND BALANCE SHEET TO DRIVE RETURN ON INVESTED CAPITAL?

My first class on distribution was a Burroughs line of business training program developed by the faculty at Michigan State University and presented by Drs. Don Taylor and George Wagenheim. It was the beginning of a long relationship with Michigan State University. I often joke that I received my bachelor's and master's degrees from Notre Dame, but I have spent more time in class at Michigan State.

That said, the second most important takeaway from that class was the introduction to the financial measures model (as illustrated in Figure 7.5) by Don Taylor and George Wagenheim. Interestingly enough, they never mentioned that the model was better known as the DuPont model for financial analysis. Regardless of the origins or evolving permutations of the model, I have used it, in its simplest form, over the years as a means for translating and communicating the benefits of operations performance improvement into financial improvements based on the operation's impact on return on capital employed (ROCE) or return on invested capital (ROIC), depending on which financial definition you want to use.

I alluded to the financial impact of supply chain operations in Chapter 2 (see Figure 2.2). However, this takes it to the level of detail where we can begin correlating specific processes and best practices to the financial measures that they impact as illustrated in Figure 7.6. The key is not to think in terms of cost when you are looking at impact, even though cost is a large measure of what we do. And I hope you have purged *spend* from your vocabulary. We don't spend; we invest.[3]

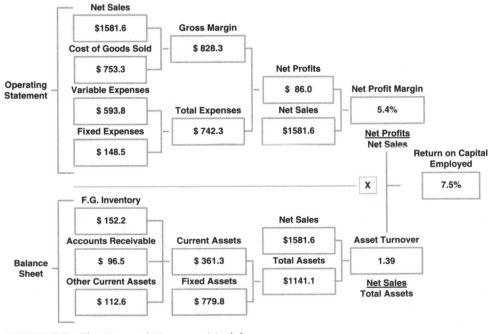

FIGURE 7.5 The Financial Measures Model

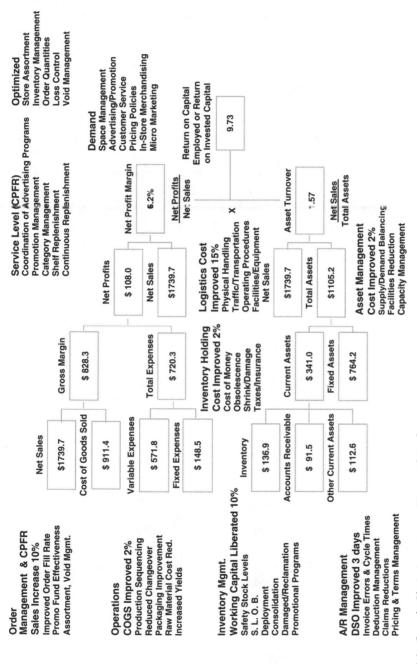

FIGURE 7.6 Supply Chain Impacts on Financial Performance

135

More often than not, operations managers don't think of themselves as revenue producers. They think that revenue is generated by sales. Wrong. Sales are converted to revenue when operations ship the orders and they are invoiced, not when the orders are taken. Operations are fully responsible for revenue, and if you and, more importantly, your executives don't think that way, please give them a copy of this book. Not to take anything away from sales, but if Lenny can't load the sale on the truck, the company will miss its revenue number. It is money being taken right out of the company's wallet. Many customers will have a policy of "ship it or kill it," meaning if the order line can't be filled, drop it from the order. You may think this is simply deferred revenue as the customer will add it to its next order, but this month's or quarter's revenue number will be missed. If the customer allows back orders, you will be taking a profit hit (reduction) on the order by incurring the additional shipping and handling costs to process and fill the back order.

I remember conducting a systems audit for a beauty and barber supply house in Wisconsin when I was with Burroughs. They guaranteed free shipment of all back-ordered items and shipped the items as they were received . . . often five to 10 items per order. Their backorder shipping costs exceeded their order revenue on 20 percent of their orders. They were losing money. It was one of the first times that I used the financial measures model. I showed the owner more than 100 percent increase in ROCE. We got the order. You can too.

Effective order management and implementing Collaborative Planning, Forecasting and Replenishment (CPFR®) can increase revenue by as much as 10 percent depending on current fill rates and forecast accuracy. In Figure 1.3, I showed the APQC benchmarks for perfect orders. Unless you are already living in Leader City, in most industries, you easily have a 10 percent improvement opportunity. And if we look at order fill rate specifically, in Figure 7.7, if you are living in Laggard City, you're letting 10 percent, give or take, of revenue go unfilled. Just as the dialogue on free cash received executive attention to get support for transformation, increasing top-line revenue is also an

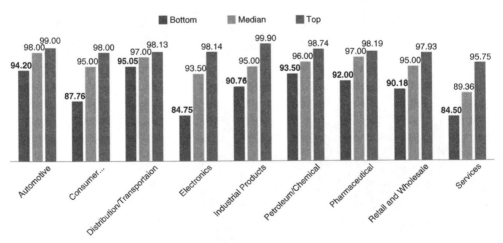

FIGURE 7.7 Order Fill Rate Benchmarks
Reprinted by permission of APQC. Excerpted from APQC Open Standards Research (www.apqc.org). Copyright © 2012 by APQC; all rights reserved.

attention grabber. Not to mention the fact that making the revenue number is a good thing to hear on Wall Street and at the next board meeting.

Implementing CPFR®, as a best practice, results in several benefits. First, any improvement in forecast accuracy results in operations improvements. AMR Research (Gartner), at its annual Supply Chain Executive Conference a few years ago, reported that companies with better demand forecasts had 17 percent better order fulfillment, 15 percent less inventory, and 35 percent shorter cash-to-cash cycle times. Collaboration, as we have seen, produces increases in forecast accuracy. CPFR® will also, especially if you are fortunate enough to do joint planning, reduce holes in retail shelf space, provide you with the opportunity to more effectively manage promotions, and improve your product assortment and space allocation. Regardless of the industry, collaboration will raise you to preferred or strategic supplier status, and the improvements to your financial performance are significant. The key takeaway is that you talk top-line revenue improvement and expanded margins, not cost reductions. Cost reduction is your job; revenue and margin increases receive strategic investments.

When speaking of costs, I like to speak of cost improvements or optimization. For example, operations can improve its cost of goods sold performance by 2 percent. Our process improvement strategy will be to implement better decision support tools to optimize production sequencing, which will reduce changeover times and costs. Our current spreadsheets constrain our capabilities, which results in lower yield rates and higher raw material costs. By investing in this strategy we will achieve an additional 2 percent gross margin expansion. As shown in Figure 7.8, the residents of Leader City enjoy a 50 percent advantage over the residents of Laggard City in cost of goods sold as a percent of revenue. Investing in this strategy will not only improve our profit margin, but will also improve our competitive advantage and free cash flow.

In the example of Figure 7.6, I assume that we will liberate 10 percent of our inventory in working capital from the balance sheet. A portion of it will come from improved production sequencing; however, reducing slow-moving, obsolete, and excess

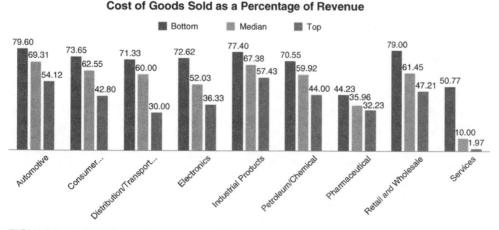

FIGURE 7.8 COGS as a Percentage of Revenue

inventory through improved forecast accuracy and regular recalculation of cycle stocks, safety stocks, and peak stock levels will contribute to more effective finished goods inventory management. CPFR® and event-driven forecasting will enable better management of promotional builds and improve our visibility to incremental lifts in demand by SKU by location. SKU by location forecast improvements will enable more effective forward deployment of inventory and provide visibility to transfer inventory between locations or ship from alternative locations to balance field-deployed inventories. A 10 percent reduction is very conservative. In my experience and based on APQC industry benchmarks for finished goods, work-in-process (WIP) inventory, and raw materials, best practice inventory management can liberate 25 to 30 percent of inventory in working capital, as I used in the example at the beginning of this chapter.

If we are liberating working capital from inventory, it stands to reason we will be improving our inventory holding costs. In the example in Figure 7.6, I assume a 2 percent improvement. You have to take into consideration cost of money, taxes, insurance, writedown of obsolescence, and shrinkage or damage, and to a lesser extent facility space. As one warehouse manager once asked me when I took a large space cost reduction in my ROIC assumptions, "What are you going to do? Tear down 20 percent of my warehouse? I pay for it whether I am using it or not." Space costs are tricky. On the other hand, when I put in an inventory management system for Simon Brothers, an institutional food distributor in South Bend, IN, (yes, one and the same), we were able to improve their turn of frozen foods enough to avoid a more than $1 million frozen foods warehouse expansion. It paid for the system. Got the order, so will you.

Let's not forget that if we are improving our order fill rates and improving service and cycle times, we will also be improving our invoicing. Assuming a three-day improvement in order cycle time, with fewer to no errors in billing, and fewer deductions based on line cuts or backorders will improve my day's sales outstanding (DSO) by at least the three-day improvement in billing date (we generally invoice the same day as ship date). Customers, if not their accounts payables systems, are creatures of habit when it comes to payment. If they receive the bill three days faster, they will pay it three days faster, improving your DSO by three days, which impacts the accounts receivables balance sheet performance. APQC benchmarks show 20 to 30 days of advantage in DSO by the Leaders over the Laggards. Go back and check out Figure 6.2 in Chapter 6 on cash-to-cash cycle times. That should get some executive attention and support for transformation.

While we're on asset performance improvement, I am also going to assume improvements of 2 percent from better capacity utilization, the capability to improve supply/demand balancing, which enables improved asset allocation and deferral of capital expenditures, and facility rationalization leveraging more third-party services for improvements in upside and downside flexibility to scale. This transformation from cost reduction thinking to focus on value creation is really getting executive attention and now response.

And we haven't even factored in my pet processes, logistics. Unless you're a Leader City resident, your logistics improvement potential is in the ballpark of 15 percent or more. The biggest improvement area I have seen at most companies is in transportation management. It is also probably your largest expenditure. Having seen the various transportation systems evolve over the years, it never ceases to amaze me how few companies model and simulate changes to their supply network. The opportunities to leverage third-party services alone for long haul, full truckload, or even rail/intermodal shipments of consolidated goods to a break bulk or cross-dock 3PL are limitless. In Chapter 9, I will suggest a methodology for evaluating outsourcing opportunities; companies that outsource select processes enjoy a significant advantage in logistics cost. Using network simulation and design tools, which you no longer have to be a PhD in operations research to do, will identify optimization opportunities that you can't identify manually.

Improvements from forecasting accuracy, order accuracy, inventory management, closer collaboration and synchronization with production and procurement, and visibility to process constraints will improve overall physical handling efficiency and cost. Customer and supplier collaboration will improve transportation utilization and cost, while synchronizing to their order cycles will improve fill rates, cycle times, predictability, and packaging. Developing and documenting operating processes and procedures will empower associates and stimulate improvements. Transforming your operations to be more customer-driven and demand-responsive yields significant improvement to return on capital employed as illustrated in the before and after performance shown in Figure 7.9. The assumptions, based on the actual industry benchmarks, are pretty conservative. In my experience, moving the needle forward is attainable at most companies.

So, there it is. Do you think you can get management attention and support if you can present a supply chain transformation strategy that is aligned to the corporate business strategy, improves the financial performance and overall health of the company by 30 percent or more (Figure 7.10 shows the APQC ROIC benchmarks),

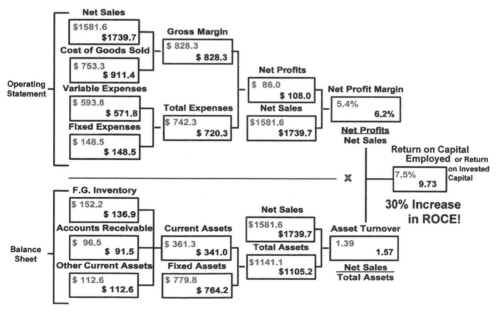

FIGURE 7.9 Transformation Yields 30% Increase in ROCE!

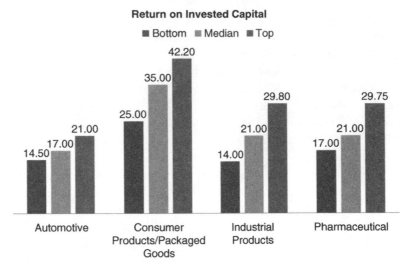

FIGURE 7.10   Return on Invested Capital Benchmarks
Reprinted by permission of APQC. Excerpted from APQC Open Standards Research (www.apqc.org).
Copyright © 2012 by APQC; all rights reserved.

funds itself through liberating working capital and improving free cash flow, and provides the foundation for sustainable continuous improvement? Do you think they will want to join you in the House of Excellence? While you think about it, let's look at the technology side of supply chain transformation in Chapter 8 and I'll come back for my answer in Chapter 9.

 NOTES

1. Information about CSCMP's Process Standards can be found at www.cscmp.org. Information about APQC's Process Classification Frameworks and Open Standards Research can be found at www.apqc.org.
2. Kaplan, Robert S., and David P. Norton, *The Balanced Scorecard: Translating Strategy into Action*, Boston: Harvard Business School Press, 1996.
3. By the way, as validation of how effective the model is, I was presenting the topic to a group of supply chain folks at Bosch Automotive in Detroit and brought up Figure 7.6 on the screen. "Hey, that's Professor Bix Cooper's (Michigan State) slide!" one of the managers said. I had presented the slide at the Health and Personal Care Distribution Conference at the Longboat Key Club that Don Bowersox and Bix Cooper organized the education program for. Bix had asked me if he could use the slide. I guess he did. So, after setting the record straight, the Bosch folks really took the rest of the presentation to heart.

CHAPTER EIGHT

Technology Drives the Waves of Change

T HE VERY FIRST ARTICLE I ever had published was in the March 1987 ICP publication, *Business Software Review*, titled "Information Systems for Distributors." Since that time I have written more articles on information technology for supply chain management than on any other topic. My intention in this chapter will not be to replicate the articles I have already published on developing enterprise system architectures. Rather, this chapter will discuss why information technology, and technology in general, is critical to your business and supply chain transformation. I will share with you some of the emerging technologies that I see converging in the market and the impact they might have on your business. I will suggest how these technologies will impact operations and why collaboration between IT and business operations is imperative to maximizing return.

If change is inevitable, then nowhere is this more evident than in technology. Over my career, I have seen more changes in technology than in any other industry. I remember when I was in my first systems class at Burroughs. At the time, the B7800 was our largest mainframe computer and rivaled the power of any business computer at the time. One of our product managers, Larry Thomas, presented to the class on the direction Burroughs would be going in. During his impassioned presentation, he placed what looked like a briefcase on the front desk and asked the class, "Do you know what that is? Can you guess? It's a B7800! That's the future." What a future it has been and continues to be. That B7800 is now in my pocket.

Remember Alvin Toffler? *The Third Wave?* He suggested we were in an information age back in 1980. Well, I am not an anthropologist, but I suggest that the information age is evolving rather quickly. There have been "sequels" to the Third Wave and, as far as I am concerned, we are being battered by the surf of change. I do think, however, that we are entering, if not already in a *Connected Age* that will dramatically change markets globally. With advances in information technology, pervasive global wireless (remember when *Wired* was the buzz?) technology around the corner, and an endless array of portable devices (do you prefer appliances?), we are in an age of always on and always connected, as I discussed in Chapter 1. It is already changing governments and society. But I'll leave that for another day. However, in my experience, the Leaders look for, pilot, and adopt technology to support best practices at a faster rate than their competitors. As we have seen, this means lower cost, expanded margins, increased revenue, and competitive leverage in the market. Technology permeates the House of Excellence. Will you be ready for smart supply network management in the Connected Age?

SCANNING THE HORIZON FOR TECHNOLOGY DEVELOPMENTS

Having been on the "bleeding edge" of technology for the past 30 years, I have learned that technology doesn't emerge disruptively. There are generally several converging technologies that cause disruption or are "game changers." Look at RFID (radio frequency identification). Lots of hype, big venture investments, and now very quiet. Why? The infrastructure to support it wasn't in place, and the infrastructure cost constrained widespread adoption. Have patience, RFID people; your day will come. It's just going to be part of a bigger disruption. Earlier I mentioned DSD and home shopping. Did they really fail? No, they morphed. The hype about DSD created consideration by many retailers that realized the futility in its hype, but they implemented it as a tactical strategy for products with the characteristics that supported DSD—dairy, high-turn beverages, cosmetics, and other pharmacy-oriented products as examples. You will frequently bump into DSD vendors in the aisles; however, it's not for every product. As Amazon.com is demonstrating, home shopping is huge; just not necessarily for grocery.

And don't think technology is only information related. If you are in the automotive industry, you have seen major changes to the bill of material of a car. Infotainment alone is a dramatic change in automobiles. What about changes to instrumentation, telematics? Mechanics are being replaced by computer technicians in the repair shop. Consumer electronics are constantly changing. Foods continually change in their composition. From unprepared, to partially prepared, to fully prepared foods and everything in between, even basic food products undergo never-ending change, not to mention all of the nutritional and sustainability compliance requirements. Regardless of your industry, technology changes the game. If you don't keep up, you'll be left behind with the typewriters and eight-tracks. Tapes, anyone? Stream on!

On one hand, keeping up with technology can seem daunting. On the other, it's why surfing the Internet isn't all that big a waste of time. It's also more justification for attending or sending your people to conferences and trade shows. Gathering market, technology, and competitive intelligence is a critical success factor in Leader City; it's a strategy you can't afford *not* to invest in. The cost of lagging, as the benchmarks demonstrate, is much greater than the cost of piloting new technologies.

Several companies I have worked with the past few years establish "sandboxes" for their people to play with new technologies. They figured out that the opportunity, time, effort, risk, and *cost* associated with the traditional technology adoption and selection process was significantly greater than if they just identified a short list of new technologies and vendors that would be *paid* to come in and pilot a solution to a priority problem or new approach in their sandbox.

Using this approach, they have streamlined their technology adoption process, identified emerging technologies that have been proved in their environment, and captured the financial rewards that come with leading-edge technologies. If the technology can't be proven in the sandbox with several vendor approaches, their risk and cost has still been less than if they had waited for wider adoption or selected the wrong solution. The vendors are satisfied as they have been paid fairly for their investment in time and proof of concept without having to go through the expense and pain of the typical selection process. It works for everyone.

 ## WHAT EMERGING TECHNOLOGIES ARE LIKELY TO IMPACT THE SUPPLY CHAIN?

So what are some of the technologies that I see on the horizon? (See Figure 8.1.) The first is a "back-to-the-future" technology, cloud computing. Early in my career, many, if not most, companies engaged "service bureaus" to support their data processing needs. Companies couldn't afford to buy mainframe computers, so they connected via dedicated lines to service bureaus and rented a slice of the bureau's mainframe. Of course, as computing power increased and price decreased, in-house computing became the buzz and the "wires" didn't have the bandwidth to support the level of data (Big Data, in a bit, pun) that the new compute power could manage.

Well, times have changed, and now we have the bandwidth and global connectivity. *Voilà!* We are seeing the emergence of software as a service (SaaS) and even data as a service (DaaS). Big Data represents datasets that are extremely large. POS data immediately comes to mind. But, when you combine POS with consumer data and location data from not just one, but many companies and sources, we are talking BIG DATA. I am on the board of advisors for a company in the Bay Area, Retailigence, which collects store inventory data, consumer data, and location data from retailers, manufacturers and other sources to make it visible to mobile apps developers both for the company's internet strategy and for independent apps companies. The benefit is that the retailer and apps developer only have to maintain a single interface to the data; it's maintained by Retailigence. As we progress into the Connected Age, there will be a blurring between traditional commerce and eCommerce. Increasingly the supply chain is a multi-channel world. In the Connected Age, it's an always on and all-channel world. Don't think it's only going to impact the consumer industry. Always on and all-channel will drive a tsunami of change in the business to business industries as well. The other benefit of SaaS and DaaS is that technology can be on-demand. You can invest based on usage. If you don't use it, you don't incur cost.

- Cloud Computing and Big Data
  - Supply Chain Visibility
  - Software as a Service (SaaS)/On Demand
  - Location-Based Technology/Mobility/Telematics
  - Business Intelligence/Decision Support
- Auto ID/Information
  - Beyond RFID
  - Voice Recognition/Response
  - Intelligent Sensors, Monitors, Devices
- Robotics Extending from Manufacturing to Logistics
  - Picking, Packing, Put Away
  - Load, Unload
- Internet Transparency & Social Media for Business
  - LinkedIn, Twitter, Blogging, Search
  - Offers, Location, Orders, Navigation, Behavior

> The Convergence of Emerging Technologies Will Lead to New Applications for Supply Chain Visibility & Integrating Planning & Execution, Resulting in a *Smart Supply Network!*

FIGURE 8.1 Technology Drivers for Supply Chain Transformation

What will make cloud computing and Big Data a game changer, though, is not just "time share" computing, it's the convergence of Connected Age technologies, such as mobility, location-based services (GPS, global positioning system), and telematics with cloud computing that change the game and create the Big Data. Application developers are no longer constrained by traditional organizational and geographic constraints. They also have more compute power available at an affordable cost. Why do you think IBM has made such an investment and popular splash with "Watson" taking on the *Jeopardy* champions? With cloud computing, you can rent a slice of supercomputer power and logic only for the time you need it.

With the level of compute power and Big Data that can be made available from affordable cloud access, business intelligence applications and mass data analysis such as Mike Saylor's MicroStrategy's relational online analytic processing (ROLAP) can be made available to even the smallest of companies. You didn't have to be a Fortune 100 company to use a service bureau. Dentists' offices were connected! Think of what on demand software does to the sandbox pilot process. Look for more new decision support and analytic applications to be developed. A new career opportunity is emerging for "data scientists." Right now, we have college students in dorm rooms developing mobile device and Web-based apps for the consumer. Business apps on a large scale are coming to a tablet or smartphone near you soon. All of this will require new thinking, new processes, and new talent and skills.

It's not limited to personal compute and communicate devices. Vehicle telematics, the technology that integrates information technology and telecommunications, will spawn new applications for the Connected Age. Some examples (not a comprehensive explanation) include the following:

- **Sensor-to-vehicle communications.** Vehicles are being built with sensors across many functions (e.g., adaptive cruise control that senses speed, grade, incline, mileage per gallon, etc.) to operate the vehicle at the optimal speed for most efficient use of fuel, lane departure signals to alert the driver that the vehicle is veering off course, automated parking operation, and so on.
- **Vehicle-to-vehicle communications.** For example, as my vehicle is approaching another too fast, it will communicate to my vehicle to automatically slow down. If two vehicles are approaching an intersection too fast, they will communicate to avoid a collision.
- **Vehicle to infrastructure.** An intelligent infrastructure is being implemented that will communicate with vehicles along a particular route that will monitor operations such as traffic control lights and warnings. The infrastructure will also integrate with GPS location-based services to assist in route guidance and vehicle monitoring. A good example of vehicle to infrastructure applications is electronic toll collection and speed cameras.
- **Vehicle to command center.** GPS and vehicle monitoring will communicate the status of the vehicle to the company's transportation control operations—the status of the vehicle, for example, when and where it is moving or stopped, whether it is on or off route; if it's off route, the engine may be cut off; monitor the operating performance of the vehicle to identify preventive maintenance or other conditions that may detain the load, and so on.

What this really means for supply chain managers and transformation is that the elusive capability that tops every supply chain capability survey every year for the past 10 years at least, supply chain visibility, is now within reach and affordability. It's being deployed as I am writing and as you are reading this book. When a couple of my former colleagues at Numetrix left following the acquisition, they founded a company to develop a supply chain integration and execution platform to connect all of Hewlett-Packard's operations and suppliers globally. VECCO International's Allegro suite enables companies to rapidly integrate their network with a plug and play technology platform to connect all of the independent nodes of a supply network for visibility and seamless collaborative execution.

In addition to the emergence of cloud computing, as telematics implies, we are seeing smarter and less costly automatic identification (AutoID) and monitoring devices emerging. So, while mobility, location-based services, and telematics are connecting everyone and everything to the cloud, we are also seeing devices for tracking, sensing, and monitoring the goods and the environment as they move through the network globally and in real time. For industries that have temperature-controlled products, products that are prone to theft or counterfeiting, high-value products, and so on, the capability to track and trace the products and the environment as products move through the supply network is already in place, and the cost is decreasing rapidly.

As traditional bar code infrastructures are being retired, new infrastructures are being deployed with lower cost: voice over Internet protocol (VoIP) technologies that support multiple AutoID methods, bar code, RFID, voice response and recognition, and other intelligent devices. As these new infrastructures are implemented, usually by the Leaders, and become more pervasive in the market, the cost will quickly become less than the benefit with the eventuality that the Laggards will be forced to adopt them, of course, after all financial and competitive leverage has been exhausted. Remember the South Bend institutional distributor? They had to make the same technology investment as GFS® did; but, having lost their biggest customer, the investment was only a short-term protective strategy versus the pre-emptive strike that GFS® levied on them.

While these technologies will converge with cloud computing and Big Data to enable greater visibility, collaboration, and synchronization to drive the smart supply network I envisioned in Chapter 1, there is also a quiet emergence, or perhaps resurgence, of more robotics and automation in the supply chain. More than 600 exhibitors packed the halls of recent Material Handling of America (MHIA)–sponsored shows, ProMat and Modex. Of those, many are touting advanced robotics for picking, packing, and palletizing, as well as loading and unloading. Combined with advanced conveyance and sortation systems, more and more companies are leveraging their facilities for greater productivity and reduced labor. Combinations of factors are at work here. The technology and intelligence of the robotic equipment is enabling the flexibility of the equipment to perform less repetitive and more directive tasks. As third-party logistics providers secure more business, they can invest more in their facilities. As retail chains grow, their networks become more defined and fixed, and they can invest more in their facilities. The reliability, fixed cost, productivity, and depreciation of automation lowers the cost and uncertainty of labor. Still not a believer that it's a game changer? With Amazon's acquisition of Kiva Systems (a provider of warehouse automation systems) and expansion of its distribution center network, Amazon will be competing with the convenience of bricks and mortar retailers. It's a good time to be in logistics automation.

Internet transparency and social networking like LinkedIn, Twitter, Facebook, and others have slightly more applicability to the demand chain. The amount of consumer behavior data becoming available is staggering. It's interesting that privacy issues, so prevalent five or more years ago, are not as prevalent today. Perhaps we are becoming comfortable with the Connected Age. *For the supply chain*, the variability associated with the demand that is generated will certainly have an impact on planning the supply chain. As you transform your operations, you have to be keenly aware of how the demand chain is leveraging the capabilities of social media for business. For example, many mobile apps are integrating with Facebook, Twitter, and LinkedIn, creating a seamless interface among shopping apps and social apps. I'd be surprised if you are a retailer and not already offering store pickup as a shipping alternative. Of course, social media will also be a great source of market and competitive intelligence. There are many supply chain communities and discussion groups that are low-cost sources of new ideas and best practices for improving your supply chain performance.

HOW DOES TECHNOLOGY IMPACT THE ORGANIZATION?

Remember the critical success factors we discussed in Chapter 7, Figure 7.1? Across all three demand management structures, the strategic deployment of information technology is a foundational critical success factor for the organization. Along with the professional recruitment, development, and maintenance of human resources, which we'll discuss in Chapter 9, IT and HR are the enablers for moving forward on the supply chain transformation journey. The two go hand in hand. Without a strategic investment in information technology and IT innovation, the House of Excellence has no power and the people would be living in the dark. That is, if we even think the journey can be made without the power to shed light on the road ahead. We need to enable the *smart* House of Excellence. It's another major reason the gap between Leaders and Laggards continues. Notice that I also added an investment in IT innovation. Many companies invest millions in their ERP systems, and yet those investments never provide the return on expectations because the companies don't invest and encourage IT innovation. They view IT as a utility, not as a competitive lever.

Supply chain management is fueled by information. We can't beam product into the hands of the customer/consumer, but we can beam information about the customer/consumer demand and the product as it flows from point of origin to point of consumption. If, as we discussed in Chapter 6, we can eliminate the time delay in the communication of demand across the channel, we can respond and synchronize the flow of goods across the channel, dampening amplification and taming the bullwhip. Narayan Laksham, founder of Ultriva (an on demand supply chain solutions provider) and I collaborated on a white paper on taming the bullwhip effect. The key, as demonstrated by the effectiveness of his company's "eKanban" capabilities is eliminating the time delay in the communication of demand signals. Synchronizing the cycles in the supply chain requires synchronizing the communication of information between cycles. The key to Leader City is collaboration. We have all of the transactional data from the ERP available to us. Now we must become innovative in how we make use of the data to improve cross-functional collaboration, analyze the data to identify potential exceptions early, and make the data actionable to the people to make the decisions that resolve the exceptions and keep the supply network in sync.

For IT innovation to take place, however, IT has to be aligned with the Demand Management structures and have an understanding and focus on the business processes and critical success factors within the structures as Figure 8.2 illustrates. Supporting the Demand Management structures, IT provides the network infrastructure to enable cross-functional communications and integration for information sharing. Timely, more effective information access and support reduces the problem to solution lifecycle and enables better decision making across the organization. IT enables and empowers the Demand Performance structure to evolve from transactional accounting to financial management. The systems provide data integrity and consistency, enabling finance to focus as much on operational measures as levers as accounting measures to ensure the financial health of the business. Finance and IT must become more aware and supportive of the Demand Creation and Demand Fulfillment operations. Investments

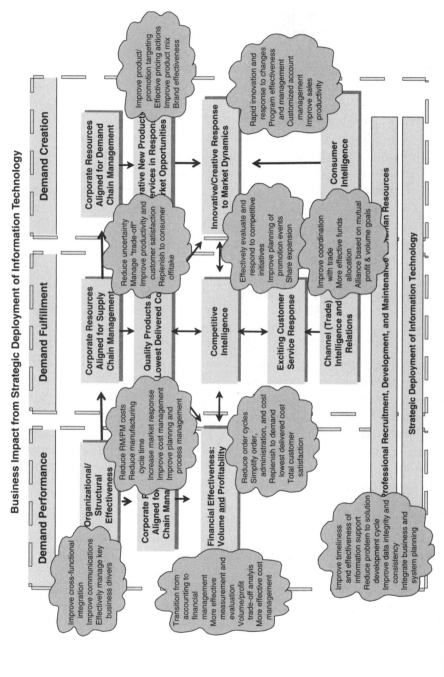

FIGURE 8.2 Strategic Deployment of Information Technology to Support the Critical Success Factors of the Business

should be analyzed on their value in meeting the company's strategy and goals, not necessarily the IT budget and goals.

In Chapter 6, I mentioned that Meijer in Grand Rapids was certainly one of the first and the only company that I worked with that actually combined IT and distribution management in the same role. Whether you place IT under the direction of supply chain or not (I am perfectly happy leaving it in the Demand Performance structure), the key learning from Meijer is that IT strategy and the business strategy must be aligned. IT is the enabler. IT innovation supports business innovation. If the IT department isn't directly involved with the organization's process improvement initiatives, it can't technologically innovate those processes. It's the reason in the ERP world that so many operations modules of the ERP are shelfware, not implemented. If IT understood, as Colgate did, the specific operations IT requirements, shelfware would not exist.

As you develop *your* critical success factors as demonstrated in Chapter 7, you should engage IT to jointly identify technologies and the impact on the business as shown in Figure 8.2. As you map your business processes, highlight where you believe existing or emerging technologies can enable process improvement and the financial impact those improvements will have on shareholder value. It's important to have a co-pilot, like IT, on your journey. Let me share an example of how working with technology can improve performance.

HOW CAN INFORMATION TECHNOLOGY ENABLE BUSINESS OPERATIONS TO MAXIMIZE RETURN?

As you read this, your supply chain operations planners and schedulers are working diligently to synchronize product flow to demand. Everyone agrees with the apple pie in supply chain management. In Chapter 6, we discussed the complexity of managing synchronization within multiple time cycles of variable demand and supply, especially without visibility or collaboration across the supply chain. Our traditional approach to this has been through ERP or "best-of-breed" planning applications; yet, my guess is that your planners and schedulers are still working with Excel spreadsheets to try to balance and synchronize supply with demand. There is a logic missing in almost all of the planning and scheduling applications that I have seen that try to plan supply chains, especially on a daily basis.

We have discussed the need for an integrated business planning process that goes beyond traditional sales and operations planning. When I was at Numetrix, I had the opportunity to work with a brilliant team of information technology and operations research engineers and with some of the most progressive companies in the global market that shaped much of my thinking about how to leverage technology to improve supply chain performance. I had the opportunity to work with Fletcher Challenge Ltd., a forestry products group of companies in New Zealand.

Fletcher Challenge, at the time, was the largest group of companies in New Zealand and has since split into four publicly traded companies. Their supply chain executive, Jeff Langley, had just taken on a corporate strategy role based on his work with the Numetrix Linx product. As I explained in Chapter 2, Linx was a quite sophisticated network modeler that companies used for many different types of analysis. In this case, Langley and his supply chain team worked with the IT folks to build out a model to simulate operations for the next 30 years. Why 30 years? Because it takes 30 years for the seedlings they plant to grow big enough to be converted to product for market, and the company wanted to make sure it was planting forests as close to the emerging forestry products markets as they could. You don't want to airship lumber any more than you want to airship axles if you don't have to.

As we were reviewing the models, Langley explained to me that they were also using Linx to model and simulate quarterly business operations based on different demand scenarios. They had literally defined every process and location in the model with the various lead times, costs, and variables to determine, based on the current plan, the optimal flow of goods through their network to meet the plan. The output would be used to set the operating performance metrics for every business unit and revise it on a quarterly basis. In those days, with models of that size, you would enter all the data from the ERP, hit the run command on Friday afternoon, and come back Monday morning hoping that it made it through the weekend. It was about as close to an integrated business planning process with supporting technology that I had seen and the basis for integrating business planning using model-based approaches.

Considering what has occurred in the past (statistical forecast) and collaborating with sales and marketing (event-based forecast) to include any current actions that may cause variation from the statistical forecast, for example, new product introductions or promotions, we can estimate demand more accurately than in the past. If we then calculate the mean average deviation (MAD) from forecast, we can identify our upside and downside risk on average. With this information, production schedules and inventories can be simulated to meet the upside deviation, showing resource/inventory cost and risk if we build to meet upside demand. Similarly, the downside deviation can also be simulated, showing customer service cost and risk if we build only to meet the downside.

Knowing the cost and risk, in the integrated business planning process, we can collaborate with our counterparts to agree on which products or categories we want to take upside or downside cost or risk based on the impact of error on our financial plan. As agreement is reached, upper and lower control limits (UCL and LCL) are set to enable visibility and process control to the flow of goods as actual demand is realized, as illustrated in Figure 8.3.

For those products already in planned production, it makes sense to build to the lower side of the forecast as there is less service risk due to lower cost and high availability. For those products that are not planned for production, it makes sense to build more inventories because the inventory cost/risk for those products is usually less than the production schedule change cost necessary to produce those products in the event that demand exceeds the plan. By setting upper and lower control limits to the plan based on potential forecast error, a business can dynamically determine its level of safety stock and service/cost risks.

When orders are received, the gap can be identified between the optimal plan and the actual order. As long as the order falls within the upper and lower control limits of the plan, then a profitable response to that order can be maintained. If orders fall

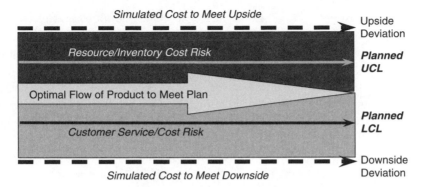

The model-based integrated business planning process sets planned ranges of performance, commitment horizons, and exception conditions based on calculated and shared risk to the plan ... applying process control techniques to synchronize the flow of goods.

FIGURE 8.3 Model-Based Integrated Business Planning

above the tolerance of the plan, they will immediately be flagged as an exception. In this case, inventory must be obtained from another location in the network; conversely, if orders fall under the tolerance of the plan, the result is excess inventory at that particular location.

Measuring the performance of the process dynamically and identifying any discrepancies (deltas) can highlight the root cause of any problem. Planners and schedulers can determine the most profitable solution considering all possible options concurrently, including rebalancing network deployment errors prior to pushing the problem back to the next level. Remember Sherman's Law of Forecast Accuracy? We are usually pretty accurate at the aggregate level. It's at the deployment level that errors bite. With visibility to the deployment errors and excess inventory, we can "move" incorrectly deployed inventory for less cost than to "make" inventory. Anheuser-Busch, for example, used network optimization simulation to determine it was less costly to trans-ship inventory between locations than it was to change their packaging schedules. Deviations from plan can be tracked, unplanned costs measured, and the event causing the deviation identified immediately . . . leading to more effective performance measurement and continuous improvement.

My aforementioned friends at Lead Time Technology use their tools to create a statistical forecast that is reviewed and recalculated daily with review by the relevant planners cross-functionally for exceptions and overrides based on current events. The collaborative forecast is then used to recalculate, based on the model of operations and inventory rules, cycle stock, peak (upside) stock, and safety (downside) stock required for each item at each location for the period of risk (period from when product was last produced or purchased to time of next scheduled production or purchase).

While you would think the daily recalculation would be the tail wagging the dog, just the opposite occurs. The bullwhip gets tamed. The bullwhip occurs based on time delay and amplification. Daily recalculation, based on actual order induction, eliminates the time delay. By capturing demand variability and measuring its impact on aggregate requirements, the amplification is eliminated because the small daily variations are captured, and the order that causes the aggregate control limit to be violated can be responded to immediately, eliminating amplification from time delay. In the Beer Game, the team that simply responds to the actual demand placed on it usually is the team with the lowest total cost.

With the improved level of forecast accuracy and the elimination of time delay and amplification, production scheduling can be optimized to determine how many production cycles or "product wheels" are needed, what should be the sequence of production to minimize changeover cost, how frequently a product should be included in the cycle, what the run length should be, and what the period of risk is for each product. Using the bill of material, purchases can be similarly analyzed. Considering deployed inventory, recommendations for interfacility transfers or shipments from alternate locations can be made to rebalance field inventory versus production replenishments.

Business process mapping provides us with the definition of our specific operations requirements. Why wouldn't we want our information technology to be modeled to enable and support those business processes? Instead, we invest millions in implementing and maintaining enterprise systems that are based on processes designed by the vendors of those systems and are mapped to an aggregate level of commonality at the industry level at best. Most companies have not realized return on investment expectations from enterprise applications because they don't meet the cycle time or process specifications to support the unique day-to-day decisions that planners and schedulers have to make based on their specific operations processes, configuration, and rules. The result is million-dollar decisions supported by tribal knowledge and custom Excel spreadsheets.

The return on investment objectives of most enterprise and supply chain applications are not realized because they don't support the decisions that are driving inventory and operations cost on a daily basis.

The Leaders integrate their information technology requirements with their specific business operations requirements to ensure that the enterprise systems support operations-level requirements either through customization or through complementary "best of breed" applications, such as advanced planning and scheduling, manufacturing execution systems, inventory planning and optimization, transportation and/or warehouse management systems, and others. The Leaders will deploy IT analyst resources into the business operations or ask that the business operations identify analyst resources to coordinate with IT for systems requirements.

Integrating IT with business operations enables the company to consistently scan the horizon for new technologies that will support continual improvements to enable the smarts for the House of Excellence. Together IT and business operations can evaluate the impact the technology may have on the business, the business processes, the IT infrastructure, and the financial value to the company. Most importantly, IT decisions and applications have to be made based on the business impact, not to support the ERP or maintain the IT budget. Too many organizations, in an effort to simplify and consolidate systems, sacrifice the value that new and operations-specific technology will have to the business. Together IT and business operations must innovate with technology to maximize IT return on investment and shareholder value. Are you still struggling with management commitment? It's time for me to hear your answer.

CHAPTER NINE

Making the Journey Happen

OKAY, YOU'VE BUILT A case for change. Putting the business into perspective, you have been able to set and align your supply chain strategy to the corporate strategy and identify your strengths, weaknesses, opportunities, and threats. With some colleagues and engaging in a little Visioneering, you've identified some of the bigger rocks you will encounter and some big bets you would like to take on to move forward on your journey. You have gotten some support from a couple of your colleagues on a game plan to start the journey. Based on market and competitive intelligence, you can see where the market drivers are for your industry, and you've opened a dialogue with some of your counterparts in sales and marketing who agree that someone has to do something to stimulate more collaboration. They are supportive, but, without a formal process or system, they won't risk much more than some chats and sharing some information about what they are up to if you ask.

Based on your structural analysis, you have mapped out an Integrated Business Planning process across the Demand Management structures that can bring the right people together on a regular basis in a formal process that doesn't overextend any one group and can be supported, at least initially, by the current enterprise system. In a meeting with senior management, you present your findings simply and precisely, focused on improvements to return on invested capital, identifying working capital that will be liberated in 90-day increments based on implementation of your transformation plan and journey to the House of Excellence in Leader City. So, as I asked at the end of Chapter 7, are they supportive of your journey?

WE GOT MANAGEMENT COMMITMENT, WHAT DO WE DO NOW?

You did get management commitment! So what are you going to do now? Well, the first thing we need to do is assess our "human" inventory. I first met Mike Gray when I was with Microsoft and he was at Dell. He was one of the early pioneers in Dell's supply chain innovation and a supply chain evangelist, speaking at scores of conferences and customers about supply chain practices at Dell. Subsequently, he retired from Dell, began teaching executive education at Penn State, and is also a consultant with the Oliver Wight organization. We have become professional friends and together support and meet with our local chapters of CSCMP, APICS, ISM, and other professional associations. Gray is also a major advocate of the "people" side of supply chain management. We both share the belief that supply chain and technology are only as good as the people that manage and execute them. Strategic deployment of information technology and the professional recruitment, training, and maintenance of human resources are the base cross-structural critical success factors for the organization.

If your management team is supportive of your transformation strategy, expect that they are going to be just that, supportive. Your success will now depend on how well you can manage and mobilize operations' human resources to execute and join you on your journey to residence in Leader City and building the House of Excellence. Creating a culture of change based on process improvement is a key pillar of your house. At one of our local CSCMP meetings, Gray introduced a process for assessing what he calls the human inventory in the supply chain as illustrated in Figure 9.1.

Look at the table in Figure 9.1. I have obviously simplified it greatly to communicate the context. You have to identify the skills and capabilities that you need in your people to successfully embark on a transformation journey and execute your supply chain operations strategy. Once you have identified all of the traits, you can either conduct the assessment with your managers or you can ask each individual to conduct a self-assessment. My recommendation is to do both as you will have data suggesting their confidence level and areas that they feel strongest and weakest in, as well as their manager's assessment.

DEVELOPING AN OPERATING PLAN AND CREATING A CULTURE FOR CHANGE

Once you have all of the individual assessments completed, you can begin the team assessments and overall function assessment. If you are going to travel the journey successfully and transform your organization, you are going to have to invest in professional development. Period. When I observed the transformation at Procter & Gamble, the one thing that stood out was their commitment to developing common knowledge platforms through common training for their people. They used these common platforms to launch change and performance improvement initiatives throughout the organization. While I happened to attend Leadership and Mastery conducted by Innovation Associates with a group of P&Gers, I subsequently learned that

Skills Rating: 1–5 with 5 High	Plan	Source	Make	Deliver	Return	ERP	Analytic Tools	Process	Individual Total/40
Bob	4	5	2	3	1	4	5	5	29
Donna	3	2	2	5	4	4	3	3	26
Ted	5	3	5	3	3	5	4	5	33
Jean	5	2	2	5	3	5	5	5	32
Joe	3	4	4	3	3	3	3	3	26
Matt	3	2	4	5	4	4	4	5	31
Team Total/ 30	23	18	19	24	18	25	24	26	

Team Total: 25-30 Great; 20-24 Average; below 20 needs development
Individual Total: 30-40 Great; 20-29 Average; below 20 needs development

FIGURE 9.1 Assessing Human Inventory and Skills
Source: Mike Gray, C.P.M./C.I.R.M., Supply Chain Evangelist—Penn State University, Oliver Wight, and former Dell director (1991–2009).

they had a "catalog" of training programs that were available to advance the culture of change throughout the organization.

Throughout my career, the companies that I have worked for and with that had the most adaptive and mature cultures were those that encouraged learning and development whether internally or externally. Over the years, I have also seen many of these professional development and training programs disappear as budgets have been cut in down and uncertain economies. I have also observed that they rarely get reimplemented as the economy or business improves. Why is best practices leadership so important? The gap in cost advantage between Leaders and Laggards enables the Leaders to continue their investments in learning and cultural maturity. They know that losing that edge, losing the competitive culture, is the beginning of the death spiral. It's when cutting and shrinking become more important than winning and growing.

Professional development programs can be implemented with as much or as little investment as you are willing to make, but you have to make the investment. As mentioned in Chapter 2, *you can pay me now, or you can pay me later.* Minimally, the various professional associations offer certification, training workshops, and educational conferences, both locally and globally, that can be leveraged to support a professional development program. Encouraging development is encouraging the culture to learn. As you conduct the transformation maturity assessment, identify the traits you would like to mature and set up programs to encourage the development of your people to adopt them.

In addition to the associations, local universities and community colleges are great sources of low-cost programs. Instructors at the academic institutions are generally quite open to developing short programs for local businesses to train their people, and they are generally not looking for huge stipends to do so. There are plenty of commercial conferences and training programs available as well. Education is not hard to find—encourage learning and a learning culture will evolve. It's a journey. The key is how you leverage the program to navigate the journey.

Working with your team and human resources, develop the program to specifically address team weaknesses first. You can even do a SWOT analysis, as we learned in Chapter 2, on your human inventory. Don't just publish a catalog of programs or trainings. Develop a professional development strategy and include your objectives and development metrics in your balanced scorecard. Your development plan should first identify trainings that will improve overall team skills first. As the team improves, so will the culture. Self-actualization is based on confidence, team learning, and shared visions of the transformation journey. Self-improvement breeds process improvement.

For example, one of my colleagues makes a point of sending each of his functional managers to one or two conferences each year. By corporate mandate, he doesn't have a formal training program. He has each of his team identify, at the beginning of each year, the professional capabilities that they individually want to improve (and he validates it with his team assessment). Together, they identify learning opportunities, such as an industry conference. As part of the approval process, the individual submits the sessions to be attended and the objectives to be gained. Upon returning from the conference, the department has a "lunch and learn" session for the attendee to present to colleagues what was learned at the conference and what performance improvement initiatives may be taken on or impacted from the learning. Big bang for the buck! Not only does the individual learn from attending, he or she also gets the experience of presenting and reinforcing the learning by sharing it with their colleagues. It may not be a formal professional development program, but it builds team learning, improves skills, and creates a culture for change.

Professional development is also a lever for maintaining/retaining and also recruiting talent. From every research source on the talent topic, all agree that we are facing talent and skill shortages in supply chain management for some time to come. A group of companies and academic institutions have formed the Supply Chain Talent Academic Initiative (www.supply-chain.org/sctai) to promote awareness of supply chain careers at the high-school level. Research indicates that most supply chain majors didn't know about supply chain as a career prior to entering college or university.

And we don't just need college grads. Despite advances in robotics, we need truck drivers, forklift operators, machine operators, technicians, and associates. As the baby boomers hit retirement age, many companies are experiencing "gray tsunamis" of employees retiring after 30 or more years of service—and with them departs 30 years of tribal knowledge and how to use the spreadsheets that they developed over those years. It's another reason for process mapping, documentation, and integrating IT with business operations execution.

Recruiting, like professional development, also doesn't have to be an expensive proposition; however, it also has to be focused on improving the team and the transformational culture maturity of the organization. If you identify skills gaps in your assessment of human inventory that can only be filled by experienced professionals, having a regular presence at industry and association conferences is a great way to identify future talent. Often the best recruits are those that you have networked with at events and have developed a professional relationship with both for themselves or to obtain references. Leveraging social media, such as LinkedIn, is another great source of talent. If your human inventory needs bolstering with entry-level people, connections with the local academic community and even the major universities is not limited only to the "big" companies.

A great way to recruit new talent from universities and colleges is to have a regular internship program for at least one or two students per year. The cost is not high; the professors will work with you to identify the right fit for your requirements. Worse case, you get a fresh look at your operations and can complete a project that you would really like done, but don't seem to have the career resource to allocate it to. It's a great way to "try and buy" resources without having to make a career commitment. If the intern fits and is an asset, then you can go after him or her for full-time employment.

The very first step of your journey is to assess your human inventory, design a professional development program that will align your human resource strategy and progress with your transformation strategy, and encourage and create a culture for change and learning. You can do it! So what about that operating plan?

At the end of Chapter 2, I tickled you with a simple "game plan" for transformation as shown in Figure 9.2. Well, it doesn't have to be complex. The plan itself should be simple so that it can be understood, easily communicated, and set forth the organization on its journey. The tough part lies in executing the plan and sustaining the journey to building your House of Excellence in Leader City.

You know that I am not a "reinvent-the-wheel" guy, especially when I have invested a lot of time and effort participating on industry committees and initiatives to invent those wheels. Lean Six Sigma SCOR® convergence is one of the best approaches that I have experienced over the years. There are ample educational materials and process support tools available to advance your people in the techniques necessary to navigate a transformational journey.

For my purposes, Six Sigma's DMAIC, define, measure, analyze, improve, and control, has been the simplest method to learn and communicate the game plan. Deming's "Plan, Do, Check, and Act" (PDCA) works as well. Lean, while great, is more difficult to learn because it can get a bit dogmatic and is often accompanied by a new vocabulary. But, certainly, the roof of the House of Excellence is a lean performance management operating system. So that's why I like to "steal" from them all. Remember my definition of "research" in Chapter 1? At the end of the day, go with what works best in your organization.

As mentioned in Chapter 6, companies don't have just one supply chain. In its most complex sense every product composed of components from every supplier to each manufacturing facility going to every customer is its own supply chain. Obviously, we

Why Should We Change?
- Assess Current Operations—***Define*** Your Supply Chain
- Determine Market Benchmarks, Environment, & Challenges—***Measure***

How Do We Change?
- Create Strategy and "Vision" for the Future—***Analyze***
- Map "As-Is" & "To-Be" Business Processes & Systems—***Improve***

What Is the Value of Changing?
- Determine Critical Success Factors & "Windows of Opportunity"
- Calculate Return on Investment

Getting Management Buy-In & Investment
- Present "Solution" Plan to Management

Getting Operations Buy-In & Commitment
- Pilot Implementation "Proof of Concept" . . . Rapid Results—***Control***

Everyone Jumps on the Bandwagon
- Deploy Transformation Plan across the Enterprise

> Executing a Game Plan for Transforming Your Supply Chain to a Culture of Change Will Lead to the House of Excellence in Leader City!

FIGURE 9.2 A "Game Plan" for Supply Chain Transformation

want to *define* our supply chain in a manageable way so that we can effectively prioritize the never-ending series of tasks along our journey. Supply chain segmentation strategy (a fancy way of saying define your supply chains) is getting a lot of play by the pundits these days.

Desiring to keep it simple, my recommendation (based on my SCOR® experience and training) is to *define* the product categories that you have that require different operational characteristics. For example, in electronics, servers may be managed differently than PCs or printers. These may represent three different product segments. After you have defined the product segments, you should now *define* your customer segments. For example, in electronics, commercial direct customers may be managed different than channel partners/distributors and consumer segments, another three different segments. As you define your customer segments, at each intersection of a customer segment with a product segment, you will have a different supply chain segment that will have different performance attributes and strategies associated with it.

To establish the priority with which to engage your transformation efforts, for each supply chain *define* the performance attributes (SCOR® Quick Reference Guide Version 10 or APQC PCF) associated with each. For example, you can consider revenue and profit, volume, cost, brand equity, service, customer level, ROIC, and others. Assess, on a scale of 1 to 10 with 10 being highest, the performance attributes in terms of their importance to achieving your corporate business strategy. Remember, the foundation of the House of Excellence is alignment of performance management to the business strategy. The supply chain or chains that contribute (sum of assessment) the most toward achieving the business strategy are the ones you should start with. At this point, as it is early in the journey, my recommendation would be to think in terms of which of the three most important supply chains to achieving the business strategy could be most quickly targeted for a pilot performance improvement project.

Once you have determined the target supply chain, the next step is to *define* the strategy for that segment. Remember, the attributes for supply chain performance management and the associated key performance indicators (SCOR® Quick Reference Guide Version 10) are the following:

- Supply Chain Reliability
  - Perfect Order Fulfillment
- Supply Chain Responsiveness
  - Order Fulfillment Cycle Time
- Supply Chain Agility
  - Upside Supply Chain Flexibility
  - Upside Supply Chain Adaptability
  - Downside Supply Chain Flexibility
  - Downside Supply Chain Adaptability
- Supply Chain Costs
  - Supply Chain Management Cost
  - Cost of Goods Sold
- Supply Chain Asset Management
  - Cash-to-Cash Cycle Time
  - Return on Supply Chain Fixed Assets
  - Return on Working Capital

For the targeted supply chain, you will determine for each attribute whether your performance needs to be top, median, or bottom based on whether your strategy requires superior, advantage, or parity performance with your competitors and/or market/industry. Superior performance isn't required for each attribute. In fact, attempting to achieve superior performance in *every* attribute may be quite costly and certainly impractical. *The attribute most important to focus on is based on what your customers are telling you.* Remember, Lean focuses on the "voice of the customer," and it's the first supply chain cycle that you need to synch up with.

I found it interesting, at the 2011 CSCMP Annual Conference, that P&G, who had pioneered the concept of the "Perfect Order," presented that they had adopted a new metric for supply chain performance: SAMBC. SAMBC is "service as measured by the customer." Always the leader, always on the journey, P&G has created a voice of the customer metric that they are using to drive their supply chain strategy. You can't get on the journey fast enough.

Let's assume that you have selected the channel partner/distributor segment of your supply chain as one of the most critical to the business strategy, and that based on customer requirements (voice of the customer), you have determined that supply chain reliability is the process attribute the customer values most and will require superior performance to compete effectively. You will want to drill down at least three levels into the metrics that comprise Perfect Order Fulfillment (SCOR® Quick Reference Guide

Version 10) to assess where process performance improvement initiatives are or need to be to achieve your strategy. Remember, the first pillar of the House of Excellence is process-oriented metrics:

- Perfect Order Fulfillment
  - Percent of Orders Delivered in Full
    - Delivery Item Accuracy
    - Delivery Quantity Accuracy
  - Delivery Performance to Customer Commit Date
    - Customer Commit Date Achievement Time Customer Receiving
    - Delivery Location Accuracy
  - Documentation Accuracy
    - Compliance Documentation Accuracy
    - Other Required Documentation Accuracy
    - Payment Document Accuracy
    - Shipping Document Accuracy
  - Perfect Condition
    - Percent of Faultless Installations
    - Percent Orders/Lines Received Damage-Free
    - Orders Delivered Damage-Free Conformance
    - Orders Delivered Defect-Free Conformance
    - Warranty and Returns

For the other attributes, you will want to drill no more than two levels down to track and improve attributes for which you have determined that you need to achieve advantage performance. For attributes requiring parity, tracking and improving no more than the first-level metric is good enough for now.

Okay, you have *defined* your supply chain segments, prioritized the segments based on alignment with the business strategy, *defined* the process-oriented metrics associated with the segment, and prioritized the metrics required to measure the performance of your targeted supply chain segment. So how are you performing? Of course, the second pillar of the House of Excellence is the Balanced Scorecard (SCOR®), as illustrated in Figure 7.3. You have defined the depth of the metrics included on the scorecard based on your strategy to collect performance data associated with each metric that you are monitoring. They include both external and internal attributes and metrics. And you are focused on providing the highest level of supply chain reliability because that's what the customer values.

So how are you performing? How do you know? No one is really complaining any more than usual, right? Our performance is as good as we can do it, right? We're trying really hard and working lots of hours, right? We are on budget and making the numbers, right? Are you living in Leader City or Laggard City? Is your House of Excellence built with sticks or bricks? Where do you stand in the industry? Are you the market share leader? Well, maybe not *the* market leader, but we're competitive. How do you know? In the absence of market or benchmark data, *how do you know how well or bad you are doing? How do you measure up?*

BENCHMARKING: PERCEPTION VERSUS REALITY

Why doesn't everyone benchmark the performance of their company? There are a lot of perceptions about the degree of difficulty in conducting benchmarking, like cost. It's free, for the most part. APQC provides its Open Standards Research (www.apqc .org) to members of CSCMP and the Supply Chain Council for free. If you are willing to submit your data to the confidential database, APQC will provide you with a report on where you stand in your industry among peer groups, regions, or other industries. You select the category for comparison based on the NAICS (North American Industry Classification System) code for your industry or industry that you would like to benchmark against.

Benchmarking can be really hard work, but it doesn't have to be. To start with, I recommend simple quantitative benchmarking. Using the metrics from APQC's Process Classification Framework or CSCMP's process standards based on the PCF metrics will provide you with a much deeper and broader dataset than using the SCOR® metrics. At this time, the Open Standards Research database has been around longer and has more active submissions. The differences between the SCOR® metrics and PCF metrics are negligible, in my opinion. Later, if you want to get into qualitative benchmarking or true competitive benchmarking, that's when it gets harder and potentially more expensive. However, benchmarking the metrics you have defined for your performance scorecard for less than 100 data points should not be arduous.

Why should you benchmark? So that you have a stake; you have a bar that can be set; you have a point of reference as to your performance relative to the Leaders. You can see what the gaps are in your performance and where you need to be to achieve your supply chain and business strategic objectives.

"But," you say, "what if we are in Laggard City and nobody knows it because we don't benchmark? I don't want to risk exposing our weaknesses."

Take the risk. As Yogi Berra said, "If you don't know where you are going, any road will take you there." You have worked too hard to build the case for transformation to take any road on your journey. Benchmarking will navigate you to two things: low-hanging fruit (quick wins) and Leader City. Benchmarking is the basis for a process improvement culture, the third pillar of the House of Excellence. You got the people and the management support to build the house with bricks . . . provide them with the blueprint by benchmarking. Many people and most executives have a competitive tendency. Show them that they are lagging and they will generally want to compete. Show them the gap and they will want to close it or extend it. Show them the money and you will have their support.

Now that you have *defined and measured* your supply chain, you should be able to evaluate gaps in performance as the basis for *analyzing* your supply chain. Based on your findings, what would you like your future to look like? Using a little Visioneering, what would you like your performance to be in the next few years? Where would you like the organization to be in terms of transformational culture maturity? What will the market environment look like, and where will you want your organization to be in that environment? What challenges will you face? What are the rocks you will encounter and bets that will be placed on your journey?

Before analyzing your processes to any degree of depth, it's important to reflect on the current reality based on the supply chain you have defined and your performance relative to the benchmarks. The gap between the current reality and your preliminary vision of where you would like to be is the source of creative tension (energy) and sense of urgency that you will have to communicate to motivate your team along the journey (or use to get management commitment, if you are still struggling with that). Are you launching the journey on a highway or a dirt road? It's good to start setting the budget for pizza parties up front.

HOW DO WE EAT THE ELEPHANT? IDENTIFYING PROJECTS AND SETTING PRIORITIES

Analysis really begins by mapping out your "as-is" processes for the target supply chain. The good news is we have segmented and prioritized our target supply chain, which, by nature, should limit the scope of the analysis and mapping exercise. For the target supply chain, develop a logical map of the nodes in your supply chain (for now, designate one node to represent the customer segment you have selected and one node to represent the supplier segment you have selected) that represent your facilities and functions in the target supply chain. The flow should go from supplier node to manufacturing and/or distribution facilities to the customer node and include any headquarters, sales, support/service, or other company-owned or outsourced nodes that perform supply chain process types: plan, source, make, deliver, return from customer, and return to supplier. It can be as simple as the one shown in Figure 9.3.

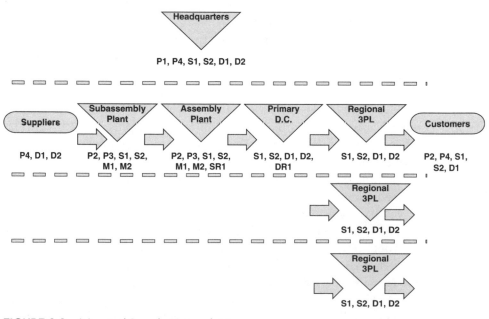

FIGURE 9.3   A Logical Supply Network Map

As you lay out the logical map (you can also map the network logically and geographically using a map as your background), you can begin to add process types and categories to the map, as I have done in Figure 9.3. Of course, I am using the SCOR® approach. If you prefer another methodology, value stream mapping, for example, you can use it. The process types are used to define the scope of your target supply chain and set the high-level performance metrics.

Process categories allow you to configure the supply chain based on the activities performed at each node in the network. Level 3 enables you to define the specific process elements (activities) performed at each network location (node), the various inputs and outputs of the process, linkages to other processes and locations, and detailed process performance metrics that are tied to your strategic metrics.

Adding in the benchmark performance data enables you to start identifying operating performance gaps, constraints, systems and tools, and other process characteristics at the activity level. The SCOR® model will also provide you with the best practices associated with the processes and environmental practices/metrics for sustainability. In addition, and the bonus, SCOR® provides, for each process, the human resource skills, education, attributes, and training requirements that you can use as part of your human inventory assessment and professional development plan.

Once you have mapped out the "as-is" processes for your supply chain with benchmark information, you can categorize the areas for "to be" *improvements* (as in DMAIC) to begin prioritizing your performance improvement projects. This can be a tricky exercise; however, the Supply Chain Council came up with a "rule of thumb" process for quickly assessing your "to be" project priorities, which I have found very useful. This is especially true when you don't have a lot of time and resources to allocate to your transformation. You may have management support, but remember, you're also funding this effort on working capital *to be* liberated, not already liberated. So my recommendation is to create a two-by-two matrix, as shown in Figure 9.4.

Process mapping, measurement, benchmarking, and analysis enable you to prioritize improvement projects and best practice implementation.

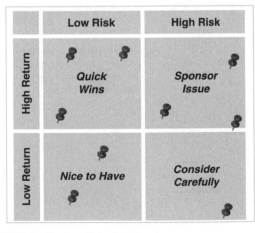

How to determine priority?
- **For each business process**
  - **Determine risk**
  - **Determine return**
- **Pin in the quadrant**

FIGURE 9.4 Project Priority Matrix
Source: The Supply Chain Council Framework and Implementation Training

Starting with any process that will potentially close an inventory performance gap or liberate working capital, determine the risk and return for each possible project that will move you from an "as-is" gap to a "to be" performance improvement. If a project has high return and low risk, it's a "quick win" opportunity. If the project has high return and high risk, you better look for a sponsor or leverage the management commitment you have received. *Reality check?* Put high-return, high-risk projects on the shelf for now. You want to select *quick win* pilot opportunities to liberate funding in the short term and garner additional management and team support. Remember, you have to *mobilize your team* to join you on your journey. Quick wins are the catalysts to launch them.

While your first inclination may be to place the low-risk, low-return "nice-to-have" projects on the shelf, and leave the high-risk, low-return "consider carefully" projects for your successor, let's not necessarily *walk away* from them. The by-product of defining and documenting your network and process mapping exercise is that you can also perform an analysis of *outsourcing* opportunities using a two-by-two matrix similar to the Project Priority Matrix as shown in Figure 9.5.

Outsourcing can also be a quick win, as the third-party firm will do much of the work and assume most of the risk (don't tell them I told you that). While it's important for you to have a definition of your requirements, avoid lengthy request for proposal (RFP) preparation and processes. Remember the sandbox in Chapter 8? Give the bidders the leeway to propose their best solutions. I can't tell you how many RFPs I have seen that require the bidder to provide features that will go away with the implementation of the solution the supplier is providing. Don't solve bad practices based on what you don't know. The requested features/requirements often actually perpetuate the problem rather than solve it. Many of *your* "requirements" will go away with the bidder's proposed *solutions.* Specify the problems of the as-is state, not features. Let them develop the solutions. Leverage their experience, knowledge, and

Process mapping, measurement, benchmarking, and analysis enable you to identify opportunities for outsourcing.

	Low Expertise	High Expertise
High Value	Performance-Based Opportunity	Core Competency/ High IP
Low Value	Traditional 3PL	Can a Third-Party Perform at a Lower Cost?

How to determine opportunity?
- **For each business process**
  - **Determine expertise**
  - **Determine value**
- **Pin in the quadrant**

FIGURE 9.5 Outsourcing Opportunity Matrix

innovation in the process as much as possible. This is a step toward achieving Kate Vitasek's vision of a "vested" relationship.

By assessing each of your network and process capabilities based on your internal expertise and the value of the process to executing and achieving your strategy, you can determine if there is an opportunity to outsource the process. Think of the bang you could get by offloading a multimillion-dollar facility and/or operation to a contract manufacturer or third-party logistics firm!

If the process has very high value to the organization and your resources and expertise are also very high, then pin the process on the matrix as a core competency. Or, if the process is based on a high level of intellectual property, you may not want to outsource it based on security issues. On the other hand, if you have great expertise in a process while contributing minimal value to the supply chain or business strategy, it may be a great opportunity to outsource through a traditional third-party relationship to reduce the cost of maintaining and/or retaining the employees. And it could be great for the employees as well.

I remember meeting with executives at ServiceMaster when they were still based in the Chicago suburbs and just starting up. Outsourcing was new to me; they were pioneering the outsourced maintenance market. When I asked them about the value proposition, it was twofold. Maintenance services were not core competencies for most companies, and yet, they had to pay the employees performing those services the same base scale, benefits, and HR opportunities that they did for employees with core competency skills and education. For firms in highly technical industries facing heavy recruitment competition for engineers, scientists, and post-graduate degree personnel, the benefits packages may be as high as the maintenance personnel's hourly salary, not to mention associated HR policy risks. For the employees, the likelihood of the maintenance person ascending through the ranks to CEO was pretty low. Where can a maintenance person be CEO? In a company staffed by maintenance people.

When I was at Microsoft, the company outsourced virtually (pun intended) every process and employee that wasn't considered a core competency to Microsoft's strategy and objectives. There were almost as many outsourced employees as full-time employees. Microsoft virtually created an outsourcing industry and companies around its campus and locations. If you ever see a Microsoft e-mail that begins with "v-", it's likely to be from a "virtual" or outsourced employee.

When you are assessing project priorities, the "nice-to-have" and "consider carefully" projects may be outsourcing opportunities. Certainly, if, as we said, it's a process with high internal expertise, but contributes little relative value with low risk and low return, definitely consider outsourcing it. Let the third party do the work and assume the risk. They are the specialists. It's what they do. If it were cheap and easy to do internally, there wouldn't be outsourcing.

If it's a process that contributes low relative value to your strategy, you have limited expertise to perform it, and it falls into the "nice-to-have" category as well, it most assuredly may be a candidate for a traditional third-party relationship.

If the process contributes very high value to your supply chain and business strategy, but in your human inventory assessment you conclude that you have very limited expertise, you may want to consider outsourcing on a performance-based third-party relationship. It may be less costly and less risky than trying to recruit or develop the expertise to undertake it internally. Kate Vitasek at the University of Tennessee and Supply Chain Visions has written a great book on what she calls "vested outsourcing" that is about as good as it gets on developing strategic third-party relationships based upon performance and value versus traditional transactional third-party relationships.[1]

For those high-risk, low-return projects that tempt you to leave them for your successor to take on, evaluate where the risk is, what the value to the business is for the process, and whether you should put them out for bid. A third party may have developed a mitigation strategy to minimize the risk, and you can be the hero.

 ## JUMP ON THE BANDWAGON: COMMUNICATING THE GAME PLAN AND BUILDING OPERATIONS SUPPORT

As you Visioneer the "as-is" and "to be" process states to support your transformation, you need to consider all approaches, systems, people, and process alternatives. It's thinking "outside the box" and collaborating with your colleagues and team that are the best vehicle for traversing the transformation journey.

As I said at the beginning of this chapter, in the previous chapters we executed the exercises determining the critical success factors, financial benefits, and returns; presented the "solution" plan to management; and received management support to initiate the transformation journey.

We have *defined, measured, analyzed*, and identified *improvement* opportunities, including outsourcing. We have evaluated and prioritized those opportunities and have selected . . . you guessed it, a "quick win" pilot "proof of concept" opportunity to serve as the *control* point to launch the team on its journey. You are a Lean (voice of the customer) Six Sigma (DMAIC and benchmarks) SCOR® (documented process map, metrics, and best practices) transformation machine! The pilot project is well within your team resources' skills, technology, experience, and training to execute successfully. In a matter of weeks, you realize your first "win" with significant *results*!

Human resources and marketing communications work with you to publish a case study on your "proof of concept" results while internally extolling your team collectively and individually for their efforts. You host a very public pizza party, and, with the team, everyone has a great deal of fun celebrating the win. Subsequent to the win, you publish a list of new prioritized projects and key personnel assignments along with a professional development program tailored to each individual. Your professional development program includes team orientation meetings and "lunch and learns" with presentations and learning from the pilot team members. You begin "poster-izing" key performance metrics and goals showing weekly progress toward achieving them.

During team orientation meetings, you and your management team/champions communicate the transformation plan to the new teams, as shown in Figures 9.2 and 9.6.

Changing the Game! With <our> Business System!

<u>Transforming From</u> ➡	<u>To</u>
Supply Chain	**Smart Supply Network**
Long and Slow	**Fast and Flexible**
Forecast-Based	**Demand Responsive**
Organization-Driven	**Customer-Driven**
Internal Focus	**External Focus**
Designed from Product Forward	**Designed from Use Point Back**
Cost Reduction	**Value Creation**
Linear, Sequential Processes	**Dynamic, Synchronized Processes**

FIGURE 9.6   Game-Changing Supply Chain Transformation

People are excited about the pilot results and enthusiastic about the program. One of your associates suggests a great idea, and you pull out a "coffee card" as a reward. You may even come up with a nickname for "The <Our> Business System" brand (for example, "The Toyota Production System" or "The Danaher Business System") for the performance management operating system roof of your House of Excellence. You and your team are taking one bite at a time out of the elephant as you launch on your journey to building the House of Supply Chain Operations Excellence and residing in Leader City.

Congratulations! The journey will be your reward.

 NOTE

1. Vitasek, Kate, *Vested Outsourcing: Five Rules That Will Transform Outsourcing*, Palgrave Macmillan, 2010.

Conclusion: Business As Usual Has Been Canceled, Now What?

WELCOME TO SUPPLY chain management in the twenty-first century! Do you remember the sidebar in Chapter 1 about the Smart Supply Network? If you don't believe now that it can be done and that the leaders aren't transforming their operations to leverage their people, processes, and technology for real-time, always on, fully visible, smart supply networks, then you can rip out the rearview mirror . . . no one's behind you. By the way, the leaders don't have rearview mirrors either . . . because what's behind them doesn't matter. They are moving forward. Their only concern is how to move anything that gets in their way.

When I first thought about actually writing a book, my real first inclination for a title was "Business as Usual Has Been Canceled, Now What?" I had been using it as the title to several presentations that I was doing that year. When I was with Burroughs, I found a great cartoon depiction of a "plumber's nightmare" that was used to show the problems with software development. It depicted a configuration of pipes, valves, buckets, sinks, and bathtubs with leaks in the flow everywhere and people trying to bail out the muck leaking through the pipes. I labeled the various muck repositories as supplier, manufacturer, distributer, and retailer and used it to illustrate the *traditional* supply chain as a pipeline and the associated plumbing. I have used it in presentations ever since. I even had T-shirts made up to give away to people attending my presentation.

Of course, I was at the 2009 CSCMP conference, and when I told Don Bowersox about my idea for the book, he gave me that "look" and reminded me about a book of his that DEC had published, *It's Not Business As Usual.* And we were both in the audience at an ECR (efficient consumer response) conference when the president of Spartan Stores (also based in Grand Rapids, MI) began his opening remarks by announcing, "Business as usual has been canceled." So much for that book title, I guess. But I am going use it as the title of my conclusion.

By the way, if you want to do some "qualitative" benchmarking of best practices, do you think a trip to Grand Rapids might work? You can also learn something from another Grand Rapids Leader, Steelcase. And, Zeeland, Michigan, the home of Herman Miller isn't too far from the Grand Rapids airport.

Every day from this day forward, you need to wake up and say, "*Business as usual has been canceled.*" You have to get away from being satisfied with the status quo. Things will change. . . . Remember the title of Chapter 1: "Change Is Inevitable; Growth Is

Optional"? Transformation is a journey. Even if you have built and are living in the House of Excellence on Collaboration Avenue in Leader City, when you get up each morning read the headline, *Business As Usual Has Been Canceled!* Boots and saddles! It's time to get back on the journey and continue building and improving the House of Excellence.

If you are new to supply chain and reading this book because someone told you supply chain is cool and you wanted to learn more about it, boots and saddles to you, too. Supply chain management isn't the only discipline impacted by change. Change is everywhere. If you're not scanning the horizon, assessing the impact that new technologies, new products, new websites, new everything that is being produced and introduced may have on your life, you may also be left behind. Remember that 80 percent of the original Fortune 500 aren't on the list any more.

Supply chain management isn't the only landscape with Leaders and Laggards. They are found in every way of life, and you have to be on a personal journey to transform yourself to build and live in the House of Excellence. Success is a great way of living and success is within you, as it is within the supply chain. The tools and techniques in this book can be applied anywhere. It's about transforming yourself and your business to work toward achieving excellence. Determine your "as-is" state and create a vision of where and what you want "to be" in the future. Leverage the creative tension generated by the gap as the energy to *Visioneer* a means to close the gap, grow, and succeed. Remember, Laggards are working as hard as Leaders. Work to Lead and you will find success.

If you are a student and had this book assigned to you, or you heard it was a good book on supply chain, consider supply chain as a career. It's vital to global commerce; in fact, it can be considered the engine of global commerce. Consider Chapter 6. Supply chain management offers a pipeline of opportunity. Regardless of your capabilities or goals, there will always be career opportunities from loading or driving trucks to managing supply chain operations. And for a growing number of supply chain professionals, it's becoming a doorway to the executive office. If you can mobilize your function to achieve excellence, you can mobilize an organization to achieve excellence.

Every organization has supply chain needs, and the supply chain discipline is becoming top of mind with more and more executives. A growing number of academic institutions are offering courses and degrees in supply chain management. Start your journey today. Strive for excellence in your studies and career. Companies are looking for talent to staff their supply chains. As it is still an emerging and developing discipline, there are yet undiscovered improvements to be uncovered by someone just like you. Challenge yourself to question everything. Ask why? Ask why? Ask why? Ask why? And then ask why one more time! Understand the whY *in You!* Dig deep enough into problems and you will uncover the solution. Remember, the devil is in the details. Do the math. Use this book to guide your first steps to architecting and building your House of Excellence.

If you are an executive or a professional in another discipline, I hope you are reading this book because you recognize the strategic leverage that supply chain management brings to your business and competitive strategy as we discussed in Chapter 7 in particular. The key is understanding the fulcrums applied to the various supply chain levers and collaboration. Again, the devil is in the details. Always challenge the pundits, including me. Transformation is for the entire organization. Or perhaps your supply chain leadership bought this book as a gift to you? *Please read between the lines.*

Regardless of your motivation, the transformation journey is a *business transformation,* not just a supply chain transformation. The roof on the House of Excellence is a business operating system that can be extended across all of the functions of your organization and guide your organization to leadership and success. The House of Excellence can serve as a residence in the Demand Creation and Demand Performance structures as well as in Demand Fulfillment. Excellence has no functional boundary.

The numbers don't lie. There are and will be Leaders and Laggards in every industry but the gap between them can be closed. Don't worry about being *the Leader, be a Leader.* Any organization can be a *best practices* leader. You will dramatically improve the performance, profitability, and overall financial and professional health of your organization by encouraging and supporting your people on their journey to excellence. Regardless of the size of your company, encourage professional development and self-actualization in your company's culture and day-to-day operations. You don't have to be the biggest to be best. You may think you are the horse that your people are riding, but the reality is that your people are the horses that have pulled your carriage to the top. The better your team is, the more successful you will be. There is no "I" in *team.* Be a leader, a coach, and a mentor. There is no substitute for the satisfaction you will earn.

It is well more than a supply chain journey as Ron Johnson, the CEO now at J.C. Penney, is demonstrating. He's just continuing on a journey toward innovation and excellence across the organization that began at Target, continued at Apple, and is now transforming JCP. Sure, he is and will be encountering rocks in the road that he will have to make bets on; but, remember "the journey is the reward." Motivate your people to build a House of Excellence and lead your organization to Leader City! Crush the competition with operations excellence.

If you are a supply chain professional, I hope you're reading this book because you want to grow, win, and succeed in your profession. Supply chain management couldn't be a better place to be right now; and I've been saying that each year for more than 30 years. It just keeps getting better. There are more opportunities in supply chain today than ever before, and there will be more opportunities emerging as technology and business processes become more aligned.

The bullwhip will be tamed and operations will become *synchronized* across the channel, enabling profitable response to demand variability in real time. The Smart Supply Network (see Figure C.1) is becoming a reality as companies define and align their processes and embrace and implement new technology to support their people's execution. The leaders are funding their initiatives from the liberation of working capital and the savings their journey is generating. They're getting farther ahead and not looking back. They wake up every morning to the revelation that *business as usual has been canceled.* They relish change and embrace it as an opportunity to distance them from the competition. They have no rear-view mirror. They are looking through binoculars with night vision and driving with a transformation culture navigation system.

They leverage their continuous improvement journey and culture of change for competitive advantage. It's like playing a video game; as you navigate your way to and

The Smart Supply Network: Key Takeaways

- **Analyze and Map End-to-End Material Flows, Nodes, & Lanes**
- **Identify Different Cycles across the Channel & Identify Pull/Push Boundaries to Synchronize Lead Times, Behavioral Metrics, & Economic Drivers**
- **Measure the Financial Impact of Daily Operating Decisions & Assess the Opportunity from Improving Decision-Making Tools**
- **Leverage Supply Chain Visibility & Analytics to Identify Outsourcing Opportunities for Flexibility & Optimization**

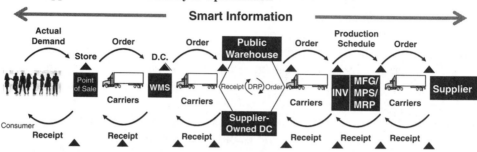

FIGURE C.1 The Smart Supply Network

through the House of Excellence to Leader City, you pick up more weapons and ammunition along the way. The more you succeed, the further you progress on the transformation journey. But it has no end.

This is the paradigm shift you are facing. It is the essence of supply chain transformation. In the new century, the *smart supply network* begins at the end. It has been interesting to me over the years that most depictions of the *supply chain* (and I am no different) begin with the supplier. In the Western side of the world, we read and think left to right. The more "important" object appears on the left and the chain's flow of goods moves to the right. We have to reverse the paradigm and start with the end buyer on the left and *respond* to their supply *consumption* by pulling supply from the point (pull/push boundary) that supply must be produced in economic order quantities, not consumption quantities. At that pull/push point, we produce supply in economic quantities to cover the product's period of risk to respond to the customer demand within the customer's lead time.

The end buyer initiates the smart supply network and a *smart* demand signal is transmitted across the channel instantaneously. The *smart* systems receive the signals from the demand sources across the channel instantaneously and interpret them. *Smart* recommendations are made to profitably respond to the demand signal based on visibility to the flow of goods being monitored by *smart* identification and whether the demand signal reaches a *critical action trigger* threshold at each *process gate* or intersection in the smart supply network.

Is the demand signal within the upper and lower process control points that have been set to *synchronize* the flow of goods through the network to profitably meet demand? If yes, no recommendation is necessary. If no, a recommendation alert is sent to the person(s) responsible for reconciling the exception. The smart supply network *technology platform* enables partners to plug their smart supply network technology platforms into one another to facilitate visibility, collaboration, and information sharing where needed.

The technology is readily available and cloud computing will make it more pervasive and affordable. Let me share a final story with you to illustrate the possibilities. Remember in Chapter 1, I shared my experience with a group of P&G managers in the Leadership and Mastery workshop. During the many discussions we had, it came out that most of them were distribution managers and were involved in the replenishment program for Wal-Mart. They relayed to me that as continuous replenishment programs (CRP) and vendor-managed inventory (VMI) were new approaches, there were no systems to support them.

What P&G did was to set up a manual distribution network solely focused on executing CRP and VMI with Wal-Mart. Their objective was to develop and document the processes for profitable execution in a pilot first. As they tested various processes and logic, they defined the technology requirements to support rollout and integration with the general distribution systems. At the end of the pilot, they had identified, documented, and resolved the issues and processes; and their IT group was able to develop the necessary technology platforms and applications to support the process and the people performing the process. The technology development was executed shortly thereafter; they were able to roll it out to a critical mass of volume and customers before it became public and an emerging trend in supply chain management. They were way ahead of the curve at that point. As the concept took hold in the market (and was now perceived as a commodity by P&G), P&G licensed the CRP applications for sale. Not only was the initiative funded by competitive advantage, the competition paid for it!

The Leaders are *investing* in their smart supply network people, process, and technology configuration based on the alignment of their *operating strategy* to the company's *business strategy* and *financial resources*. They are on the transformation journey. Where are you? *Business as usual has been canceled*. While we can't beam products to customers at the speed of light, we can beam information instantly and simultaneously across the smart supply network to synchronize the flow of goods to profitably respond to demand. Boots and saddles, my friends. Beam us a beer, Scotty.

References

ABC Television Network. "Castle," Episodes: *Pandora*, Season 4, Episode 415, Aired 02/13/2012, and *Lynchpin*, Season 4, Episode 416, Aired 02/20/2012 (http://beta.abc.go.com/shows/castle/episode-guide).

Abraham, Magid M. and Lodish, Leonard M. *Promoter: An Automated Promotion Evaluation System*, Marketing Science, Spring 1987, vol. 6, no. 2, pp. 101–123.

Barker, Joel Arthur. *Future Edge*, William Morrow & Company (1992).

Bolstorff, Peter and Rosenbaum, Robert. *Supply Chain Excellence: A Handbook for Dramatic Improvement Using the SCOR Model*, Second Edition, AMACOM (2007).

Bowersox, Donald J., Daugherty, Patricia J., Droge, Cornelia L., Germain, Richard N., and Rogers, Dale S. *Logistical Excellence: It's Not Business as Usual*, Digital Press (1992).

Daugherty, Patricia J., Autry, Chad W., and Ellinger, Alexander E. "Reverse Logistics: The Relationship between Resource Commitment and Program Performance," *Journal of Business Logistics*, vol. *22*, no.1, Spring 2001 Council of Supply Chain Management Professionals, pp. 107–123.

D'Innocenzio, Anne. "New J.C. Penney CEO's Challenge: Bring Life Back to an Iconic Brand," Associated Press, *Austin American Statesman* (January 31, 2012, online version).

Editorial Staff. "The Courage to Change,"*Inbound Logistics* (January, 2002), Thomas Publishing Company, pp. 90–92.

Elwin, Toby. *The Cost of Culture: A 50% Turnover of the Fortune 50*, blog, 2011, www.tobyelwin.com/the-cost-of-culture-a-50-turnover-of-the-fortune-500/.

Forrester, Jay. "Industrial Dynamics—A Major Breakthrough for Decision Makers," *Harvard Business Review* (1958) vol. *36*, no.4, pp. 37–66.

French, J. P. R., Jr., and Raven, B., "The Bases of Power," adapted from "The Bases of Social Power" in D. Cartwright and A. Zander (eds.), *Group Dynamics* (pp. 607–623). New York: Harper and Row (1960).

Friedman, Thomas. *The World Is Flat*, Farrar, Straus, and Giroux (2005).

Fritz, Robert. *The Path of Least Resistance*, Fawcett Columbine, Ballantine Books (1989).

George, Michael L. *Lean Six Sigma: Combining Six Sigma Quality with Lean Speed*, McGraw-Hill (2002).

Harps, Leslie Hansen. "Hitting the Mark: Supply Chain Best Practices,"*Inbound Logistics* (December 2003), Thomas Publishing Company, www.inboundlogistics.com.

Kaufman, Jr., and Draper L., *Systems 1: An Introduction to Systems Thinking*, Future Systems, Inc. (1980).

Keebler, James, Mandrodt, Karl B., Durtsche, David A., and Ledyard, D. Michael. *Keeping Score: Measuring the Business Value of Logistics in the Supply Chain*, Council of Logistics Management (1999).

Krauss, Lawrence M. *The Physics of Star Trek*, Basic Books (1995).

Larson, Paul D., and Rogers, Dale S. "Supply Chain Management: Definition, Growth, and Approaches," *Journal of Marketing Theory & Practice*, Vol. 6, No.4 (Fall 1998), M.E. Sharpe, Inc., pp. 1–5.

Levitt, Theodore. *The Marketing Imagination* (Expanded Edition), Free Press (1986).

Martin, Andre. *DRP: Distribution Resource Planning*, Oliver Wight (1983).

Maslow, Abraham. "A Theory of Human Motivation" (originally published in *Psychological Review*, 1943, Vol. *50*, no.4, pp. 370–396).

Mercer Management Consulting, *New Ways to Take Costs out of the Retail Food Pipeline: Making Replenishment Logistics Happen: A Study*, Coca-Cola Retailing Research Council, Atlanta (1993).

Rogers, Everett. *The Diffusion of Innovations*, Simon and Schuster (1962).

Savage, Charles. *5th Generation Management*, Digital Press (1990).

Senge, Peter. *The Fifth Discipline: The Art and Practice of the Learning Organization*, Currency Doubleday (1990).

Sherman, Richard J. "8 Steps to Info Systems Happiness,"*Inbound Logistics* (January 2002), Thomas Publishing Company, pp. 206–218.

Sherman, Richard J. "A Fulfilling Experience,"*DCVelocity* (March 2004), Agile Business Media, www.dcvelocity.com.

Sherman, Richard J. "Improving Customer Service through Integrated Logistics," *Annual Conference Proceedings*, Council of Logistics Management (Oakbrook, 1991), vol. 2, pp. 293–314.

Sherman, Richard J. "Information Systems for Distributors,"*Business Software Review* (March 1987), ICP Publication.

Sherman, Richard J. "Collaborative Planning, Forecasting & Replenishment (CPFR): Realizing the Promise of Efficient Consumer Response through Collaborative Technology," *Journal of Marketing Theory & Practice*, vol. 6, no.4 (Fall 1998), M.E. Sharpe, Inc., pp. 6–9.

Sherman, Richard J. "Leveraging People, Processes, and Technology for Optimal Response," *Auto Focus Asia* (Issue 4, 2008), Ohcre Media, www.autofocusasia/magazine.

Sherman, Richard J. "Look Ahead to Integrated Channels,"*Transportation and Distribution* (March, 1989), Penton, p. 46.

Sherman, Richard J. "Need a Breakthrough? Try Business Process Outsourcing,"*Supply Chain Management Review* (September/October 2010), Peerless Media LLC, pp. 44–51.

Sherman, Richard J. "The Process of Creating Strategic Plans: Creating Customer Value for Competitive Advantage," *Annual Conference Proceedings*, Council of Logistics Management (Oakbrook, 1992), pp. 519–531.

Sherman, Richard J. "Softening the Bullwhip's Sting,"*DCVelocity* (February 2004), Agile Business Media, www.dcvelocity.com.

Sherman, Richard J. *Supply Chain Management for the Millennium*, Warehousing Education & Research Council (WERC) (1998).

Sherman, Richard J. "Survival of the RFID-fittest,"*DCVelocity* (January, 2004), Agile Business Media, www.dcvelocity.com.

Sherman, Richard J. "Why Has CPFR Failed to Scale,"*CSCMP's Supply Chain Quarterly* (Quarter 2, 2007), Supply Chain Media, LLC, www.supplychainquarterly.com.

Vitasek, Kate, Ledyard, Mike, and Manrodt, Karl. *Vested Outsourcing: Five Rules That Will Transform Outsourcing*, Palgrave Macmillan (2010).

About the Author

Richard J. Sherman is an internationally recognized author, researcher, and speaker on trends and issues in supply chain management, technology, marketing, and organizational change. As president and CEO of Gold & Domas Research, *a Visioneering company*, Mr. Sherman assists clients worldwide through speaking, training, and consulting to implement game-changing strategies for supply chain transformation. He also serves as director of strategic development for the Council of Supply Chain Management Professionals (CSCMP) and is a professional member.

As a research director, he successfully launched the supply chain management advisory services for AMR Research and was a founding member of the team that developed the SCOR® model and founded the Supply Chain Council. Throughout his career, Mr. Sherman has served in executive positions with visionary technology firms such as EXE Technologies, Syncra Systems, Numetrix, Ltd., and marketing leading corporations such as Microsoft Corporation, Information Resources, Inc., Mercer Management Consulting, Digital Equipment Corporation, and Unisys Corporation, serving clients in retail, distribution, manufacturing, and third-party services. He is a frequent contributor of articles and speaks at conferences, symposiums, and universities worldwide.

He has served on leadership committees for several industry initiatives such as DAMA/Quick Response, Efficient Consumer Response, Continuous Replenishment, and VICS's Collaborative Planning, Forecasting and Replenishment (CPFR®).

Mr. Sherman serves on the board of directors for Lead Time Technology and the advisory boards of several technology firms. He has served on the board of directors (SCORBoard) and North American Leadership Team of the Supply Chain Council and the National Advisory Board to the Center for Logistics Management at the University of Nevada–Reno. He has served as an executive-in-residence at the universities of Alabama and Tennessee, Michigan State University, Texas A&M University, Tuskegee University, and The Ohio State University, among others.

An alumnus of the University of Notre Dame for both undergraduate and graduate degrees, Mr. Sherman has attended executive development programs at Michigan State University, Miami University, and the universities of Tennessee and North Florida.

A writer for *IndustryWeek* magazine once wrote, "Visionaries come from a variety of molds. Some paint future scenarios by examining that which is technologically possible today and then projecting a world in which the possibilities have become reality. Others go a step beyond. Richard Sherman seems to fit both categories."

Index